D0139842

PARALLEL
PROCESSING

INTERNATIONAL COMPUTER SCIENCE SERIES

Consulting editors   **A D McGettrick**   University of Strathclyde

                        J van Leeuwen   University of Utrecht

SELECTED TITLES IN THE SERIES:

PARALLEL PROCESSING

Principles and Practice

E. V. Krishnamurthy

University of Waikato, New Zealand

ADDISON-WESLEY
PUBLISHING
COMPANY

Sydney · Wokingham, England · Reading, Massachusetts
Menlo Park, California · New York · Don Mills, Ontario
Amsterdam · Bonn · Singapore
Tokyo · Madrid · San Juan

© 1989 Addison-Wesley Publishers Ltd.
© 1989 Addison-Wesley Publishing Company, Inc.

All rights reserved. No part of this publication may be reproduced, stored in a retrieval system or transmitted in any form or by any means, electronic, mechanical, photocopying, recording or otherwise, without prior written permission of the publisher.

The programs presented in this book have been included for their instructional value. They have been tested with care but are not guaranteed for any particular purpose. The publisher does not offer any warranties or representations, nor does it accept any liabilities with respect to the programs.

Many of the designations used by manufacturers and sellers to distinguish their products are claimed as trademarks. Addison-Wesley has made every attempt to supply trademark information about manufacturers and their products mentioned in this book. A list of the trademark designations and their owners appears on page xii.

Cover designed by Crayon Design of Henley-on-Thames.
Typeset by Times Graphics, Singapore.
Printed in Singapore.

First printed 1989.

British Library Cataloguing in Publication Data
Krishnamurthy, E.V.
  Parallel processing: principles and
  practice. – (International computer science
  series)
  1. Computer systems. Parallel-processor
  systems
  I. Title   II. Series
  004′.35
ISBN 0–201–17532–0

Library of Congress Cataloging in Publication Data
Krishnamurthy, E.V.
   Parallel processing: principles and practice/
 E.V. Krishnamurthy.
      p. cm. –– (International computer science series)
   Bibliography: p.
   Includes index.
   ISBN 0–201–17532–0
   1. Parallel processing (Electronic computers)   I. Title.
 II. Series.
 QA76.5.K765   1989
 004′.35––dc20   89–31529
                                                                      CIP

The endless cycle of idea and action,
Endless invention, endless experiment,

T.S. Eliot – Choruses from 'The Rock'
Selected Poems. London: Faber and Faber

Preface

Overview

This book introduces the principles and practice of parallel processing. Research in parallel computing has been very active in the last decade, as indicated by the tens of thousands of publications in this area. It was therefore quite difficult to make a choice of the topics that were to be covered and was still more difficult to decide the depth of presentation in each topic. In addition, I had to cope with the problem of reading and understanding exponentially growing literature in linear time and presenting it in linear space. The choice of topics I have made is subjective and I take the blame for any injustice done.

The topics covered in this text have been taught at both undergraduate and graduate levels at various universities over several years. I am glad that I have been able to collect these materials and knit them together in a coherent framework suitable for the next generation of computer scientists.

Readership

This book is intended for senior undergraduates and graduates in computer science, electrical engineering and mathematics as well as for computer professionals.

The style and presentation are kept simple so as to initiate new readers in this area and also to provide a good background for advanced study.

About the book

About half of this book is devoted to the theory and principles while the other half is devoted to the practice. Chapter 1 essentially presents the many facets of parallelism while Chapter 2 considers the basic properties of parallel processes and their interaction. Chapters 3, 4 and 6 provide the necessary theoretical framework – modelling, semantics and complexity. Chapter 5 deals with the parallel processor architecture. In Chapter 7, a brief introduction to parallel programming is given. Chapter 8 deals with the aspects of parallel processing of databases. Exercises are given at the end of each chapter; some of these exercises are from research papers and the required references are cited. A list of references appears at the end of each chapter.

Acknowledgements

Certainly a text of this type cannot be written without deriving many valuable ideas from several different sources. I express my indebtedness to all the authors, too numerous to acknowledge individually, from whose specialized knowledge I have benefited.

I wish to acknowledge the contributions of those who, in various ways, influenced this book: Richard Brent, Heiko Schröder, Australian National University; Azriel Rosenfeld, University of Maryland; Nicholas Metropolis, Los Alamos Scientific Laboratory; Michael Lynch, University of Sheffield.

I am thankful to Azriel Rosenfeld, University of Maryland, and Geoff Fox, California Institute of Technology, for facilities provided in the fall of 1988 to gain programming insight on the Butterfly, Warp, Hypercube and the Connection Machine.

I also wish to record my indebtedness to the University of Waikato for the facilities provided; in particular, I thank the Vice-Chancellor, Wilf Malcolm, for his unfailing support and encouragement. I express my gratitude to Rhonda Wright for her patience and skill in the production of this manuscript through its several drafts during the last two years. I am also thankful to Lorraine Dun for assisting in the final stages of the manuscript and to Frank Bailey for providing the necessary artwork.

Finally, it is my pleasant duty to thank the reviewers and the Addison-Wesley Publishing Company for their help and friendly advice throughout this project.

E.V. Krishnamurthy

University of Waikato
Hamilton, New Zealand
December, 1988

Contents

Trademark notice
UNIX™ is a trademark of AT&T.
occam™ is a trademark of the INMOS group of companies.
Smalltalk™ is a trademark of the Xerox Corporation.
IBM™ is a trademark of the International Business Machines Corporation.
Intel™ is a trademark of the Intel Corporation.
CYBER™ is a trademark of the Control Data Corporation.

Chapter 1
Parallelism – its Many Facets

1.1 Introduction

Many of today's advanced research problems need greater computing power at high speeds. Examples of this kind include artificial intelligence, robotics, signal processing, fluid mechanics, weather forecasting, high energy physics, molecular physics and space sciences.

A simple-minded approach to gain speed, as well as power, in computing is through **parallelism**; here many computers would work together, all simultaneously executing some portions of a procedure used for solving a problem. Such an approach rests on the following assumptions:

(1)   the availability of many low-cost, high-speed computers that can be put together to work in unison, as in a concert;

(2)   the existence of a strategy to partition a problem into smaller problems, such that most of these can be solved simultaneously, and from which we can easily construct the solution to the entire problem: this is popularly known as the 'divide-and-conquer strategy'.

Fortunately, the first of these assumptions is facilitated by the recent advances in microelectronics, solid state and superconducting devices technology. Using very large scale integration (VLSI) it is now possible to fabricate millions of transistor-equivalent devices on a single 4 mm square silicon chip. Several hundreds of thousands of such chips can be put together to build several thousands of processors within a few cubic centimetres at a reasonable cost.

The second of these assumptions, namely the application of the divide-and-conquer strategy, raises three basic issues:

(1)   decomposability,

(2)   complexity, and

(3)   communication.

We shall consider these issues below.

Decomposability

The nature of those computational problems that can be split, solved in parallel and recombined is at present not known. Some problems appear to be inherently serial in nature and not amenable to parallel processing, although it is not quite obvious which problems are of this type. Thus we may ask: can all computationally solvable problems be decomposed, solved piecewise in parallel and reassembled to obtain the solution? If the answer to this question is 'no', then can one identify a subclass of problems that are amenable to solution through a divide-and-conquer strategy?

Complexity

How effective is the divide-and-conquer strategy in obtaining the maximum gain in speed when several processors are used to process the decomposed tasks? To answer this question one should study how well a problem can be partitioned for solution by a given computer architecture or by an algorithm. For instance, let T be the total time taken by an algorithm in which there is a serial portion taking time T_s and a parallel portion taking time T_p, so that $T_s + T_p = T$; then, no matter how many processors are used, the serial portion would limit the increase in speed by a factor of at most T/T_s; this is because at best T_p can go down to near zero! Thus, if an algorithm has a 10% serial portion, the speed increase that can be achieved by putting infinitely many processors to work would still be limited to ten times.

Therefore a judicious choice is needed in partitioning an algorithm and minimizing the serial portion.

Communication

When a large problem is broken into smaller tasks, it is necessary to set up a coordination between these tasks. To do this coordination we need communication links between the different tasks. The larger the number of pieces a problem is split into, the more communication links the resulting algorithm requires. In fact, the number of directed two-way communication links between any two tasks among n tasks could be $n(n - 1)$ and so the communication complexity grows quadratically. The communication problem introduces a new dimension to parallel programming and parallel architecture design. This means that in addition to the computing time and memory space requirements of an algorithm, we must also consider the communication costs and set a bound on the complexity of communication. This would imply that communication between tasks which are not close enough (closeness being measured by a suitably defined criterion for an architecture or for a program) should be avoided; that is, the communication should preferably be confined to only those processes that are very close neighbours.

When a large number of processors are assigned to carry out the split tasks, it is possible that simultaneous request or access to certain data or tasks may create a conflict or collision. This could slow down the anticipated speed advantage resulting from the multiple processors, or may even lead to a state of inactivity or standstill when two processes or processors wait for each other indefinitely (deadlock), or may delay some process indefinitely (lockout). Since the computational speeds for different tasks are unpredictable (non-deterministic), the different processes may become unsynchronized, leading to a total breakdown of the tasks.

The communication problem is therefore concerned with the minimization of communication complexity, prevention of deadlocks and improved coordination.

In recent years, the models and techniques employed to solve the three basic issues, namely decomposability, complexity and communication, have grown into a major interdisciplinary science of parallel processing. This science deals with both the theoretical studies and the practical aspects of design to achieve the best results. In this chapter, we shall present an overview of these studies in order to understand the many facets of parallelism. In later chapters, we shall make a more detailed study of these different facets.

1.2 Practical realization of parallelism

In the introductory section, the notion of parallelism was introduced by the informal statement 'many computers are put together to work, all simultaneously executing some portions of a procedure'. This statement is imprecise and requires further elaboration on the different practical ways in which several processors can be coupled together and the nature of the tasks that are handled. We shall now provide a more detailed explanation of these concepts.

1.2.1 Coupling of the processors

The task of assembling the processors to work together is called **coupling**. Two major methods are available for this purpose:

- tight-coupling method;
- loose-coupling method.

The tightly coupled network of processors shares a common or global memory and has centralized control. The processors are physically linked by a circuit or permanently wired switching mechanism.

The loosely coupled processors usually do not share memory and do not have a centralized control. They usually consist of a network of completely separate computers each with its own memory, control unit and central processing unit (CPU) connected via a message transfer system without establishing a physical connection path. For example, one may use a cable (called a **bus**) onto which all the computers are interfaced; sometimes a ring (a **circular bus**) is preferred so that the messages can be cycled until received by the specified processors. Also, a packet switching mechanism that transmits data in a packet may be used.

1.2.2 Nature of the tasks

There are two major categories in which computational tasks can be classified:

- mutually independent or non-interacting tasks;
- mutually dependent and interacting tasks.

In the case of mutually independent tasks, the input consists of many non-interacting or disjoint sets of data; on this data a common (or a different) set of operations is to be performed. To carry out these operations each processor works independently by dividing the problem suitably. The following are examples:

(1)   elementwise addition of several arrays;

(2)   A := B + C

        D := E – F

        G := B * H + F

When the tasks are mutually dependent, different tasks may be simultaneously executable, sometimes on common data. However, it is possible that a succeeding task is dependent on the outputs generated from one or more of the preceding tasks. In such a case there is a need for a mechanism to coordinate the arrival of the inputs with the succeeding tasks from the preceding tasks. For instance, one or more of the several required inputs may arrive at different time intervals, some earlier and some later; then the succeeding tasks have to wait before any action; otherwise, the computed input–output relations would not be the desired relations. To coordinate such a dynamic or time-varying situation, a synchronization mechanism of some kind has to be introduced. Such a mechanism should have the following properties:

(1)   the ability to detect actions performed by the interacting pro-
        cesses;

(2)   the ability to permit the data transfer at the appropriate time.

These two properties require that the communication between dependent processes and their synchronization go hand in hand and are, in general, inseparable.

The design of a parallel machine with many processors and the design of a program with many processes are critically dependent on the manner in which synchronization and communication take place. Several methods are available for the design of a parallel machine and for the design of parallel languages. These methods are essentially dependent on the methods used for coupling the processors, the nature of the tasks and the types of parallelism involved. We shall now, therefore, introduce the different types of parallelism that are currently known together with the terminology used for each type. Such an introduction will be useful for studying aspects of parallelism in greater detail later.

1.2.3 Different types of parallelism and terminology

1.2.3.1 Concurrency

Concurrency is an alternative term used to describe parallelism among a set of mutually dependent processes which communicate among themselves using some well-defined mechanisms. These mechanisms help to synchronize and permit data transfer between the different processes.

1.2.3.2   Multiprocessing–distributed multiprocessing

Multiprocessing is the execution of independent jobs in parallel using many computers. Usually a multiprocessor system consists of two or more computers executing different programs using the same memory. The processors and memory are interconnected through multiple memory ports or using a centralized switch.

The saving of time results from the sharing of the memory, tape drives and other expensive resources. The several processors are also designed to **time-share**; that is, to execute a number of programs at the same time – the processor does a bit of work on one, then goes on to the next, and so on, so that each program proceeds; however, at the level of the processors only one program is executed at each time unit called a **slice**. The user gets the impression of parallel execution, although at the machine level it is still serial.

When a centralized switch is used it is difficult to add new processors. To allow flexibility a distributed multiprocessor system in which each processor has a local storage is used. The local storage of every processor is accessible to other processors. Thus all processors share a common address space but storage units are physically distributed, each unit connected to one processor.

Here, each processor can access its local storage directly but to access other storage it must go through packet switching. In packet switching there is no direct electrical connection but the communication is through messages.

1.2.3.3   Pipelining

Many computers, especially the so-called supercomputers, use pipelines to increase their speed for number crunching. A **pipeline** is somewhat like an automobile assembly line, in which there are several processing stages. Each processor repeatedly executes the same instruction on successive pieces of data received from a preceding processor. This approach is useful when a procedure or an instruction can be broken down into small components, so that each component can be assigned to a different stage in the pipe; thus the results (output) of one processor become the input of the next processor. This is also known as multiple-instruction single-datastream (MISD) processing. Using this terminology, a conventional single-processor computer that works on one set of data may be called a single-instruction single-datastream (SISD) processor.

The pipelining technique is appropriate for applications in which the major functions are dependent on each other and the data sets are very large, for example signal processing of real-time data.

1.2.3.4 Multipass algorithms, interleaving, pipes and co-routines

A multipass algorithm consists of several subalgorithms or tasks. Each task can communicate with its adjacent task and conversely. Hence the communication between the two tasks takes place in a symmetrical manner. This permits us to interleave the execution of two or more tasks; such an interleaving is sometimes called **quasiparallelism**. When a collection of concurrent processes has processes in which the output of each process is used as the input to another, the information flow resembles a pipeline. An example of this kind occurs in the UNIX operating system. UNIX uses the concept of pipes for connecting programs or interleaving the execution of processes.

Co-routines are autonomous programs for executing multipass algorithms. They have some similarities to subroutines; however, the differences are more striking. A subroutine is a hierarchial structure. The relationship between the main procedure and the subroutine is an asymmetric or master–slave relation. The subroutine always starts at the beginning, completes its work and returns to the main procedure. A subroutine may call itself or other subroutines. In each case a subroutine completes its task and returns the control to its main procedure.

Co-routines have a symmetric relationship between the calling and called parts of the program and are not hierarchical. When a co-routine is invoked for the first time it starts from the beginning, executes for a period of time, and then transfers the control to another co-routine. After that, if called, a co-routine again starts where it left off the previous time. Co-routines do not require parameters, since they may not necessarily start from the beginning each time they are called. Also, it is not useful to have a co-routine call itself.

Co-routines are useful for interleaving tasks and hence in the design of operating systems. They are also useful for simulating concurrent processes where switching between processes is completely prespecified.

1.2.3.5 Vector–array processing

In vector–array processors, several tightly coupled processors arranged in a rectangular grid execute the same instruction, each on a disjoint set of data under a centralized control, for example vector addition. This kind of processor is called a single-instruction multiple-datastream (SIMD) processor. Such a processor is used as an attachment to a host supercomputer called the **front end**.

1.2.3.6   Network processors and distributed computing

In the network of processors, several processors are loosely coupled via a bus or a ring or telephone lines. Unlike the distributed multiprocessor, here each processor has its own local storage and there is no shared storage. In other words, we say the processors are loosely coupled. Usually, here the communication takes much longer than the processing time involved.

Typical examples are the ARPANET which connects computers in the US and Europe and the ETHERNET.

Here each processor can execute a different sequence of instructions on a different set of data. This kind of processing is also called multiple-instruction multiple-datastream (MIMD) processing. MIMD processing can be done together with multiprogramming, to be described in the next subsection.

Some MIMD computers can be tightly coupled, sharing a common memory. If, however, the shared memories are disjoint, the system is called multiple single-instruction single-datastream (MSISD) processing. This is nothing but a set of several independent SISD uniprocessor systems.

1.2.3.7   Multiprogramming (scheduling)

When two or more programs share the resources of a single CPU, we call it multiprogramming. When two or more processors are involved it is called multiprocessing. Thus multiprocessing is a hardware concept while multiprogramming is a software concept. Multiprogramming increases the CPU utilization by always having something for the CPU to execute by properly scheduling the jobs or suitably interleaving them. Essentially such a concept evolved for the design of multiuser operating systems. Thus multiprogramming handles a queue of jobs and schedules them to maximize the performance of the computer system.

When several processors are loosely coupled in a network, it is obviously necessary to improve the performance and to balance the load in each processor by properly routing the jobs to the various processors. Multiprogramming techniques are therefore useful for the design and optimization of systems that work in parallel.

We now turn our attention to the description of parallel processes.

1.3   Description of parallel processes

Traditionally, computer users are taught to program for processes which are essentially sequential. In such sequential computer programs, a list of statements is sequentially executed. The sequential nature gives rise to a deterministic set of operations. Therefore, a sequential program is easily described with the help of flow diagrams containing the following well-known structured primitive deterministic constructs (or boxes) (Alagic and Arbib, 1978):

(1)   begin (start);

(2)   assignment (set);

(3)   if B then S else T (decision);

(4)   while B do S (indefinite loop);

(5)   for i = 1 to n (definite loop);

(6)   end (halt).

In the case of parallel or non-sequential programs, in addition to the above constructs we need the following mechanisms:

(1)   parallel initiation and termination mechanisms;

(2)   synchronization, protection and communication mechanisms.

We shall describe these mechanisms and their functions below.

1.3.1 Initiation and termination mechanisms

When a set of processes are non-sequential we need to have constructs that can begin a list of processes simultaneously and end a list of processes when all of them terminate. These are respectively called cobegin and coend constructs.

1.3.2 Synchronization mechanism

Also, when a set of processes are non-sequential, the processes may have several simultaneous inputs or outputs and they may need to pass data to one another or to communicate. Since the speed at which each process works is not determinable, non-determinism arises in linking the processes. For instance, even if several processes begin together they may not all end simultaneously. Therefore we say there is a **race condition** and the parts of computation containing such processes are **time critical**. A need therefore arises to introduce a mechanism to coordinate and control the temporal order in which processes are executed to realize a given non-sequential algorithm. Such a mechanism is called a **synchronization mechanism**.

The synchronization mechanism is essentially meant for handling the non-determinism that arises in the execution of different processes by providing choice and delay among the processes to coordinate them. Here two additional constructs, that is one for non-deterministic choice (selection) and another for delay (wait), are introduced to describe non-sequential programming in addition to the sequential constructs described above.

1.3.3   Protection mechanism

The synchronization mechanism alone is not adequate to carry out non-sequential programming. In order to coordinate the processes it is also necessary to prevent clashes among them. That is, we must restrict the access of a shared variable or a resource to one process at a time. This is achieved by using another mechanism called the **protection mechanism**. This protection mechanism prevents interference or clashes from other processes when a particular process is using a shared variable or a resource.

The sequence of statements in which access to a shared variable or a resource is to be exclusively provided to a process is called a critical section or critical region. When a process is about to execute its critical section we avoid a clash by ensuring that no other process is executing its own critical region at the same time. Then once an access is given to a process, the access by another process should again be excluded by a locking arrangement. When the process completes its work and leaves its critical region, the access by another process should be allowed by an unlocking process. In other words, the protection mechanism should provide a locking facility for each process to do its critical section and to unlock and come out to let the other processes do their own critical sections.

1.3.4   Synchronization methods

Two distinctly different methods are used for synchronization among processes.

(1)   **Shared-variable method**
      In this method, synchronization and communication among the processes are achieved using shared mechanisms under a centralized control.

(2)   **Message-passing method**
      In this method the processes are autonomously controlled in sending and receiving messages, without sharing data; they are coordinated by using delay and wait operations among them.

These two methods have contributed to the development of new styles of programming languages for concurrent programming. These will be outlined in Section 1.7 and studied in detail in a later chapter.

The design of methods for the description of parallel processes and the synchronization and protection mechanisms has been a very active area of research during recent years. As a result of these studies, new concepts and analytic models have been developed for the programming, complexity and analysis of parallel and concurrent processes. We shall study these aspects in the following sections.

1.4 Modelling computational power and complexity of parallelism

The theory of computation is concerned with the study of different formal models of computation such as (Denning *et al.*, 1978):

(1)   machine models (for example finite state machines, Turing machines);
(2)   recursive function models;
(3)   production or grammatical models;
(4)   Markov algorithms.

These models evolved with a view to understanding the relative computing power of the various machines, algorithmic solvability, language recognition and generation capabilities, and the study of complexity of computations.

To extend these models for parallel computation, it becomes necessary to understand the effect of adding non-deterministic choice and coupling of actions in the above sequential models. These studies have been directed to understanding the following basic questions.

(1)   **Expressive power**
Can one design certain functions by parallel programs which cannot be expressed by sequential programs? In other words, are there functions that can only be associated with a concurrent system?

The question of expressive power has practical importance in specification, verification and modelling for concurrent programs.

(2)   **Linguistic constructs**
What are the basic constructs for a concurrent programming language?

(3)   **Complexity**
Which problems can be solved substantially faster in parallel computers? What are the effects of non-determinism and parallelism in speeding up algorithms whose time for execution grows exponentially with the input size?

(4)   **Architecture**
What are the most satisfactory models for parallel computation which reduce complexity and are easily buildable? What are the different kinds of mechanisms that are needed in a parallel architecture in contrast to the original von Neumann architecture?

In the following sections we briefly deal with some of the above aspects; they are discussed in later chapters in greater detail.

1.5   Modelling parallel control and data mechanisms

Two mechanisms are basic to any program organization. These are:

(1)   the control mechanism: this mechanism is responsible for the execution of instructions;
(2)   the data mechanism: this mechanism is responsible for providing the required data objects to an instruction as well as communicating the data objects to other instructions.

In the classical architecture, known as the von Neumann architecture, the control mechanism is sequentially organized. This mechanism executes the instructions one by one. The data mechanism uses named memory cells as a means to pass data objects between instructions. In other words, a common name is shared by the instruction generating the data object and the instruction consuming it. This common name is embedded in these instructions; so, when the control mechanism executes an instruction, the embedded names are referenced for the input to an instruction and also to the output from an instruction. Therefore this data mechanism acts 'by reference'. Also, the control steps together with the embedded data objects flow sequentially. In other words there is 'one-dimensional' or 'single-thread' control flow.

When parallel computations are involved, there is no sequential flow of instructions embedded with data objects. First, the data objects in the parallel computation are generated and consumed concurrently and non-deterministically. Therefore the control mechanism needs to be decentralized. Further, an instruction is to be executed only when either all the required input data objects are **available** or as and when a **need** arises. Also, the data mechanism in such cases need not necessarily act by reference. It may be preferable to pass the data objects 'by value' directly between the selected instructions rather than storing them and then referencing. Such a direct communication would eliminate read–write in memory cells, thus saving time in the computation. Furthermore, it would also avoid 'side effects' that may otherwise arise from the collisions of names among shared objects or program variables.

With these basic ideas we can now classify the different models based on control and data mechanisms.

(1) **Multithread control flow model**

This model is based on the program's explicitly containing the special parallel instructions for initiation, termination and synchronization of processes such as fork, join and wait to control the order of execution of the operations. There is a centralized control and the sequence of instructions is handled by program counters. Data objects are passed between instructions via references to shared memory cells. Hence this computation is known as **control-driven** computation.

(2) **Dataflow model**

In this model there is decentralized control. The instructions are executed as soon as the required input data objects are available. The program is explicitly structured in terms of flow of information between various instructions. In other words, the communication between instructions is direct without sharing memory. Also, no program counters are used. The intermediate output values are consumed and not available for re-use. The data dependences constrain the order of computations. Hence it is known as a **data-driven** computation.

(3) **Reduction model**

This model denotes the computation organization where instructions are only selected when the value they produce is needed by another already selected instruction. Usually the by value data mechanism is used and the result is directly passed between instructions (see Peyton Jones (1988)).

A **demand-driven** computation performs only those computations required to produce whatever output is demanded. Therefore it is in general more economical.

Associated with each of the above models one can design a particular class of programming languages and a particular class of supporting architectures because of the different ways the data and control mechanisms work (see Chapters 5 and 7).

In the following section we consider some of the issues concerning efficient architectures for parallelism.

1.6   Efficient architectures for parallelism

Having outlined the fundamental concepts involved in parallel computation, we now consider the more practical aspect of the design of efficient parallel computer architectures. Here the main issues that need consideration are as follows (see Uhr (1984) and Treleaven and Vanneschi (1987)).

1.6.1   Special- or general-purpose systems

This concerns whether the parallel system is meant for only specialized tasks or for a general purpose (for example, the array and vector processors are special-purpose parallel machines).

1.6.2   Grain size (granularity)

The capability and the number of the basic processors used in a system determine the grain size. Machines with a few tens of large processors (large word size and large memory capacity) are called coarse grained, while machines with several hundreds of smaller processors (small word size and small memory capacity) are called medium grained. Those with several thousands of processors (small word size and very small memory capacity) are called fine grained.

1.6.3   Interconnection (topology)

The general communication network through which the processors are interconnected plays a very important role. For example, the processors could be connected by rings or as elements in trees or as a mesh or as a torus. It is necessary to determine the best interconnection pattern for a given algorithm or alternatively to achieve the desired interconnection by either switching or programming.

1.6.4   Tightness of coupling

This factor determines whether the processors share a global memory and a clock (tight coupling) or they do not share a global memory or a clock (loose coupling). The natures of the control and data mechanisms are determined by the tightness or looseness of the coupling.

1.6.5 Control and data mechanisms

As mentioned in Section 1.5, there are three different control and data mechanisms: these are control-driven, data-driven and demand-driven mechanisms. The use of each one of these mechanisms is dependent on the programming language used and the supporting architecture. Which one of these mechanisms is best suited?

1.6.6 Task allocation and routing

This is one of the most difficult issues. Having chosen the interconnection pattern and the control–data mechanisms, we must now find the most effective way to allocate the tasks to the different processors for implementing a given algorithm. This problem is also known as the **mapping** of the program onto the machine architecture.

There are two strategies for task allocation – static and dynamic. In static allocations, the tasks are allocated once for all initially as determined by the topology and coupling or by an external control. In dynamic allocation, the tasks are varied from processor to processor to balance the load. This is analogous to 'dynamic programming' and 'scheduling'. Also, one could devise a combination of the dynamic and static strategies.

Another important issue is whether to perform the task allocation when the program is run or when it is compiled. If the program is not well suited for a specific architecture the task allocation may take excessive amounts of time. Alternatively, one can allocate the tasks during compilation. In this case the best results are achieved if the compilation produces a program that is best suited for the given architecture. The procedure to determine whether a given program is best suited involves the comparison of the flow of the activities of a program with the communication activities of the machine. For this purpose, the activities of a program are represented by a directed graph (program graph) and the communication activities of the machine are also represented by another directed graph (machine graph). The best results are achieved when the program and the machine graphs have the greatest resemblance (in mathematical terminology, **isomorphism**); the greater the difference between these two graphs, the greater the cost of communication.

1.6.7 Reconfiguration

We just mentioned that the best way to do parallel computation is to find a best match between the machine graph and the program graph. Since it is a very difficult problem, it has been suggested that the pattern of connections in a machine should be changeable under external program control. This principle is used in a new architecture called the 'connection machine' architecture (Hillis, 1985).

1.6.8 Programming languages

Several types of programming languages are currently used – imperative (for example FORTRAN, Pascal), applicative or functional (for example LISP) and logic (for example PROLOG) languages. Should one modify these languages to cope with the new architectures or design new languages with appropriate architectures?

1.6.9 Nature of technology

VLSI technology is currently the most used for building a large number of processors. At present, new holographic optical computing elements are available and are making an impact on the newer computer architectures (Feitelson, 1988). Which will be the most suitable technology for a given type of architecture?

1.6.10 Performance evaluation

There are numerous parallel computer architectures currently. What are the measurement units (**metrics**) as predictors of machine–algorithm performance? This study will be useful for the commercial production of architectures; see Stone (1988).

1.7 Parallel–concurrent programming styles – evolution

The classical von Neumann architecture had a central processor that was strictly sequential. Thus, when the central processor initiated an external operation, it simply monitored some register and idled until the operation was complete. To have a better utilization of the central processor, the interrupt-driven hardware facility was later introduced. This facility permits the processor to engage in other activities until the external operation is complete, thus improving the processor utilization.

Later operating systems were introduced to take advantage of high speed asynchronous architectures. These operating systems were written in high level sequential programming languages and permitted several independent 'user processes' to be run in an interleaved fashion. The introduction of time sharing then gave the illusion of parallelism while at the same time achieving a high degree of processor utilization.

Further advances in hardware created coordination and scheduling problems. Therefore the operating system design became more demanding from the programming point of view. Since the sequential programming languages have no specific constructs for creating and managing interactions among the concurrent processes, new *ad hoc* low level mechanisms (operating close to hardware) such as test set and semaphores (see Chapter 2) were used for synchronization and mutual exclusion among the processes.

Also, the well-known UNIX operating system, introduced two basic mechanisms known as fork and join. The fork operation splits a parent process into two processes, each of which can run concurrently until required. The join operation recombines the two processes into one process with a provision for waiting (delay) if needed. The synchronization and communication is then achieved by using the join operation appropriately (Section 2.4).

The fork–join and other related low level mechanisms are too primitive and are not structured syntactic constructs. Further, they were *ad hoc* mechanisms specifically tailored for use in operating systems that do not demand a very high degree of communication among processes. In other words, the bandwidth requirement for communication (number of messages sent or received by a processor in one instruction execution time) is low. To improve the bandwidth as well as clarity in programming and for efficient compilation it is therefore essential to introduce new syntactic constructs (in programming languages) that can handle the three common features of concurrency:

(1)   the ability to express concurrent execution;
(2)   process synchronization;
(3)   interprocess communication.

Depending on the techniques used for incorporating the above three features, parallel programming styles can be classified (Perrott, 1987).

1.7.1   Classification

Two major classifications arise from whether the languages are control driven or data driven (Section 1.5). There are, of course, combinations of these two aspects suggested recently.

1.7.1.1   Control-driven languages

The control-driven languages are again classified as

(1)   synchronous parallel languages;
(2)   asynchronous parallel (concurrent–distributed) languages.

Synchronous parallel languages   The synchronous parallel languages are meant for handling mutually independent or non-interacting tasks (Section 1.2). They are used for performing the same computations on different sets of data. They are also known as 'supercomputer languages' since they are meant for processing large amount of data which can be processed in parallel in supercomputers. Examples of this kind occur in tightly coupled vector and array processors, where the same operation is applied simultaneously and repeatedly to a sequence of operands.

Most existing supercomputer languages are based on FORTRAN. Modifications are made to FORTRAN for expressing parallel execution (called 'vectorization') on a disjoint set of data. There are no special facilities for interprocess communication. The synchronization is achieved by using parallel expressions for DO loops and assignments; hence they are called synchronous languages.

Asynchronous parallel–concurrent languages   Asynchronous languages are used for concurrent and distributed programming. Therefore the following facilities are to be added over and above those instructions available in the sequential programming languages:

(1)   A way to separate sections of code which can be executed in parallel.
(2)   A method of saying that a process can now be executed.
(3)   A way to guarantee mutual exclusion of data which is shared. The sequence of statements that refer to a variable which is shared by another process is called a critical region. The mutual exclusion facility prevents one process from tampering with the data when the other is using it.
(4)   Synchronizing the processes using wait and signalling.
(5)   Mechanism for delaying a process by a fixed amount of time.
(6)   Assigning priorities to processes.

The asynchronous languages fall under three classes:

(1)   procedure-oriented languages;
(2)   message-oriented languages;
(3)   operation-oriented languages.

The procedure-oriented languages are extensions of the sequential procedure-oriented languages, such as Pascal. In these languages the process interaction is based on shared variables. Ada, concurrent Pascal, Pascal Plus and Modula-2 belong to this class.

The message-oriented languages provide for interprocess communication by using instructions such as send and receive for messages. Languages such as CSP (communicating sequential processes), Ada and occam belong to this class.

The operation-oriented languages provide for remote procedure call as the primary means for process interaction. These languages combine aspects of the message-oriented and procedure-oriented languages. When shared memory is available, an operation-oriented language can be implemented like a procedure-oriented language; otherwise it can be implemented using message passing. Languages such as Ada and StarMod belong to this type.

We shall study these languages further in Chapters 2, 3 and 7.

1.7.1.2 Data-driven languages

The dataflow and reduction models decribed in Section 1.5 provide the basis for these languages. Example of dataflow languages are Irvine dataflow (ID) and the value algorithmic language (VAL) (see Chapter 7).

There are also demand-driven languages (reduction) currently under development.

In addition, there are languages such as PARLOG, concurrent PROLOG, and GHC which use PROLOG as the basis and with added features of non-determinacy and dataflow-like synchronization (see Chapter 7).

Associated with the design and use of each of the programming languages is its semantics and the validation of programs written in that language. We shall study these aspects in the next section.

1.7.2 Parallel language implementation

New programming styles require new methods for language design, system and compiler design. Also, they require a wide range of new support tools for productive software development. This is a rapidly growing research area; see Hilfinger (1983).

1.8 Semantics of parallel programs

The complete definition of a programming language is divided into syntax, semantics and pragmatics. Syntax defines the grammatically valid sentences; semantics assigns the meaning of these sentences in the respective domains. Pragmatics is concerned with the usage of the language.

A very important aspect of a programming language is to provide the users with a concise, mechanical method to interpret the meaning of a program and to establish its correctness. To say that a program is correct means that it meets the specifications. In other words, we are interested in properties such as

(1)   does the program compute correct values for all permissible input values?

(2)   does the given program terminate for all possible permissible input values?

1.8.1   Correctness of sequential programs

Two important methods that have been developed for proving the correctness of sequential programs are (Krishnamurthy, 1983; Alagic and Arbib, 1978):

(1)   the method of inductive assertion;
(2)   the functional method.

1.8.1.1   Method of inductive assertion

The method of inductive assertion works as follows. Attach the assertion $A(D)$ describing the imput data D to a program P; also attach assertion $A(P)$ describing what the program is supposed to accomplish. Then the program P is said to be partially correct (with respect to $A(D)$ and $A(P)$) if the program when executed with D either terminates with $A(P)$ true or fails to terminate. Thus a program is partially correct even if it fails to terminate for some (or all) values of the input data D that satisfy $A(D)$. All we need to prove is that, if the program terminates, the results are correct.

A program is called totally correct with respect to $A(D)$ and $A(P)$ provided that it is partially correct with respect to $A(D)$ and $A(P)$ and P terminates for all values of D satisfying $A(D)$. In other words, we must prove that the program terminates and the results are correct.

1.8.1.2   Functional method

The functional method uses the recursive definition for the functions computed by the program. Recursion is a very compact and natural way to describe all computable functions. Also, the recursively defined functions can be interpreted as fixed points of a set of functions and we can use the induction rule to prove their properties.

The functional method to prove termination relies on the existence of least fixed points over a partially ordered set of sequences. Every program is treated as a finite description of a function. Thus as a sequential computation proceeds the program produces better and better approximations (under a suitable measure or ranking) to the result that improve monotonically and continuously (see Section 3.3.6.8). Eventually a least fixed point is reached at which stage computation can be terminated, with the desired interpretation for the result.

The assertional method leads to what is known as 'axiomatic semantics' while the functional method leads to 'denotational semantics' for the sequential programming languages (Allison, 1987).

1.8.2 Correctness of parallel programs

In the case of sequential programs, it was adequate to prove only the correctness and termination properties. When dealing with parallel programs, we need to consider several other properties.

(1) **Continuous programs**

Some concurrent programs such as operating systems and real-time systems such as airline reservation systems and on-line database systems are supposed to run forever. A halt in these programs is an error condition. Thus in this case we have to modify our definitions of correctness for these types of program. The continuous or cyclic behaviour is called **responsiveness**. Responsiveness ensures readiness of the program to work forever.

(2) **Mutual exclusion**

We need to ensure that in the critical regions the mutual exclusion of processes holds.

(3) **Deadlock absence**

When there are several concurrent processes, all these processes may end in a tie, competing for the same resources. Then all the processors will idle. This is called **deadlock**. There should be a proof for the absence of such a deadlock.

(4) **Livelock absence**

In deadlock all affected processes are suspended indefinitely. Another acute condition arises when a collection of processes are inhibited from proceeding, but are still executing. This is called **livelock**. A typical example would be a collection of interacting processes stuck in loops in which they are not doing any useful work (see Sections 2.5.3 and 2.6.1). We must ensure that there is no livelock.

(5)   **Accessibility**
A complementary property to mutual exclusion is accessibility. When two processes are mutually excluded from a critical region, and one process gets access, we must show that eventually the other process will get there without the protection mechanism's holding it forever. Accessibility guarantees that every process will eventually enter its critical region.

(6)   **Lockout**
Sometimes it may happen that certain processes cannot proceed even though the other processes are proceeding. For example, if processes are given priorities then a low priority process may never gain access to a busy resource. This is called a lockout or **individual starvation**. Absence of lockout ensures that individual starvation will not arise.

(7)   **Fairness**
When there is a repetitive choice among alternatives, fairness means that no alternative will be postponed forever. This means that all processes get just or fair treatment with respect to the choices that may occur.

In order to prove all the above properties we need to introduce several different models. A graph model known as a Petri net is one of the earliest models. Recently several other models have been proposed. We shall study these models in Chapter 3.

Also there have been attempts to extend the approaches of axiomatic semantics and denotational semantics. We shall describe the studies related to semantics of parallel programs in Chapter 4.

Having reviewed the many facets of parallelism, we now briefly comment on the design of parallel algorithms.

1.9   Devising parallel algorithms

The act of devising an algorithm is believed to be an art and may never be fully automated. Devising a parallel algorithm is much more than an art and requires, on the part of its designer, the precision of a mathematician, the skill of an engineer and the training of a scientist; for this is the meeting point of all disciplines – art, mathematics, computing and VLSI technology. While the concept of a sequential algorithm is an ancient one, independent of the notion of modern computing machinery, the concept of parallel algorithms is clearly of recent origin (1970s) and evolved together with the emergence of large-scale integration and the availability of computers at low costs. The design of a parallel algorithm is very intricately woven with the new technology used for the basic processor design, grain size, nature of interconnections, tightness of coupling, control and data mechanisms used and programming styles. It is therefore essential that every practical parallel algorithm provides a clear specification of the nature of the architecture used, the data structures chosen and the mode of synchronization and communication, as well as the computation and communication complexities.

1.9.1 Design strategies

There are no clear-cut design methods that are known for devising algorithms to any specific problem. However, experts in algorithm design classify nine major strategies (see Horowitz and Sahni (1983), Baase (1988), Aho *et al.* (1983), Quinn (1987), Jamieson *et al.* (1987), Paull (1988) and Harel (1987)).

1.9.1.1 Divide-and-conquer strategy

Decompose the problem into subproblems, solve the subproblems, then combine the resulting solutions to the subproblems into a solution to the problem. This is a very widely used strategy.

EXAMPLE 1.1 _____

Consider the problem of multiplying two $n \times n$ matrices $\mathbf{A}$ and $\mathbf{B}$, where $n = 2^k$. Let $\mathbf{A}$ and $\mathbf{B}$ be partitioned as four $2^{k-1} \times 2^{k-1}$ matrices $\mathbf{A}_{ij}$, $\mathbf{B}_{ij}$ as shown below and the product $\mathbf{C}_{ij}$ be computed thus:

$$\begin{bmatrix} \mathbf{A}_{11} & \mathbf{A}_{12} \\ \mathbf{A}_{21} & \mathbf{A}_{22} \end{bmatrix} \begin{bmatrix} \mathbf{B}_{11} & \mathbf{B}_{12} \\ \mathbf{B}_{21} & \mathbf{B}_{22} \end{bmatrix} = \begin{bmatrix} \mathbf{C}_{11} & \mathbf{C}_{12} \\ \mathbf{C}_{21} & \mathbf{C}_{22} \end{bmatrix}$$

The products

$$\mathbf{C}_{11} = \mathbf{A}_{11}\mathbf{B}_{11} + \mathbf{A}_{12}\mathbf{B}_{21}$$
$$\mathbf{C}_{12} = \mathbf{A}_{11}\mathbf{B}_{12} + \mathbf{A}_{12}\mathbf{B}_{22}$$
$$\mathbf{C}_{21} = \mathbf{A}_{21}\mathbf{B}_{11} + \mathbf{A}_{22}\mathbf{B}_{21}$$
$$\mathbf{C}_{22} = \mathbf{A}_{21}\mathbf{B}_{12} + \mathbf{A}_{22}\mathbf{B}_{22}$$

can be simultaneously computed in parallel using eight processors, each processor carrying out 2^{3k-3} multiplications. Thus instead of a total of 2^{3k} multiplication time units in a single processor, we can carry out this matrix multiplication using eight processors eight times faster.

In this example, the divide-and-conquer strategy is useful, since it breaks the problem into mutually independent tasks with no need for interprocess communication.

1.9.1.2   Greedy method

Here one makes as many possible attempts as one can to search for the solution without considering any potential drawbacks (heuristic search).

EXAMPLE 1.2

A well-known example for the use of the greedy method is the knapsack problem. We are given n objects and a knapsack. Each object i has a weight w_i and the capacity of the knapsack is W. If a fraction x_i of object i, $0 \le x_i \le 1$, is placed in the knapsack then a profit $p_i x_i$ is earned.

The aim is to maximize the profit by filling the sack to its capacity. In other words, the problem is to find x_i that maximizes

$$\sum_{i=1}^{n} p_i x_i$$

subject to

$$\sum_{i=1}^{n} w_i x_i \le W, \, p_i > 0, \, w_i > 0$$

This problem can be solved using search strategy.

1.9.1.3   Dynamic programming method

This method is used when the solution of a problem involves a sequence of decisions.

EXAMPLE 1.3

The knapsack problem may be viewed as the result of a sequence of decisions. Here we need to find the optimal sequence of decisions to maximize the profit.

1.9.1.4   Search and traversal method

This method is useful for problems involving graphs and trees.

EXAMPLE 1.4

The creation of a spanning tree of a graph by depth-first search is a typical example.

1.9.1.5   Backtracking method

This is a very general technique which involves searching for a desired solution. If an attempt fails, the algorithm backtracks and searches in a different direction for a possible solution. This technique is useful for problems involving trees, paths and mazes.

EXAMPLE 1.5

A well-known example of the use of searching and backtracking is in the graph colouring problem. Here we want to find whether the nodes of the graph can be coloured using k colours so that no two adjacent nodes receive the same colour. The least integer k for which this is possible is called the chromatic number of the graph.

1.9.1.6   Branch and bound method

This method is a variant of the exhaustive search method but is more efficient since it utilizes the information obtained in earlier searches to avoid wasteful searches.

EXAMPLE 1.6

A typical example of the application of this method is for the travelling salesman problem. Here a salesman has to walk through all the nodes of a graph in such a way that the cost of travelling through the edges in minimized.

1.9.1.7   Algebraic transformation

The problem is transformed from one domain into another and solved; the resulting solution is then inversely transformed to obtain the solution in the original domain.

EXAMPLE 1.7

A typical example is the use of prime modular or residue arithmetic for parallel carry-free addition, subtraction and multiplication of integers.

The integer operands in a positional representation are first transformed to the residue form for different primes; then the arithmetic operation is performed in parallel and the results are combined using the Chinese remainder theorem (Section 1.9.4.6).

For example, if $a = 19$, $b = 17$ are two integers, and we choose three primes $p_1 = 5$, $p_2 = 7$, $p_3 = 11$, we carry out the parallel multiplication using the residues thus:

$$19 = (4 \bmod 5, 5 \bmod 7, 8 \bmod 11)$$

$$17 = (2 \bmod 5, 3 \bmod 7, 6 \bmod 11)$$

$$(19 \times 17) = (3 \bmod 5, 1 \bmod 7, 4 \bmod 11)$$

Using the Chinese remainder algorithm (Section 1.9.4.6), the right-hand side evaluates to 323.

1.9.1.8 Random trial methods

These methods are based on the use of random numbers for probabilistic searching or estimation.

EXAMPLE 1.8

A well-known example is the Monte Carlo method for inverting a matrix.

1.9.1.9 Approximation methods

These methods do not generate exact results. They generate an approximate solution in a much shorter computing time.

EXAMPLE 1.9

A well-known example is for finding the chromatic number of a graph within a bounded value.

The above-mentioned strategies are not mutually exclusive and a combination of these may be needed together with a suitable choice of data structures and architectures to devise a parallel algorithm. It should be noted that for any specific problem it may often be possible to design algorithms for various choices of data structures and architectures.

1.9.2 Choice of architectures

The standard architectures used are classified under two major classes (Uhr, 1984):

(1)   synchronous computers;
(2)   asynchronous computers.

1.9.2.1 Synchronous computers

Synchronous computers can have either a central control or a distributed local control mechanism. The SIMD machines have central controls. There is another class of synchronous computers known as 'systolic processors'. These processors have distributed local control mechanisms (Kung and Leiserson, 1980) (see also Chapter 5).

The systolic machines have regular structures and a fine grain size. The name 'systolic' refers to the rhythmic act of the performance of the machine in pumping data in and out analogous to that of the heart. In systolic processors, each processor has a small memory and the communication paths are simple and regular.

The SIMD and systolic machines are designed with different interconnection geometries. Some of the well-known geometries are (Uhr, 1984):

(1)   linear arrays;
(2)   square arrays;
(3)   hexagonal arrays;
(4)   triangular arrays;
(5)   tree structures;
(6)   other specialized networks such as pipelines, butterflies, cubes, shuffle networks, pyramids, prisms and hypercubes.

The main issue here is the choice of a suitable interconnection network for implementing a given algorithm.

1.9.2.2 Asynchronous computers

The MIMD computers are composed of a number of independent processors sharing the primary memory by a connection network. These computers are called 'asynchronous' since they have a distributed control. Usually they have a coarse grain size.

Asynchronous processors are the most suitable ones for performing concurrent computations which consist of a collection of co-operating or interacting processes that communicate with each other.

The choice of a suitable class of architecture needs a careful evaluation. Some evaluation criteria are available.

1.9.3   Evaluation criteria

An important topic for research is to study the relation between the algorithms and the supporting multiprocessor communication structures to understand the run-time performance. There are several important factors that are to be considered by the designer:

(1)   Diameter: this is the worst-case time to get a message from one processor to another in a network.

(2)   Bandwidth: total number of messages that can be sent or received by processors in one instruction execution time.

(3)   Message capacity: this gives a measure of congestion in the network.

(4)   Complexity and speed-up: for each type of architecture one has to evaluate the complexity of the algorithm with respect to input size and comparison of speed-up with respect to sequential computing.

We shall consider these aspects in Chapter 5.

1.9.4   Some parallel algorithms

In this section we provide some examples of parallel and concurrent algorithms. These will be described in an informal style, in order to highlight some of the key issues involved in programming.

1.9.4.1   Parallel carry-free addition and multiplication

The use of residue arithmetic provides a parallel carry-free addition–multiplication algorithm for integers. Here the problem of addition–multiplication is broken into n mutually independent tasks which are simultaneously carried out in parallel using n processors.

Here no synchronization or communication between the processors is needed.

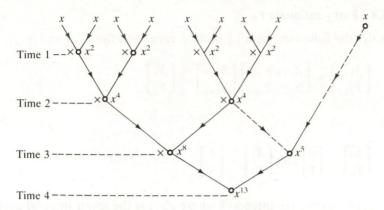

Figure 1.1   Computing powers of x.

1.9.4.2   Computing the power x^n

We can compute x^n where n is an integer by using $[\log_2 n] + 1$ processors (where [ ] denotes the lower integral part) in $[\log_2 n] + 1$ time units.

For example, if $n = 13$, the tree of processors shown in Figure 1.1 can be used to compute x^{13}. Note that in this example there is a mutual dependence between processes and precedence constraints, for example x^4 cannot be computed unless x^2 is computed by the earlier processors. There is a need for synchronization and interprocessor communication from the leaves of the tree to the root.

1.9.4.3   Computing the binomial coefficient

Consider the computation of the binomial coefficient

$$c(n, k) = \frac{n!}{(n - k)!\,k!} = \frac{n(n - 1)\ldots(n - k + 1)}{1 \times 2 \times 3 \ldots k}$$

for integers n and k such that $0 \leqslant k \leqslant n$. Here we use two processors, one for the numerator and another for the denominator computation.

The synchronization condition is needed to ensure that the division of the numerator by the denominator happens only after both the numerator and the denominator have performed $k - 1$ multiplications, that is after the numerator is multiplied by $n - k + 1$ and the denominator is multiplied by k.

Since the two processors may run at different speeds the synchronization condition is needed to ensure even divisibility. (The use of co-routines for this problem is given in Chapter 7.)

1.9.4.4   Farey rationals F_N

Consider the following parallel mutual recursion for X_{k+2} and Y_{k+2}.

$$\begin{bmatrix} X_{k+2} \\ Y_{k+2} \end{bmatrix} = \begin{bmatrix} Z_{k+1} & 0 \\ 0 & Z_{k+1} \end{bmatrix} \begin{bmatrix} X_{k+1} \\ Y_{k+1} \end{bmatrix} - \begin{bmatrix} X_k \\ Y_k \end{bmatrix}$$

given

$$\begin{bmatrix} X_0 \\ Y_0 \end{bmatrix} = \begin{bmatrix} 0 \\ 1 \end{bmatrix} \text{ and } \begin{bmatrix} X_1 \\ Y_1 \end{bmatrix} = \begin{bmatrix} 1 \\ N \end{bmatrix}$$

for a specified positive integer N where Z_{k+1} is the lower integral part of

$$\frac{Y_k + N}{Y_{k+1}}$$

For a specified N, the above recurrence computes reduced rationals ≤ 1 with denominator $\leq N$ arranged in increasing order of magnitude. The resulting sequence is called a Farey sequence F_N of order N. For example, given $N = 5$, we obtain

$$F_N = \{ 0/1,\ 1/5,\ 1/4,\ 1/3,\ 2/5,\ 1/2,\ 3/5,\ 2/3,\ 3/4,\ 4/5,\ 1/1 \}$$

To generate F_N the computation of Z_{k+1} needs to be carried out and the two processes for X_{k+1} and Y_{k+1} wait until Z_{k+1} is computed to proceed for the matrix vector product.

1.9.4.5   Sieving for prime numbers

One of the well-known methods for listing prime numbers less than N is the Eratosthenes sieve method.

In this method the integers from 2 to N are first listed; then in this list the multiples of 2 are crossed out; the remaining elements are again scanned and successively we remove all multiples of uncrossed numbers, starting from 3 and so on.

It is possible to use many processors to carry out this task; here the first process crosses out multiples of 2 and the second process crosses out multiples of 3 and so on with each successive processor trailing behind the preceding processor to remove multiples of uncrossed numbers.

This requires a synchronization among the different processors: that is, each succeeding processor starts its task as soon as the first uncrossed number is available and at the same time it does not overtake any preceding processor to do a wasteful task.

For example consider the case $N = 12$:
then we have the sequence

2, 3, 4, 5, 6, 7, 8, 9, 10, 11, 12

Let us label by p the processor which crosses out prime p. The synchronization must be such that processor 5 does not cross out 10 before processor 2 crosses it out; also, processor 5 should start as soon as processor 3 has not crossed it out.

For an implementation of a multiprocessor algorithm see Bokhari (1987).

1.9.4.6   Chinese remainder algorithm

This algorithm reconstructs an integer r given its n residues r_i (= r modulo p_i) with respect to n primes p_i ($i = 0, 1, \ldots, n - 1$) where

$$r \leqslant \prod_{i=0}^{n-1} p_i - 1$$

(Gregory and Krishnamurthy, 1984).

This example is chosen to illustrate the communication between processors. We assume that there are n processors labelled P_i each with four registers R_i (to hold r_i), D_i (the intermediate digits), S_i and M_i ($i = 0, 1, \ldots, n - 1$). It is assumed that each processor performs arithmetic addition, subtraction, multiplication and inversion over the field modulo p_i.

To describe the parallel algorithm we use the term 'in parallel' for parallel operations on all processors.

This algorithm is illustrated in Table 1.1 in tabular form for the choice $r_0 = 1, r_1 = 5, r_2 = 9, r_3 = 11$, and $p_0 = 5, p_1 = 7, p_2 = 11, p_3 = 13$:

```
For i = 0 to n − 1 do
  R_i := r_i ;
For j = 0 to n − 1 do
begin
  D_j := R_j ;
  For k = j + 1 to n − 1 in parallel do
  begin
    S_k := R_j ;      (interprocessor communication)
    R_k := R_k − S_k ;
    M_k := p_j^{-1} ;
```

$$R_k := R_k \cdot M_k \, ;$$
end
end

Remark
Then

$$r := D_0 + \sum_{j=1}^{n-1} D_j \prod_{k=0}^{j-1} p_k$$

where D_j are the mixed-base digits, is then accumulated by another processor P, in its register R, in parallel (not included in the above algorithm).

Table 1.1 illustrates how the various processors cooperate towards the solution. For instance, the second, sixth and tenth rows do $S_k := R_j$ and transfer data between processor j and all other processors $k \geq j + 1$. The manner in which this transfer is achieved depends on how we synchronize – whether by shared memory or message passing. The other rows perform computations which are mutually independent.

Table 1.1 Chinese remainder algorithm.

Operations	p_0 mod 5	p_1 mod 7	p_2 mod 11	p_3 mod 13	D_i	$r = P$
$R_i := r_i$	1	5	9	11	$D_0 = 1$	$R := 1 = D_0$
$S_k := R_0$		1	1	1		
$R_k := R_k - S_k$		4	8	10		
$M_k := p_j^{-1} = 5^{-1}$		3	9	8		
$M_k \times R_k$		5	6	2	$D_1 = 5$	
$S_k := R_1$			5	5		$R := R +$ $D_1 p_0 = 26$
$R_k := R_k - S_k$			1	10		
$M_k := p_j^{-1} = 7^{-1}$			8	2		
$M_k \times R_k$			8	7	$D_2 = 8$	
$S_k := R_2$				8		$R := R +$ $D_2 p_0 p_1 = 306$
$R_k := R_k - S_k$				12		
$M_k := p_j^{-1} = 11^{-1}$				6		
$M_k \times R_k$				7	$D_3 = 7$	
Result						$R := R +$ $D_3 p_0 p_1 p_2$ $= 3001$

The above algorithm demonstrates the fact that, for efficient parallel solution of a problem, efficient synchronization and communication are needed between the processors.

SUMMARY

In this introductory chapter we explored the many facets of parallelism. We started with the notion of parallelism and the basic issues of problem decomposability, complexity and communication. Following this we covered the basic concepts of practical realization of parallelism and the terminology used for the description of parallelism. Then we briefy discussed the modelling of the power and complexity of parallelism. The basic control and data mechanisms for program organization were then introduced. Then, we outlined the basic principles of the design of efficient architectures, styles of programming languages and their semantics. Finally, we described the design strategies for parallel algorithms, illustrated by simple examples.

EXERCISES

1.1   Consider the addition operation of two n-digit integers in a base of representation p.

    (1)   Break up the addition problem into sequential and parallel tasks.

    (2)   Which task limits the speed of addition?

1.2   Consider the multiplication operation of two n-digit integers in a base of representation p.

    (1)   Arrange the scheme into sequential and parallel tasks.

    (2)   What task limits the speed of multiplication?

1.3   Consider the euclidean algorithm for finding the greatest common divisor (GCD) of two positive integers m and n given by the conditional expression:

$$GCD (n, m) = [m > n \rightarrow GCD (m, n), m = 0 \rightarrow n,$$
$$GCD (m, REM (n, m)]$$

where REM (n, m) = positive remainder when n is divided by m.

    This is a sequential process. Can you think of any way to improve its speed by using a parallel method? (See Kannan *et al.* (1987).)

1.4   Describe how you can compute x^n where x and n are positive integers sequentially and in parallel when you have many processors. What is the best speed you can achieve by using many processors?

1.5   Consider a sequence of left and right parentheses.

(1)   Describe a sequential algorithm to match the left and corresponding right parentheses.

(2)   Is there a parallel algorithm to do this matching? (See Chapter 3.)

1.6   Is there a faster algorithm for obtaining only the remainder of a division of an n-digit decimal number by an m-digit decimal number ($m < n$) than the conventional long division method? Can it be parallelized?

1.7   The conventional matrix multiplication algorithm uses the inner (row by column) product of vectors as the basic operation. Think of a parallel algorithm for matrix multiplication based on the outer (column by row) product of vectors. (See Chapter 5.)

1.8   Describe a practical method used for multiplication or division of two decimal numbers based on the algebraic transformation.

1.9   How could the divide-and-conquer strategy be used for multiplication and division of two high precision (multiple-length) integers? (See Knuth (1981).)

1.10   Describe an algorithm for multiplication of matrices of size $2^n \times 2^n$ based on partitioning the given matrices into 2×2 matrices. Can we parallelize this algorithm?

1.11   Describe how you can use several processors to sieve primes using the Eratosthenes sieve method. (See Bokhari (1987).)

1.12   A set of n positive numbers are to be sorted in ascending order using n processors. Can you suggest an algorithm that takes the input unsorted datastream and sends out the output sorted datastream? If there are less than n processors will the scheme work? (See Section 2.7.2.6).

1.13   A very well-known method for parallel addition and multiplication of integers a, b within a range $0 \leq a, b \leq M - 1$ is the use of congruence arithmetic with respect to several primes $p_1, p_2, \ldots,$

p_n such that $M \leqslant p_1 p_2 \ldots p_n$. The results are then converted back to integers using a well-known theorem called the Chinese remainder theorem. Read about this and work out some examples. (See Gregory and Krishnamurthy (1984).)

1.14 Draw a synchronous (clock-controlled) scheme using two processors for computing the recurrences:

$$f_n = f_{n-1} + g_n$$
$$g_n = f_{n-1} + g_{n-1}$$

given $f_0 = 1, g_0 = 0$. Merge the two sequences in the order g_i, f_i ($i = 0, 1, \ldots$). (The resulting sequence is called a Fibonacci sequence.)

1.15 Draw a synchronous (time-stepped) scheme using three processors for computing the recurrences:

$$f_n = f_{n-1} + g_n + h_n$$
$$g_n = f_{n-1} + g_{n-1} + h_n$$
$$h_n = f_{n-1} + g_{n-1} + h_{n-1}$$

given $f_0 = g_0 = 1$ and $h_0 = 0$. Merge the three sequences in the order h_i, f_i, g_i ($i = 0, 1, 2, \ldots$).

1.16 Assume that an unlimited number of processors are available. Then how fast can you evaluate

$$P(x) = a_n x^n + a_{n-1} x^{n-1} + \ldots + a_0$$

for a given value of x. Compare with the conventional sequential method:

$$P_n = a_n$$
$$P_i = p_{i+1} x + a_i \text{ for } i = n - 1, \ldots, 0$$

with $P_0 = P(x)$ (Horner's rule).

References

Aho A.V., Hopcroft J.E. and Ullman J.D. (1983). *Data Structures and Algorithms*. Reading MA: Addison-Wesley

Alagic S. and Arbib M.A. (1978). *The Design of Well-structured and Correct Programs*. New York: Springer

Allison L. (1987). *A Practical Introduction to Denotational Semantics*. Cambridge: Cambridge University Press

Baase S. (1988). *Computer Algorithms*. Reading MA: Addison-Wesley

Bokhari S.H. (1987). Multiprocessing the Sieve of Eratosthenes, *IEEE Computer*, **20** (April), 50–8

Denning P.J., Dennis J.B. and Qualitz J.E. (1978). *Machines, Languages and Computation*. Englewood Cliffs NJ: Prentice-Hall

Feitelson D.G. (1988). *Optical Computing – A Survey for Computer Scientists*. Cambridge MA: MIT Press

Gregory R.T. and Krishnamurthy E.V. (1984). *Methods and Applications of Error-free Computation*. New York: Springer

Harel D. (1987). *Algorithmics – The Spirit of Computing*. Reading MA: Addison-Wesley

Hilfinger P.N. (1983). *Abstraction Mechanisms and Language Design*. Cambridge MA: MIT Press

Hillis W.D. (1985). *The Connection Machine*. Cambridge MA: MIT Press

Horowitz E. and Sahni S. (1983). *Fundamentals of Computer Algorithms*. Rockville MD: Computer Science Press

Jamieson L.H. Gannon D. and Douglas R.J. (1987). *The Characteristics of Parallel Algorithms*. Cambridge MA: MIT Press

Kannan R., Miller G. and Randolph L. (1987). Sublinear parallel algorithm for computing the gcd of two integers. *SIAM J. Computing*, **16**, 7–16

Knuth D.E. (1981). *The Art of Computer Programming*, 2nd edn., Vol.2. Reading MA: Addison-Wesley

Krishnamurthy E.V. (1983). *Introductory Theory of Computer Science*. New York NY: Macmillan

Kung H.T. and Leiserson C.E. (1980). Algorithms for VLSI processor arrays. In *Introduction to VLSI Systems* (Mead C. and Conway L., eds.), pp. 271–92. Reading, MA: Addison-Wesley

Paull M.C. (1988). *Algorithms Design*. New York NY: Wiley

Perrott R.H. (1987). *Parallel Programming*. Wokingham: Addison-Wesley

Peyton Jones S.L. (1988). *The Implementation of Functional Programming Languages*. Englewood Cliffs NJ: Prentice-Hall

Quinn M.J. (1987). *Designing Efficient Algorithms for Parallel Computers*. New York NY: McGraw-Hill

Stone H.S. (1988). *High Performance Computer Architecture*. Reading MA: Addison-Wesley

Treleaven P.C. and Vanneschi M. (1987). Future parallel computers. *Lecture Notes in Computer Science*, **272**

Uhr L. (1984). *Algorithm Structured Computer Arrays and Networks*. New York NY: Academic Press

Chapter 2
Processes – Interaction and Description

2.1 Introduction

In the previous chapter (Section 1.2.2) we mentioned that processes can be divided into two major categories:

(1) those which are mutually independent or non-interacting, and
(2) those which are mutually dependent and interacting or co-operating.

These two categories require further elaboration in the context of practical situations arising in the design of parallel programs, real-time computing systems and operating systems. Such an elaboration of the variety of processes that occur in a parallel computing environment will be useful for the modelling and analysis of parallel computing systems. These in turn would aid the improvement in reliability and the efficiency of parallel computing systems. With this in mind, we now study the basic principles of concurrent processes in relation to general program design.

2.2 Processes and their events

A typical program in a higher level language contains components such as:

(1)   assignment statements;
(2)   iterations;
(3)   conditionals;
(4)   execution of procedures.

We may use the term **process** to describe these components. A process itself may be composed of other processes. The size of the processes chosen for the introduction of parallelism is quite arbitrary and may vary widely depending on the resources, time complexity and the available technology.

The basic size of a process chosen for parallelism is called the **granularity** or **grain size**. The granularity can be at the following three levels:

(1)   *Data level:* here the parallelism results in effecting the same operation on multiple data items simultaneously, for example vector addition. We also call this 'fine granularity'.

(2)   *Operational level:* here the parallelism arises by the execution of independent instructions simultaneously, for example consider (a + b) * (c/d); here we can execute + and / simultaneously. We call this 'medium granularity'.

(3)   *Task level:* here the parallelism is at a specific task level or program level, for example simultaneous reading from a database. We call this 'coarse granularity'.

2.2.1 Interleaving

A convenient way to think of parallelism between different processes is by using the logical notion of interleaving. Let a_1; a_2; a_3 and b_1; b_2 be the basic instruction (or event) sequences of processes P and Q respectively. Then by interleaving of these instruction (or event) sequences we mean that the given precedence orders a_1 precedes a_2 precedes a_3 and b_1 precedes b_2 are to be retained while introducing events b_1 or b_2 between events a_1, a_2 or a_3. Thus, for example, the following interleavings are possible:

a_1; a_2; a_3; b_1; b_2
a_1; a_2; b_1; a_3; b_2

$a_1; b_1; b_2; a_2; a_3$
$b_1; b_2; a_1; a_2; a_3$

Naturally the number of possible interleavings can grow very rapidly (exponentially) if no constraints are placed on the interleaving modes. The nature of parallelism is dependent on the constraints placed on the interleavings. As the number of constraints increases, the number of possible interleavings is reduced. These may be precedence constraints introduced by process interactions and communication.

For example, interaction among processes introduces certain precedence constraints. Also, when some resource is used by a sequence of events of one process, this process is in its critical section and so one should not permit the interleaving of other processes involving the shared resource. This is called mutual exclusion of processes and it places constraints on the interleaving of processes. In some contexts, the process P may be producing some message or data in one of its events and process Q may have to consume this message or data as soon as it is available. This places yet another kind of constraint on the interleaving of the events.

2.2.2 Non-determinacy

We saw earlier that, when there are many basic events in each process, the number of possible interleavings of events grows very rapidly. When we deal with sequential programming, the selection of events from processes is precisely determined, leading to a deterministic behaviour of the compound process. Thus in a single-thread control the interleaving of events is constrained to a specific determinate sequence.

Non-determinacy means that there exist multiple possible sequences of operations. Sometimes we may not be able to prescribe or influence the choice of interleaving of events. The compound process then exhibits a non-deterministic behaviour. The correct behaviour of the compound process can be interpreted in two ways:

(1)   There exists a sequence of events that produces a result (of the compound process) satisfying certain specified conditions; otherwise the result is undefined.

(2)   The result (of the compound process) is the same for all permissible interleavings which satisfy specific constraints.

In concurrent computing, interpretation (2) is used for non-determinacy; in fact the proofs of correctness of concurrent programs and transaction processing in databases are based on this interpretation. (See Sections 3.7.2 and 8.4.)

2.3   Independence of processes

Informally, the term 'independence' means that one process or its execution does not directly depend in any way on the execution of another process. In other words, independent processes can be executed without any necessity for communication or synchronization between them until each one finishes and reaches a common end. Usually such processes have their own set of resources and do not share any of these or other data objects.

An example of this kind is the addition of two vectors, where each vector has n components which are added in parallel using n processors.

As another example, consider the assignments

    a := 5; b := 4; c := 3

With three processors, these assignment statements can be executed concurrently. Also, they can be executed in another order since there is not time dependence between them.

However, consider the assignments

    x := 5; x := 4

These cannot be made concurrently. Thus we see that, for the processes to be independent, they should not share common resources at the same time and should not have name collisions (that is, each different process receives a different name). Conversely, it is the sharing of the names or resources that introduces dependence and interaction among the processes.

2.4   Specifying concurrent execution

When several independent processes $P_1, P_2, \ldots, P_n$ are to be executed simultaneously on multiple processors, it is required to have a notation for the compound command that initiates all the processes, executes them and, when all the processes terminate, shifts the control to other processes. For this purpose the command

    cobegin $P_1, P_2, \ldots; P_n$ **coend**

is used. This command causes $P_1, P_2, \ldots, P_n$ to start simultaneously and to proceed concurrently until they have all ended. An equivalent compound command is **parbegin** $P_1, P_2, \ldots, P_n$ **parend**.

A more powerful notation is **fork** and **join**. The **fork** operation creates a new process – that is, two processes continue from one initial process. In **join** the two processes are recombined into one process. For example, we may use **fork** and **join** as below:

Program P	Program Q
. . .	. . .
fork Q	. . .
. . .	. . .
join Q	**end**.
. . .	

Execution of Q is initiated when the **fork** in P is executed. Programs P and Q then execute concurrently until either P executes the **join** Q statement or Q terminates. If P executes the **join** Q first, it will wait until Q completes execution. After P reaches the **join** and Q terminates, P executes the statements following the **join**.

The **fork–join** technique is appropriate for applications in which no major function requires the results of any other; that is, each major function is independent of the others, for example one may compute the mean and the median of some set of data simultaneously.

The UNIX operating system makes extensive use of variants of **fork** and **join** for specifying concurrent processes (Bourne, 1980). There are several differences, however, between **fork–join** statements and **cobegin–coend** (or **parbegin–parend**) statements. The **fork–join** statements provide a direct mechanism for dynamic process creation including multiple activations of the same process. The **cobegin–coend** statements provide a structured single-entry, single-exit control structure and are not as powerful as **fork–join**.

2.4.1   Identical independent processes

When the programs $P_1, \ldots, P_n$ are identical, it is desirable to reduce the burden of declaring the subtasks to be carried out in each program. Thus provision should be made in the programming notation to have a common task declaration and indicate specific instances of this task in $P_1, \ldots, P_n$.

As an example for parallel independent and identical processes consider the simultaneous searching for the n real roots of a polynomial along the real line by using the divide-and-conquer strategy (Maeder and Wynton, 1987). Let us assume that n processors are available. We divide the given search interval into n equal subintervals. Then the process of determining at each such subinterval whether the function contains a zero is an independent and identical task. Using this method we can reject those subintervals in which no zeros exist. Then repeat this process of *n* subdivisions and searching in those subintervals containing zeros. In this way the intervals shrink and ultimately we can simultaneously reach a smallest subinterval where each root lies (subject to a suitable tolerance).

2.4.2   Non-identical independent processes

In this case the programs $P_1, P_2, \ldots, P_n$ have different tasks to perform; in other words, the basic atomic instructions which are needed for each of $P_1, \ldots, P_n$ are not identical and vary very widely. Therefore each program or process needs to have its own declarative part for each of these tasks.

A simple example of this situation arises in the realization of the three parallel independent processes such as reading, processing and writing; also, in such a situation it may be required to perform concurrently the operations of reading and writing, by reading the *n*th line when the $(n - 1)$th line is printed and so on.

Remarks
(1)   The programming language Ada (Perrott, 1987) has the facilities to carry out both identical and non-identical tasks.
(2)   The programming language occam (Perrott, 1987) uses the parallel constructor PAR followed by the component processes. This construct causes the component processes to execute simultaneously and terminates when its component processes have finished.

2.5   Dependent processes

When two or more processes are brought together to cooperate and each process operates only on its local objects (that is resources, variables and events that exclusively belong to that process) no interaction occurs and independence is preserved. However, when processes operate on shared objects at the same time, a collision is bound to result, unless some kind of control is imposed on the manner in which the objects are to be shared between the processes.

A real-world example of this situation arises in road traffic. Here the shared object is a portion of the road. Mutual exclusion can be introduced for traffic flow on a straight road in the two opposite directions by using either the 'keep left' or the 'keep right' rule. However, when two roads intersect, we need a system of priority (such as the vehicles coming from the right have the right of way) or traffic lights (semaphore) or a traffic policeman to control the traffic flow; these devices ensure mutual exclusion of the shared parts of the road.

It must be remembered, however, that these devices such as semaphores or policemen are indirect external mechanisms for control and these mechanisms are themselves shared.

Another way to achieve mutual exclusion is by providing each vehicle with its own signalling device or a message-passing communication system (such as a two-way radio) to tell the other vehicle drivers which portion of the road is being used. Such a system is too sophisticated to be of practical use for the road traffic. However, this system is needed for air traffic control where a lot of information needs to be communicated; here each aircraft in flight can autonomously and directly communicate the relevant details, such as coordinates, speed and direction, to other aircraft in the vicinity in order to ensure mutual exclusion and to avoid collisions.

Note that the message communication method for control is autonomous and direct (unlike the semaphore-like mechanisms) to achieve mutual exclusion. Thus the message-passing method is well suited for distributed computing systems and data-driven systems with autonomous control.

2.5.1 Synchronization

From the above real-world analogies, we see that basically two methods are available for the mutual exclusion of processes to allow access to a common resource without collisions:

(1)   use of shared mechanisms that indirectly control access to shared objects (shared-variable method);

(2)   use of direct autonomous or distributed communication (message-passing method).

Using either of or a combination of these methods, we can introduce an order restriction to avoid collisions. This order restriction is given the name **synchronization**. It must, however, be remembered that the indirect mechanisms that control access to shared object do not themselves transfer data, whereas the use of direct communication can transfer data as well as implement synchronization.

The synchronization mechanism (whether direct or indirect) can control the traffic flow in two distinct ways:

(1)   by delaying the execution of a process (as in the use of horn or hand or hazard signals in a vehicle); this is called **conditional synchronization**;

(2)   by treating a group of events as an indivisible unit so that no

interference is possible when these events are executed together (as in a traffic flow when the green signal is on); this is called **mutual exclusion**.

2.5.2 Conditional synchronization

When two processes share a data object which is in a state inappropriate for executing a particular operation, such an operation should be delayed. For example, consider the recursion (Section 1.9.4.4) for generating Farey rationals. We need to compute Z_{k+1} before computing X_{k+2}.

Similarly in computing the ratio $C(n, k)$ in Section 1.9.4.3 we must synchronize the product formation in numerator and denominator before the division operation.

2.5.3 Critical section problem

The notions of mutual exclusion and critical section were briefly introduced in the previous chapter. We now elaborate these notions further.

Let two processes P and Q be executed in parallel. Let each contain a critical section in which no interleaving of processes should be permitted. For example, the process P might access a shared device (such as a disk); in such a case this task should not be performed by both processes simultaneously. The property stating that the processes will never simultaneously execute their respective critical sections is called **mutual exclusion** with respect to the pair of critical sections.

When n processes are cooperating, no more than one process should be allowed to execute in its critical section. This is called the **critical section problem**. A solution to this problem should preferably be independent of the hardware features or the number of processors or relative speeds of the processes. Also, such a solution should ensure that the following conditions are satisfied:

(1)   When any one process is in its non-critical section or not attempting to enter its critical section, it does not prevent any other process entering its own critical section; that is, there is no blocking or livelock.

(2)   When a number of processes are waiting to execute their critical section, no process is neglected for ever (that is, there is no lockout). There is a bound on the number of time each process is allowed to enter its critical section after a process has made a request to enter its critical section and before that request is

granted. When there are n processes, there must be an assurance that each will enter its critical section within $n - 1$ times; this is called **fairness** (Francez, 1986).

(3) Two processes about to enter their critical sections cannot, by entering infinite waiting loops, postpone the decision on which one actually enters indefinitely (that is, there is no deadlock).

2.5.4 Devices for synchronization

The devices used for synchronization depend on whether the shared-variable method or the message-passing method is used for interprocess communication.

The shared-variable method communicates through sharing of variables. Here the responsibility for providing the communication rests usually with the user; the operating system only provides the shared memory. Hence we say the communication is **indirect**.

The message-passing method allows each process to be autonomous and to exchange messages directly; here the operating system is directly responsible for communication. We say the communication is **direct** since there is no need for shared variables.

2.6 Shared-variable synchronization mode

There are five principal devices used for synchronization in the shared-variable mode (Andrews and Schneider, 1983; Peterson and Silberschatz, 1983; Raynal, 1986):

(1) busy waiting;
(2) semaphores;
(3) conditional critical regions;
(4) monitors;
(5) path expressions.

2.6.1 Busy waiting technique

This technique is useful when hardware provides a single test and set instruction. Usually this method is applicable to only two processes. Each process can test or set a value for a shared variable.

To provide for mutual exclusion of two concurrent processes P and Q, a common integer variable LOCK is introduced. LOCK is set to 0 (or 1) initially. If LOCK = 0, then P is allowed to execute its critical section. When P finishes its critical section, it sets LOCK = 1 to allow Q to execute its critical section. This means that each process should test the variable LOCK as to whether it is 1 or 0 to enter its critical section; otherwise, it has to wait until its turn arrives. This is called **busy waiting**; the process waiting for access to its critical section is said to be **spinning**. The variable LOCK is called a **spinlock**.

To describe the algorithm SPINLOCK, we use the following notation:

SPINLOCK :: I; [P ∥ Q]; F

in which :: denotes 'consists of' and ; denotes 'followed by' which means that SPINLOCK consists of an initial part I, a set of two communicating processes P and Q, and a final part F. The processes P, Q are component processes whose concurrent composition forms the main body of the program; only when P and Q both terminate is F executed. In other words,

P ∥ Q means **cobegin** P, Q **coend**

Also, for the loop construct we use the statement **repeat** . . . **forever** which has the same meaning as **repeat** . . . **until false**. The **repeat** . . . **forever** statement also indicates that these programs are to run forever cyclically as in typical operating or real-time systems.

An equivalent construct is loop . . . end used in Modula 2. Also while B do S or repeat S until B where B is a boolean expression and S is the body of the loop has the following meaning: while takes a single statement and repeat takes a sequence of statements (separated by semi-colons); while tests whether B is true before the body S is done and repeat tests whether B is true after the body S is executed at least once.

The statements such as while B do, or while B do spin, or while B do skip, or while B do delay, or while B do nothing, where the loop body S is empty are all equivalent, testing whether B is true on each iteration. When B turns false the loop terminates and execution continues with the next statement. Thus these statements represent wait or delay loops.

Using this notation the SPINLOCK algorithm with the shared variable LOCK reads as follows:

var LOCK: integer
SPINLOCK :: LOCK := 0; [P∥Q]

where

P :: **repeat**
    Execute non-critical section;

```
        while LOCK ≠ 0 do
            spin;
        Execute critical section;
        LOCK := 1
    forever;
Q :: repeat
        Execute non-critical section;
        while LOCK ≠ 1 do
            spin;
        Execute critical section;
        LOCK := 0
    forever;
```

There are three drawbacks in using the spinlock:

(1)   If the process P is much faster than process Q and P has to enter its critical section more often then Q, it still needs to wait for Q and follow the frequency of Q, since Q controls the entry of P and conversely.

(2)   If for some reason process Q halts and fails to return then P is blocked; this is a livelock since P is stuck without doing any useful work.

(3)   If for some reason P enters its critical section and loops forever then Q can never enter its critical section and gets blocked forever. This situation is also a livelock, since neither P nor Q is doing any useful work.

There have been several attempts to obviate the above difficulties in solving the critical section problem for two processes and for the general case of n processes. An ingenious solution for the case of two processes was given by Dekker and for the case of n processes by Dijkstra. These solutions ensure three constraints, that is mutual exclusion, no blocking and fairness, on all the processes.

Remark
The theory of locking is one of the most important areas of study in database concurrency control. (See Chapter 8; also see Papadimitriou (1986).)

2.6.1.1 Dekker's algorithm

The use of the spinlock device as explained earlier has three drawbacks which arise because each process on its own turns the variable LOCK on and off to let the other process enter its critical section. These drawbacks are removed in Dekker's algorithm by using an external umpire to control the two processes.

To explain Dekker's algorithm we use a real-world example in which two aeroplanes are competing to land or take off in a small airport with one runway.

Let us denote the two landing (or taking-off) processes of the aeroplanes by P and Q and let the umpire be the control tower. Let the processes P and Q have flags (or indicators), call FLAGP and FLAGQ respectively, each of which can be set to GREEN or RED. We also assume that each aeroplane can express its intention to use the runway (or enter its critical section) by setting its flag GREEN. Upon termination of the operation it can set the flag to RED to indicate that it is out of its critical section.

The control tower (TOWER) assigns priority among the processes by setting LANDP or LANDQ to indicate respectively whether P or Q is granted permission to use the runway.

In this algorithm each process can inspect the intention of the other process to see whether a conflict arises; each process enters its critical section only if the other process is outside its critical section. The TOWER resolves the conflicts by assigning the priority. When a process exits from its critical section, the TOWER changes its priority to permit the other process to perform its critical section; if, however, the other process does not want to enter, the priority is altered.

Dekker's algorithm

```
var (to be declared suitably);
    SAFELAND :: (TOWER, FLAGP, FLAGQ) := (LANDP, RED, RED); [P‖Q]
    (This is the main program in our convention)
```

where

```
P :: begin
        repeat
            FLAGP := GREEN;
            while FLAGQ = GREEN do
            begin
                If TOWER = LANDQ then
                begin
                    FLAGP := RED;
                    while TOWER = LANDQ do
                    delay using runway;
                    FLAGP := GREEN;
                end (if );
            end (while);
            P uses runway;
            TOWER := LANDQ;
            FLAGP := RED;
        forever
    end;
```

and

```
Q :: begin
       repeat
           FLAGQ := GREEN;
           while FLAGP = GREEN do
           begin
               If TOWER = LANDP then
               begin
                   FLAGQ := RED;
                   while TOWER = LANDP do
                   delay using runway;
                   FLAGQ := GREEN;
               end (if );
           end (while);
           Q uses runway;
           TOWER := LANDP;
           FLAGQ := RED;
       forever
       end;
```

The proof of the correctness of this algorithm is available in Peterson and Silberschatz (1983) and Francez (1986).

Dekker's algorithm was extended to *n* processes by Dijkstra. However, such an extension is not of much practical use when compared with the solution offered by another synchronization device called semaphores, which we shall describe in the next section.

2.6.2 Semaphores

Semaphores are very powerful synchronization devices. These were suggested by Dijkstra (1968a, 1968b) as an alternative means to reduce the complexity involved for achieving mutual exclusion of *n* processes using busy waiting.

A **semaphore** S is an integer variable than can be altered in its value by two operations P (for the Dutch word 'passeren' meaning 'pass') and V (for the Dutch word 'vrijgeven' meaning 'release'). P and V are also sometimes called 'wait' and 'signal' respectively.

The operations are defined thus:

P(S): **while** S $\leq$ 0 **do** skip (nothing);
        S := S − 1;
V(S): S := S + 1;

The modifications (test and decrement) to the integer values are executed atomically as an indivisible operation. This means that, when any one process is modifying the value of a semaphore, another process cannot modify the same semaphore value. If, however, two processes execute P(S) and V(S), these operations will be sequentially executed in an arbitrary order. It is to be remembered that assignments or tests of value of S are prohibited except for the initial assignment in the main program.

A semaphore is called a binary semaphore if it assumes only binary values 0 or 1. A semaphore is called a general or counting semaphore if it assumes arbitrary non-negative integer values.

To implement a solution to the mutual exclusion problem, each critical section is preceded by a P operation and followed by a V operation on the same semaphore. All mutually exclusive critical sections use the same semaphore which is initialized to 1.

For implementing conditional synchronization, shared variables are used to represent the condition and a semaphore associated with the condition is used to achieve synchronization. After a process has made the condition true, it signals by using the V operation; a process delays until a condition is true by executing a P operation (see Section 2.6.2.2).

For controlling resource allocation general semaphores are useful. The initial value of S is then set to the number of units of resource available; P or V is respectively executed when a unit of resource is utilized or is returned. A semaphore can be thought of either as a shared variable or as a message-passing device. In this sense the semaphore can be fitted into both the procedure-oriented and message-oriented languages.

2.6.2.1   Mutual exclusion

To illustrate the use of a binary semaphore SEMA consider the program Q with two concurrent processes: Q1 which reads from a common database and Q2 which writes to a common database.

var SEMA: semaphore;

Q :: SEMA := 1; [Q1∥Q2]

Procedure Q1 ::	Procedure Q2 ::
begin	**begin**
repeat	**repeat**
P(SEMA);	P(SEMA);
read;	write;
V(SEMA);	V(SEMA);
forever	**forever**
end;	**end**;

Here whenever Q1 or Q2 is executing its critical section read or write respectively they are mutually exclusive.

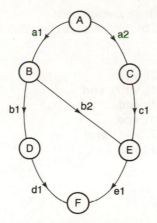

Figure 2.1   Precedence of processes.

2.6.2.2 Precedence constraints and conditional synchronization

One important application of a semaphore is for indicating the precedence order and synchronization of two or more processes. Hence the use of a semaphore together with the cobegin and coend statements becomes as powerful as the fork–join statements. This is explained below.

Let Q1 and Q2 be two processes such that a statement q2 in Q2 should be executed only after the statement q1 in Q1 has been executed. Then we use a common semaphore (COSEM) initialized to 0 and insert the statements:

    q1;
    V(COSEM);

in Q1 and the statement

    P(COSEM);
    q2;

in Q2. Since COSEM is 0 initially, Q2 can execute q2 only after Q1 has invoked V(COSEM).

The above concept can be used for executing a complex program containing may processes with precedence constraints.

For example, consider the precedence of processes given by the directed graph Figure 2.1. The process names are the nodes and the seven semaphores used to control the precedence order are named across the directed edges: a1, a2, b1, b2, c1, d1, e1. The program PRECEDENCE can then be written in the extended notation thus:

```
var a1, a2, b1, b2, c1, d1, e1: semaphores;
PRECEDENCE :: (a1, a2, b1, b2, c1, d1, e1) := (0, 0, 0, 0, 0, 0, 0);
begin
  cobegin
    begin A; V(a1); V(a2); end;
    begin P(a1); B; V(b1); V(b2); end;
    begin P(a2); C; V(c1); end;
    begin P(b1); D; V(d1); end;
    begin P(b2); P(c1); E; V(e1); end;
    begin P(d1); P(e1); F; end;
  coend;
end.
```

2.6.2.3   Producer–consumer system

Some systems consist of two parts that are dependent on each other only through one variable called BUFFER that appears in both parts. One part, called the producer, puts a product in BUFFER each time when it is called. The other part, called the consumer, consumes the product each time it is called. Obviously, for this system to be useful, the two parts have to be called alternately by a control process. It should be ensured that the producer stores the product until the consumer is ready and the consumer does not starve; also, if the producer produces a surplus quantity, the storage is able to store and release the product for the consumer at an appropriate rate. The BUFFER acts as a storage for this purpose.

To allow concurrent production and consumption processes there must be a synchronization. If the BUFFER has unlimited capacity there is no difficulty for the producer in storing items. However, if the BUFFER is limited in size, the producer has to wait when the BUFFER is full; if the BUFFER is empty, the consumer has to wait until an item arrives. For the sake of simplicity we do not assume any structure within the buffer, except that it has a finite capacity.

The semaphore device turns out to be useful to describe the producer–consumer system. We assume that the BUFFER size is limited to holding n items. In the program PROCON below three semaphores are used:

(1)   OCCUPANCY – a general semaphore to count the number of items occupying the BUFFER;

(2)   VACANCY – a general semaphore to count the number of vacancies in BUFFER;

(3)   EXCLUSION – a binary semaphore to provide mutual exclusion for access to the BUFFER.

var OCCUPANCY: semaphore (general);
   VACANCY: semaphore (general);
   EXCLUSION: semaphore (binary);
PROCON :: (OCCUPANCY, VACANCY, EXCLUSION) := (0, n, 1); [Q1||Q2]

(PRODUCER) Q1 ::	(CONSUMER) Q2 ::
begin	**begin**
repeat	**repeat**
Produce item	P(OCCUPANCY);
P(VACANCY);	(reduces occupancy)
(reduces vacancy)	P(EXCLUSION);
P(EXCLUSION);	. . .
. . .	Remove item from BUFFER
Add item to BUFFER	. . .
. . .	V(EXCLUSION);
V(EXCLUSION);	V(VACANCY);
V(OCCUPANY);	(increases vacancy)
(increases occupancy)	Consume item
forever	**forever**
end.	**end**.

2.6.2.4 Uses of semaphores for other problems

We shall for the sake of completeness mention other classical problems of concurrency such as the readers–writers' problem and the dining philosophers' problem for which semaphore devices can be applied, although not efficiently.

The readers–writers' problem This problem arises in an airline reservation system. Several operators, each using a terminal, issue boarding passes for a flight. Flight reservations are in a shared file. Reading the file (called **a reader process**) permits an operator to check a reservation. Writing the file (called a **writer process**) allows a clerk to include a new passenger who had no reservation. Thus the reader process never modifies a shared file, while a writer process modifies it. Hence writer processes must mutually exclude all the other reader and writer processes, but multiple reader processes can access the shared file simultaneously. The constraints are therefore:

(1)   Waiting readers are given priority over the waiting writers after a writer finishes.

(2)   A waiting writer is given priority over the waiting readers after all the readers finish.

There are several variants to this problem.

The dining philosophers' problem The dining philosophers' problem (Hoare, 1985; Ben-Ari, 1982) is as follows. Five philosophers share a common table and five chairs. Each chair is reserved for one philosopher. At the table there is a perennial food dish and there are five forks and five plates. Usually a philosopher's life is one of thinking and eating. A philosopher who feels hungry sits in the correct chair and picks up the two forks on either side of the plate. (We assume that a philosopher needs two forks to eat.) If the philosopher's neighbours have already picked up the two forks the philosopher cannot eat. If two forks are available the philosopher takes the food from the perennial food dish, eats and places the forks back (Figure 2.2).

The problem is to devise a protocol (a code of conduct) that will allow the philosophers to eat. The protocol must satisfy the following requirements:

(1) Mutual exclusion: no two philosophers fight for the same fork.

(2) Absence of deadlock: if all the philosophers sit and each one takes the right-hand fork simultaneously then every one is delayed forever and a deadlock results; this should be avoided.

(3) Absence of starvation: a philosopher who never gets right and left forks starves. This must not be allowed. For example, if philosophers 1 and 3 conspire, they can lock out and starve to death philosopher 2. We shall consider this problem later in Section 2.6.3.2.

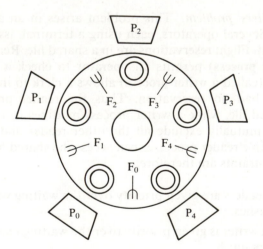

Figure 2.2 Dining philosophers' problem.

2.6.2.5   Limitations of semaphores

The use of semaphores can lead to errors. For example, if a process interchanges the operations of a semaphore EXCLUSION and we have

    V(EXCLUSION);
    . . .
    critical section
    . . .
    P(EXCLUSION);

several processes may enter the critical section.

Also, if by mistake we exchange V(EXCLUSION) with P(EXCLUSION) and write

    P(EXCLUSION);
    . . .
    critical section
    . . .
    P(EXCLUSION);

a deadlock will result.

Similarly, omission of P(EXCLUSION) or V(EXCLUSION) or both will violate mutual exclusion and result in deadlock.

Further, the semaphores are not structured devices. Both mutual exclusion as well as conditional synchronization are described by the same P and V notation.

Also, the semaphore operation is very primitive in its semantic content. A process can only test whether an integer variable is zero and if so the process is suspended. Thus we have no way of making a compound test on several semaphores.

To overcome these limitations, a more powerful construct critical region (CR) was introduced by Hoare and Brinch Hansen and later this was improved to the conditional critical region (CCR) construct (Brinch Hansen, 1973, 1977; Hoare, 1972).

2.6.3   Critical region construct

A CR is a primitive construct for mutual exclusion. Here a variable r (for resource) of type T which is to be shared among many processes can be declared:

    var r: **shared** T;

the variable r can be accessed only inside a region statement:

region r **do** S;

which means that, while S is executed, no other process can access r; the other processes are placed in a queue. When a process leaves a CR, another process from the queue is allowed to enter its CR.

To solve more difficult problems the construct CCR is used. Here the entry to a CR is allowed only if an entry condition (a guard) is satisfied. Thus we have here

region r **when** B **do** S;

where B is a boolean expression; B is to be evaluated and S is a statement list. A CCR statement delays executing the process until B is true; S is then executed. It must be remembered that regions referring to the same shared variable exclude each other in time. If B is false, the process must enter the queue of waiting processes.

The CCR construct separates the two distinct concepts of mutual exclusion and conditional synchronization. The mutual exclusion is provided by ensuring that the execution of different CCR statements each naming the same resource is not overlapped. Conditional synchronization is provided by the explicit boolean condition B. Thus CCR provides a structured notation that enables us to understand the concurrent program easily in terms of its component sequential programs and reduces the possibility of errors. Also, it enables us to prove the correctness of the concurrent program using the axiomatic method.

Brinch Hansen (1977) suggested an improvement in the CCR construct that permits the placement of a synchronization condition anywhere within the CR rather than only at the beginning. This is given below:

region r
  do begin
    S1;
    await (B);
    S2;
  end.

When a process enters the region it executes statement S1 (S1 may be null). Then B is evaluated. If B is true then S2 is executed; otherwise, the process relinquishes mutual exclusion and is delayed until B becomes true and no other process is in the region associated with r. As before, the region referring to the shared variable is declared thus:

```
var r: shared T
    . . .
end ;
```

2.6.3.1   Mutual exclusion

The mutual exclusion is obtained for the problem of Section 2.6.2.1 thus:

```
var r: Shared record
    . . .
end ;
Q :: [Q1‖Q2]
```

Procedure Q1 ::	Procedure Q2 ::
begin	**begin**
. . .	. . .
region r **begin** read **end**	**region** r **begin** write **end**
. . .	. . .
end	**end**

Remark

The construct **region** r **do** S can be implemented using the semaphore r thus:

```
P(r) ;
S ;
V(r) ;
```

2.6.3.2   Dining philosophers' problem

In Section 2.6.2.4 we briefly mentioned the dining philosophers' problem. It mirrors a fundamental case of competition for limited resources. We are required to design a protocol which does not deadlock and which does not lead to starvation.

We can use binary semaphores for this problem. This ensures that there is mutual exclusion in accessing the forks. The safety can be assured by permitting eating only after two forks on either side are available for each philosopher.

Thus the following program DINPHIL can be written using five binary semaphores declared as an array to denote the five forks; each philosopher is denoted by PHILi, i = 0, 1, 2, 3, 4.

```
var fork: array [0..4] of (binary) semaphore:
     i:     integer;
DINPHIL :: (fork: array [0, 1, 2, 3, 4] := [1, 1, 1, 1, 1]);
               [PHIL0‖PHIL1‖PHIL2‖PHIL3‖PHIL4]
```

where

```
Procedure :: PHILi (i  =  0, 1, 2, 3, 4)
            begin
               repeat
                  think;
                  P(fork[i]);
                  P(fork[i + 1] mod 5);
                  eat;
                  V(fork[i]);
                  V(fork[i + 1] mod 5);
               forever
            end.
```

This procedure results in a deadlock if all the philosophers take their left forks simultaneously. This is because the first P(fork[i]) operation sets all fork[i] to 0 so that no philosopher can do P(fork[i + 1]).

In order to avoid deadlock, we must make sure that each philosopher does not take a fork unless both of the forks are available. This would mean testing for a compound condition on the availability of two forks.

Also, one can solve the problem by restricting the number of philosophers entering the dining room (see Hoare (1985)). For instance, we can impose the condition that no more than four philosophers can enter the dining room. This would enable at least one philosopher to have two forks. Thus, by using an additional general semaphore to keep count of the number of philosophers entering the room, a procedure can be written (see Exercise 2.11).

We can, however, use a CCR construct (Brinch Hansen, 1973). In this solution a philosopher 'awaits' for the availability of two forks before picking up the two forks; having 'picked up' the two forks the philosopher is in a CR and reduces the 'fork availability count' of the right and left neighbours by one. This would keep others waiting.

A philosopher whose eating cycle is complete 'puts down' the two forks, again entering a CR. Now this philosopher increases the 'fork availability count' of the right and left neighbours by one. This would enable others to eat, under suitable conditions.

The procedure based on this logic is given in the next subsection.

2.6.3.3   Dining philosophers' problem – CCR application

The new procedure DINPHIL-CCR is given below; it uses an array of five general semaphores and CCR.

```
var r: shared record
          fork: array [0..4] of integer;
       end;
```

```
            i: integer;
  DINPHIL-CCR :: (fork array [0, 1, 2, 3, 4] := [2, 2, 2, 2, 2]);
                [PHIL0 ‖ PHIL1 ‖ PHIL2 ‖ PHIL3 ‖ PHIL4]
```

where

```
        Procedure :: PHILi (i = 0, 1, 2, 3, 4)
        begin
          repeat
            think;
            await fork[i] = 2;
            region r begin (pick up forks)
                fork[(i + 1) mod 5] := fork[(i + 1) mod 5] − 1;
                fork[(i − 1) mod 5] := fork[(i − 1) mod 5] − 1;
            end
            eat;
            region r begin (put down forks)
                fork[(i + 1) mod 5] := fork[(i + 1) mod 5] + 1;
                fork[(i − 1) mod 5] := fork[(i − 1) mod 5] + 1;
            end
          forever
        end.
```

A trace of the above procedure is given in Table 2.1. In this table, the rows indicate the names of philosophers engaged in their activities. The columns indicate the number of available forks called 'status': here fork[i] = 2 indicates that PHILi has two available forks and is eligible to eat. Initially all fork[i] = 2 to indicate that all PHILi are eligible to eat. The * notation indicates that PHILi is picking up the two forks.

Notice that it is possible that there is a lockout for PHIL3 if PHIL4 again picks up the forks at the last row. It is possible that under a suitable dynamic configuration PHIL3 always starves. This will not result in 'fairness'. When two of the philosophers, say PHIL2 and PHIL4, alternatively pick up their forks they can conspire a lockout for PHIL3.

2.6.4 Monitors

The devices described so far for mutual exclusion and synchronization will be dispersed throughout a concurrent program. Thus it is not easy for a reader of a program to understand all the different ways in which a resource is used. In this sense we may call these devices unstructured.

When dealing with large concurrent programs it is desirable to introduce a structuring device for data, as well as accesses to data; this device would then function as a centralized mechanism that controls or monitors certain types of critical functions. Such a device was suggested

Table 2.1 The dining philosophers' problem.

	Status					Summary of events
	fork[0]	fork[1]	fork[2]	fork[3]	fork[4]	
Start	2	2	2	2	2	All forks on table
PHIL0*	2	1	2	2	1	PHIL0 picks up forks
PHIL2*	2	0	2	1	1	PHIL2 picks up forks
PHIL1 PHIL3 PHIL4	2	0	2	1	1	PHIL1,PHIL3,PHIL4 think, expecting to eat; no change in fork status
PHIL0	2	1	2	1	2	PHIL0 puts down forks
PHIL4*	1	1	2	0	2	PHIL4 picks up forks
PHIL2	1	2	2	1	2	PHIL2 puts down forks
PHIL1*	0	2	1	1	2	PHIL1 picks up forks
PHIL4	1	2	1	2	2	PHIL4 puts down forks
PHIL1 PHIL3 PHIL4						Who will pick up forks?

by Brinch Hansen and Hoare to achieve this goal; it is called a **monitor** (Hoare, 1974).

The monitor is designed as a programming primitive. It consists of a collection of declarations of permanent variables which store the resource's state, followed by a set of procedure declarations which implement operations on the resources. The monitor has a body (**begin** ... **end**) which is a sequence of statements that is executed when the program is initiated. Once the initial values are assigned, the monitor functions as a package of data and procedures.

The important property of a monitor is that it permits only one of its procedure bodies to be active at a given time, thereby ensuring mutual exclusion. Even if two processes (the same or different) are called simultaneously, one of the calls will be delayed until the other is completed. Hence the procedure body functions like a critical region protected by the 'same' semaphore. Also the variables in the monitor are directly accessible only within the monitor procedures. Further, the only way to execute a monitor is to call a monitor procedure.

The synchronization is achieved explicitly by using two primitives 'wait' and 'signal' as follows. When a process is granted access to a monitor, it may request access to a resource. If the resource is busy, a wait command is generated; if the resource is released by another task, a signal command is generated. To achieve this, we introduce in the declaration part of the monitor a condition variable C. Two commands are applicable to C:

- wait(C)
  Current process is suspended and kept in a first-in-first-out queue until another process invokes signal(C).
- signal(C)
  Resumes a suspended process that has been waiting first in the queue.

The signal(C) operation has no effect if no process is suspended, that is the queue is empty.

Semaphores can be used to simulate monitors and conversely monitors can be used to simulate semaphores. Thus it is possible to transform a program containing monitors to one containing semaphores and conversely (Peterson and Silberschatz, 1983; Ben Ari, 1982).

2.6.4.1 Monitor simulating a semaphore

In order to illustrate the concept of a monitor, we simulate a semaphore. The monitor uses a boolean variable engaged and a condition state. If the semaphore is engaged, a wait condition is given; otherwise, a signal condition is given. Thus this monitor treats the semaphore as a resource and uses it. It is declared thus:

```
monitor semasimu;
var      engaged: boolean;
         state: condition;
procedure P; (acquire semaphore)
begin
   if engaged then wait (state);
   engaged := true
end;
procedure V; (release semaphore)
begin
   engaged := false
   signal (state)
end;
begin (monitor)
   engaged := false
end.
```

2.6.5 Path expressions

While the monitors are able to provide mutual exclusion, we still need to put in the wait and signal operations on condition variables for synchronization. This results in wait and signal operations being dispersed throughout the monitor. In order to avoid this difficulty it is desirable to collect all the constraints at one place. This is achieved by using a device called **path expression**, which defines allowable sequences of actions on shared resources. A path expression takes care of the mutual exclusion and enforces a specific order in which resources can be shared (Cambell and Habermann, 1974).

The path expression consists of a path list and a list of path operators. The path list contains the process names; the path operator specifies the linking of processes – whether sequencing, selection or concurrency. Thus the path expression provides an operational approach to synchronization, without explicitly coding it in the procedures. The path expression is not well suited for condition synchronization, since it is not always possible to predetermine the constraints on the use of resources. However, the path expressions are useful for studying the semantics of concurrent programs. Also, since the programmer need not explicitly specify the semaphores, errors are minimized.

2.7   Message-passing synchronization (or handshaking) mode

The message-passing mode of synchronization provides a greater flexibility for a large number of interacting processes – called distributed processes. This mode of synchronization is also known as **handshaking** since it involves the exchange of information.

2.7.1   Basic issues in handshaking mode

The basic operations needed for message passing are:

(1)   send (message);
(2)   receive (message).

For any two processes to communicate using these operations the following basic issues are to be considered:

(1)   Naming of processes so that the processes know each other's identity.

(2)   Size of the message – fixed or variable?

(3)   Capacity of links – is there a buffer storage?

(4)   Symmetric or asymmetric – can two processes communicate with each other symmetrically or only one way?

(5)   Introduction of non-determinism: to deal with a set of events whose order cannot be predicted in advance.

(6)   Termination: although each process communicates with others for a finite unbounded number of times, the program terminates.

(7)   Deadlock absence: no two processes should wait for each other for communication.

(8)   Chattering free: two processes do not communicate infinitely, ignoring other processes.

(9)   Fairness – there are three types of fairness:

  ● process fairness – each process will infinitely often communicate with others and conversely;

  ● channel fairness – each pair of processes is mutually willing (symmetric) to communicate;

  ● communication fairness – for specific communication between two processes there is no restriction.

(10)   Starvation free: no process is locked out as a result of the absence of any one of the three possibilities described in (9). In particular, we must ensure that several of the processes do not conspire against some of the other processes to lock them out.

2.7.2 Use of guarded commands

When two concurrent processes want to communicate they must go through two basic steps:

(1)   Synchronization: each process must contain in its program a statement that expresses its intention to exchange information with another process. If one of the processes arrives at its statement of intention earlier and the other arrives at its statement of intention later, the former has to wait until the latter reaches its proper point to synchronize.

(2)   Communication: once the processes are synchronized as above, they exchange messages.

In order to accomplish these two basic steps, special programming constructs are required. We will now indicate how the two concurrent programming languages CSP (communicating sequential processes) and

Ada accomplish these two steps using the guarded commands of Dijkstra (1975).

A guarded command is a statement list prefixed by a boolean expression. Only when this boolean expression is initially true is the statement list eligible for execution. The boolean expression is also known as a **guard** as it signals the execution of the statements following when true; when the guard is true we say the following statement is **open** for execution.

A set of guarded commands can be assembled together, separated by a punctuation symbol [ ]. This is useful for defining alternative and repetitive constructs.

The alternative construct begins with an **If** followed by the guarded command set and a **fi**. It also exhibits non-determinacy of choice. For example the alternative construct to output max(a, b) is given by:

```
If a ⩾ b → max := a
[ ] b ⩾ a → max := b
fi.
```

If in the initial state none of the guards is true, the program aborts; if several guards are true, an arbitrary choice will be made among one of the true guards, and the corresponding **'open statement'**, or **'open alternative'** will be executed.

The repetitive construct begins with **do** followed by guarded commands and **od**. When no guards are true the program leads to a termination. In other words, the repetition terminates if none of the guards is true; during the repetition any command may be selected for evaluation provided that its guard is then true. Since it is not required that the guards be mutually exclusive, non-deterministic selection is allowed: parallel execution corresponds then to the execution of two guarded commands whose guards are both true and which do not modify common variables. If no guard ever becomes false the program is non-terminating.

An interesting example is that for the determination of the greatest common divisor of two positive integers a and b:

```
a := A; b := B
while a ≠ b  do while a > b do a := a − b od;
                  while b > a do b := b − a od;
              od
```

This program is due to Dijkstra (1975) and formulates the euclidean algorithm into two cooperating sequential (cyclic) processes which are synchronized in such a way that $a > 0$ and $b > 0$ would be kept invariantly true.

2.7.2.1   CSP constructs

The language CSP was developed by Hoare (1978, 1985). This language is based on the following concepts:

Disjointness of state space   A program consists of $n > 1$ communicating processes

$$[P1 \parallel P2 \parallel \ldots \parallel Pn]$$

(note that $\parallel$ is associative; hence we may omit []) disjoint in their state spaces, that is there are no shared variables or common addresses.

Synchronous message passing   This is achieved through input–output constructs. Process P1 (called the **source process**) **sends** a message to process P2 (called the **target process**) by executing an **output command** of the form P2!x (meaning, send x to P2). The name x identifies the type of message supplied from P1's variable x (source variable) and is received in target variable y of P2. In effect this is an assignment statement x := y. We refer to P1 and P2 as partners exchanging messages. Complementarily, an equivalent input command has the form P1?y (meaning, receive y from P1). Here the target variable y of P2 **receives** the message from the source variable x of P1.

Selective communication   This specifies selection of one of the alternative processes for communication subject to some condition. This construct is based on Dijkstra's guarded commands:

⟨guard⟩ → ⟨command list⟩

A guard consists of a list of declarations and boolean expressions optionally followed by a semi-colon and a message-passing statement. A guard fails if any one of its boolean expressions has the value false, or if the process named in its input command has terminated; the guard (temporarily) neither fails nor succeeds if the boolean expression is true, but the message-passing statement cannot be executed without causing a delay. The process form P_i is

$$P_i :: [\textbf{If } B_i1;\ \alpha_i1 \rightarrow S_i1$$
$$[]\ B_i2;\ \alpha_i2 \rightarrow S_i2$$
$$\vdots$$
$$[]\ B_in;\ \alpha_in \rightarrow S_in$$
$$\vdots$$
$$\textbf{fi}].$$

Here $B_i1, \ldots, B_in$ are guards or boolean expressions over the local state of P_i; $\alpha_i1, \ldots, \alpha_in$ are communication commands naming some target process P_j, $j \neq i$, $1 \leq j \leq n$ either for input or for output. $S_i1, \ldots, S_in$ are loop-free and communication-free statements.

The process works as follows. If more than one guard B_in is true, an arbitrary one is non-deterministically selected and the corresponding open command (also called an 'open alternative') is executed. If all the guards fail the command aborts. If all the guards neither fail nor succeed, execution is delayed until some guard succeeds.

Repeated selective communication   In some problems it may be required to execute a selective communication repeatedly. The repetitive process has the form

$P_i ::$ *** [if** B_i1 ; $\alpha_i1 \rightarrow S_i1$
   [] B_i2 ; $\alpha_i2 \rightarrow S_i2$
   $\vdots$
   [] B_in ; $\alpha_i \, n \rightarrow S_in$
   fi];

Here the inner part which is an alternative command is executed repeatedly until all the guards fail. When all the guards fail, the repetitive command terminates and transfers the control to a succeeding statement.

2.7.2.2   Examples

(1)   As an example of the repetitive command consider the following communication-free non-deterministic process for sorting in ascending order:

ASORDER ::*** [If** $a_1 > a_2 \rightarrow (a_1, a_2) := (a_2, a_1)$
       [] $a_2 > a_3 \rightarrow (a_2, a_3) := (a_3, a_2)$
       [] $a_3 > a_4 \rightarrow (a_3, a_4) := (a_4, a_3)$
       fi]

If $(a_1, a_2, a_3, a_4) := (1, 4, 3, 2)$, we then have the possibility of two sequences owing to non-determinism:

$$(1, 4, 3, 2) \rightarrow (1, 3, 4, 2) \rightarrow (1, 3, 2, 4) \rightarrow (1, 2, 3, 4)$$

or

$$(1, 4, 3, 2) \rightarrow (1, 4, 2, 3) \rightarrow (1, 2, 4, 3) \rightarrow (1, 2, 3, 4)$$

(2)   Consider the sequential computation of the lower integral part of the quotient (quo) of x/y where $x, y > 0$, using the primitive recursion (Section 3.3.6.4):

quo(x, y) = [x < y → 0, sum (quo(x − y, y), 1)]

Let us write x = num; y = den.

The above primitive recursion can be written in CSP using repeated selective communication with user thus:

```
DIVISION :: * [x, y: integer; user? (x, y) →
                num, den, quo: integer;
                quo := 0; num := x; den := y;
            *[If num ≥ den → quo := quo + 1;
                             num := num − den
             fi];
            user! quo
           ]
```

2.7.2.3 Producer–buffer–consumer problem

We now illustrate the message-passing scheme for the simple producer – buffer–consumer (PBC) problem (Section 2.6.2.3) with a buffer that can hold a maximum of n items. This problem is illustrated in Figure 2.3.

As in Section 2.6.2.3, for the sake of simplicity we assume that the inner structure of the buffer is not known except that it has a finite capacity. Thus the process PBC is as defined below:

```
PBC :: P‖B‖C
```

where

Process P   Process C
(generates item in p)   (receives item in c)
begin   **begin**
  repeat   **repeat**
    generate item in p   B?c
      B!p   Use c
  forever   **forever**
end.   **end**.

Process B
    (stores item in b)
```
B :: OCCUPANCY := 0, SIZE := N
    * [If OCCUPANCY < SIZE; P? b → OCCUPANCY := OCCUPANCY + 1;
       [] OCCUPANCY > 0, C!b → OCCUPANCY := OCCUPANCY − 1;
       fi]
```

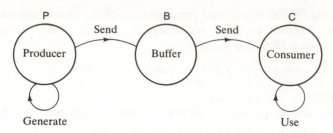

Figure 2.3   Producer–buffer–consumer.

Note that if producer process P fails after a finite time, OCCUPANCY will eventually become zero and items cannot be despatched to C from B; however, B will be waiting to receive from P and will delay its communication with C.

2.7.2.4   Ada constructs

Ada is a programming language developed for the United States Department of Defense. This language has the following basic constructs (Barnes, 1980; Burns, 1985; Nissen and Wallis, 1984) (see also Chapter 7):

(1)   **accept** statement: a combination of procedure calls and message transfer for achieving synchronous message passing.

(2)   **select** statement: a non-deterministic control structure based on Dijkstra's guarded command as in CSP, to handle selective communication.

The **accept** statement provides a process with a mechanism to wait for a predetermined event in another process. The **select** statement, in contrast, provides a process with a mechanism to wait for a set of events whose order cannot be predicted in advance.

In Ada processes are called tasks. The transfer of information between two tasks at a predetermined point is known as a **rendezvous**.

The **accept** statement is of the form:

```
accept <entry-name> [ <formal parameter list> ]
       [do <statement> end;]
```

Ada uses [. . .] to denote an alternation construct and {. . .} for a repetitive construct (zero or more times).

An **accept** statement can be executed only if another task invokes the entry name. The rendezvous takes place between the **do** and the corresponding **end** statements. The body of the **accept** statement is like a critical section. The calling process is blocked for the duration of the rendezvous to prevent it from changing the values of parameters until the exchange of information is complete (see Chapter 7).

Choices among several entry calls are accomplished using the **select** statement which has the form

```
select
    when B1 → accept <A1> do
                statements end;
                other statements
    or
    when B2 → accept <A2> do
                statements end;
                other statements
    else statements
    end select;
```

The **select** statement works as follows:

(1) The guards B_i are evaluated to find which alternatives are open.

(2) Among these open alternatives, it determines which **accept** statements have processes waiting for rendezvous.

(3) When several open alternatives arise, it selects one of the processes arbitrarily.

(4) If there are neither open alternatives nor waiting processes, it executes the **else** clause, if there is one.

(5) If there are neither waiting processes nor **else** clauses, it waits for the first process to attempt a rendezvous with an **accept** statement in one of the open alternatives.

Remarks
(1) The **else** clause is optional.

(2) When there is no **else** clause and no open alternative, error is indicated.

(3) When a guard is identically true, the **when** clause can be omitted.

2.7.2.5 Producer–buffer–consumer problem

We now illustrate how Ada constructs are used for the producer – buffer – consumer problem (PBC; see Section 2.7.2.3):

```
Select
    when OCCUPANCY < SIZE →
    accept put p in b do
    end;
    OCCUPANCY := OCCUPANCY + 1
```

or

```
    when OCCUPANCY > 0 →
    accept put b in c do
    end;
    OCCUPANCY := OCCUPANCY − 1
end select;
```

2.7.2.6 Pipeline sorting

The producer–buffer–consumer model can be used to sort n numbers using the pipeline principle in $o(n)$ time with n processors (Brinch Hansen, 1978).

The principle is illustrated in Figure 2.4. A producer inputs the stream of unsorted numbers to n processors connected as a pipeline in succession; the consumer is connected to the first processor at the receiving end with the n processors connected in a reverse-order pipeline.

When inputs arrive, each processor retains the smaller of the values it has received so far and passes on the rest to its successors in the forward direction. When the n inputs cease, the processors contain the values in ascending order. Note that each processor needs to store only two values.

The consumer can now receive the sorted values through processor 1, in ascending order, by the reverse pipeline, after a delay of n time steps used for communication.

2.8 Mixed-style synchronization modes

Languages in which process interaction is based on shared variable synchronization mode are called procedure-oriented concurrent languages. These are also known as monitor-based languages since they use monitors for synchronization. Examples of this kind are Modula-2

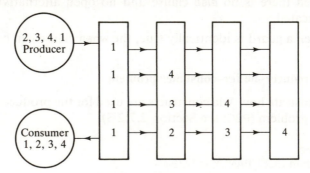

Figure 2.4 Pipeline sorting.

(Wirth, 1985) concurrent Pascal (Brinch Hansen, 1975) and Pascal Plus (Perrott, 1987).

Languages in which process interaction is based on message passing are called message-oriented languages. Examples of this kind are CSP and occam (Perrott, 1987) (see Chapter 7).

In recent years, new languages have evolved which combine the aspects of the procedure- and message-oriented languages. These are called operation-oriented languages. These languages have the advantages of both message-oriented and procedure-oriented languages. If shared memory is available, they can be used in a procedure-oriented style; if, however, communication is possible, they can be used in a message-oriented style.

From the point of view of expressive power both procedure- and message-oriented languages are equivalent. In fact it is possible to transform programs from one class to another.

Examples of operation-oriented langauges are Ada and StarMod (Cook, 1980). The rendezvous concept of Ada uses the mixed style of synchronization – based on what is called a **remote procedure call** (Lampson, 1981) to be explained below.

In the remote procedure call a process P invokes a predefined procedure at site A. The invoked procedure executes appropriately and then returns the needed parameters to P. Alternatively, a process P can send a message to site A. The operating system creates a new process Q to carry out the specified task. When Q is completed, it sends the result back to P by the message system.

The remote procedure calls are also called client–server procedure calls. This is because the client and server execute message-passing statements; also, at the same time the client's request for executing a procedure is carried out by a server at a remote machine.

The mixed-style synchronization modes are more efficient for designing distributed database systems. For example, if a summary of a large number of files is needed when the files are at different places, it is more efficient to access the files at their corresponding places and then to return the desired results to the place of enquiry rather than transferring all the files. Since several server processes can run concurrently at different places, efficiency is achieved.

2.9 Modelling and analysis

In this chapter we described processes, their interaction and how they may be described during the execution of computational steps in a program. Also, the different devices used for synchronization and communication were introduced from a practitioner's point of view.

In order to develop new understanding and to design new

techniques for the analysis of parallel processes, analytic models have been developed. These models are abstract in the sense that the actual details of the computation are ignored, only the principles of the basic control structure being examined. A comparison of these models is useful to study the interrelationships between the systems they model. From this study one can also understand the expressive power and complexity of a given model.

The following models have been proposed for parallel computation:

(1)   finite state transition systems;
(2)   Petri nets–marked graphs–computation graphs;
(3)   vector addition systems;
(4)   dataflow models;
(5)   P–V systems;
(6)   calculus of communicating systems;
(7)   communicating sequential processes;
(8)   partially ordered multiset systems;
(9)   tree automata, cellular automata, mesh automata;
(10)   alternating Turing machines, parallel RAM models.

We shall study aspects of these models in the following chapters.

SUMMARY

In this chapter we studied the interaction among various processes and their description. We explained the notion of processes, the events in processes, interleaving and non-determinacy. Then we outlined the methods for specifying the concurrent execution of independent and dependent processes. While dealing with dependent processes, the concepts of mutual exclusion, critical sections and conditional synchronization were introduced. We then considered the two modes of synchronization, namely the shared-variable mode and message-passing mode.

The five principal devices used for shared variable synchronization, namely busy waiting, semaphores, conditional critical regions, monitors and path expressions, were described. The deficiencies of each device were mentioned and we also explained how such deficiencies may be removed by using a better synchronization device.

In the message-passing or handshaking mode we considered the two principal methods used in CSP and Ada which are based on sending and receiving messages and selective communication based on Dijkstra's guarded commands.

Finally, we introduced the concept of a mixed style of synchronization called an operation-oriented system based on both procedure- and message-oriented systems.

EXERCISES

2.1   Consider the multiplication of two three-digit decimal integers. Draw a precedence graph for the different operations involved in generating individual digit products, partial products and the total product.

2.2   Draw the precedence graph for computing the greatest common divisor of two positive integers using the euclidean algorithm.

2.3   Draw the precedence graph for the computation of the recurrences

$$f_n = f_{n-1} + g_n, f_0 = 1$$
$$g_n = f_{n-1} + g_{n-1}, g_0 = 0$$

2.4   In the mutual recursion of Section 1.9.4.4 draw the mutually dependent–independent task graphs.

2.5   Take any program. Can you reformulate it as a producer–consumer problem? Illustrate by a few examples.

2.6   Convert the problem of finding both of the roots of a quadratic equation

$$ax^2 + bx + c = 0$$

into a producer–consumer system. Use the rule

$$x = \frac{-b \pm \sqrt{b^2 - 4ac}}{2a}$$

How do you solve this problem using the message-passing mode?

2.7   Given a finite continued fraction

$$a_0 + \cfrac{b_0}{a_1 + \cfrac{b_1}{a_2 + \cfrac{b_2}{a_3 + \dots}}} = [a_0, a_1, \dots, a_n]$$

the various approximants P_0/Q_0, P_1/Q_1, ... are given by

$$\begin{bmatrix} P_0 \\ Q_0 \end{bmatrix} = \begin{bmatrix} a_0 \\ 1 \end{bmatrix}; \quad \begin{bmatrix} P_1 \\ Q_1 \end{bmatrix} = \begin{bmatrix} a_1 a_0 + b_0 \\ a_1 \end{bmatrix}$$

and

$$\begin{bmatrix} P_{i+1} \\ Q_{i+1} \end{bmatrix} = \begin{bmatrix} P_i & P_{i-1} \\ Q_i & Q_{i-1} \end{bmatrix} \begin{bmatrix} a_{i+1} \\ b_i \end{bmatrix}$$

Convert this problem into a producer–consumer problem.

2.8   Let A be an $m \times n$ matrix with real elements. Let A be written in terms of its column partitioning as

$$\mathbf{A} = [\, \mathbf{a}_1 \,|\, \mathbf{a}_2 \,|\, \ldots \,|\, \mathbf{a}_n \,]$$

where $\mathbf{a}_i$ ($i = 1, 2, \ldots, n$) denote the ith column each of size $m \times 1$. We also write

$$\mathbf{A}_i = [\mathbf{a}_1 \, \mathbf{a}_2 \ldots \mathbf{a}_i] = [\mathbf{A}_{i-1} \,|\, \mathbf{a}_i]$$
$$(i = 2, 3, \ldots, n)$$

Then the Moore–Penrose inverse $\mathbf{A}_i^+$ of $\mathbf{A}_i$ is given by the recursion

$$\mathbf{A}_i^+ = \begin{bmatrix} \mathbf{A}_{i-1}^+ - \mathbf{d}_i \mathbf{b}_i \\ \mathbf{b}_i \end{bmatrix}$$

where

$$\mathbf{d}_i = \mathbf{A}_{i-1}^+ \mathbf{a}_i$$

and

$$\mathbf{b}_i = \begin{cases} \dfrac{1}{\mathbf{c}_i^T \mathbf{c}_i} \cdot \mathbf{c}_i^T & \mathbf{c}_i^T \mathbf{c}_i \neq 0 \\[2ex] \dfrac{1}{1 + \mathbf{d}_i^T \mathbf{d}_i} \cdot \mathbf{d}_i^T \mathbf{A}_{i-1}^+ & \text{otherwise} \end{cases}$$

where

$$\mathbf{c}_i = \mathbf{a}_i - \mathbf{A}_{i-1} \mathbf{d}_i$$

Here T denotes transpose and + denotes the Moore–Penrose inverse. To start with,

$$\mathbf{A}_1^+ = \begin{cases} 0 & \text{if } \mathbf{a}_i = 0 \\[2ex] \dfrac{\mathbf{a}_1^T}{\mathbf{a}_1^T \mathbf{a}_1} & \text{otherwise} \end{cases}$$

Devise a producer–consumer algorithm for computing the Moore–Penrose inverse of **A** with an unbounded number of columns.

2.9 Study the various errors that can arise due to interchange of P and V operations in semaphores.

2.10 Study the dining philosophers' problem for the simpler case of three philosophers, three plates and three forks. Examine the various cases by enumeration.

2.11 Extend the dining philosophers' problem (Exercise 2.10) to the general case of odd numbers of philosophers $(2n + 1)$ with $2n + 1$ plates and $2n + 1$ forks where n is a positive integer.

2.12 Simulate in Ada the problem of sorting n positive integers as a producer–consumer problem using n processors (Section 2.7.2.6).

2.13 Read about the programming languages Modula, Ada and CSP and find how synchronization is achieved.

2.14 Read about the UNIX operating system of the AT&T and the use of fork and join statements.

2.15 Examine the differences between cobegin . . . coend and fork and join constructs.

2.16 If you have facilities for using Modula, try to simulate the semaphores and apply this to the producer–consumer problem.

2.17 Rewrite the producer–consumer problem with a bounded buffer using the guarded command repetitive construct.

2.18 The following predicate function determines whether a number $N \geq 4$ is a prime:

PRIME (N) = P(N, N div 2)

where N div 2 is the lower integral part of the quotient when N is divided by 2 and

P(N, I) = if N mod I = 0 then false
else if I = 2 then true
else P(N, I − 1).

Write this predicate using the guarded commands.

2.19   Study the features of concurrent Pascal. How does it ensure that no deadlock occurs?

2.20   Study the features of an object-oriented language such as Small-talk. How does the message-passing mechanism work in Small-talk?

2.21   There are three resources: a card reader R, a line printer P and a tape drive T and three processes *A*, *B* and *C*. *A* requires R and P, *B* needs P and T, and *C* needs R and T. Represent this situation using semaphores.

2.22   Assume that there are three readers and three writers. Use the constraints of Section 2.6.2.4 and explain how to solve this problem.

2.23   Solve the producer–consumer problem when there are two buffers each of capacity *m* and *n*. When one of the buffers is empty, add a new condition that it can take items from another buffer.

2.24   Draw the precedence graph for Exercise 1.15.

References

Andrews G.R. and Schneider F.B. (1983). Concepts and notations for concurrent programming. *Computing Surveys*, **15**, 3–43

Barnes J.G.P. (1980). *Programming in Ada*. Wokingham: Addison-Wesley

Ben-Ari M. (1982). *Principles of Concurrent Programming*. Englewood Cliffs NJ: Prentice-Hall

Bourne S.R. (1980). *The UNIX System*. Wokingham: Addison-Wesley

Brinch Hansen P. (1973). *Operating System Principles*. Englewood Cliffs NJ: Prentice-Hall

Brinch Hansen P. (1975). The programming language concurrent Pascal. *IEEE Trans. Software Engineering*, **1**, 199–207

Brinch Hansen P. (1977). *The Architecture of Concurrent Programs*. Englewood Cliffs NJ: Prentice-Hall

Brinch Hansen P. (1978). Distributed processes: a concurrent programming concept. *Comm. ACM*, **21**, 934–41

Burns A. (1985). *Concurrent Programming in Ada*. Cambridge: Cambridge University Press

Cambell R. and Habermann A.N. (1974). The specification of process synchronization by path expressions. *Lecture Notes in Computer Science*, **16**, 89–102

Cook R.P. (1980). MOD – a language for distributed programming. *IEEE Trans. Software Engineering*, **6**, 563–71

Dijkstra E.W. (1968a). The structure of the 'THE' multiprogramming system. *Comm. ACM*, **11**, 341–6

Dijkstra E.W. (1968b). Cooperating sequential processes. In *Programming Languages* (Genuys F., ed.). New York NY: Academic Press

Dijkstra E.W. (1975). Guarded commands, nondeterminacy and formal derivation of programs. *Comm. ACM*, **18**, 453–7

Francez N. (1986). *Fairness*. New York NY: Springer

Hoare C.A.R. (1972). Towards a theory of parallel programming. In *Operating Systems and Techniques* (Hoare C.A.R. and Perrott R.H., eds.), pp. 61–71. New York NY: Academic Press

Hoare C.A.R. (1974). Monitors: an operating system structuring concept. *Comm. ACM*, **10**, 549–57

Hoare C.A.R. (1978). Communicating sequential processes. *Comm. ACM*, **21**, 666–7

Hoare C.A.R. (1985). *Communicating Sequential Processes*. Englewood Cliffs NJ: Prentice-Hall

Lampson B. (1981). Remote procedure calls. *Lecture Notes in Computer Science*, **105**, 365–70

Maeder A.J. and Wynton S.A. (1987). Some parallel methods for polynomial root finding. *J. Computational Applied Mathematics*, **18**, 71–81

Nissen J.C.D. and Wallis P.J.L. (1984). *Portability and Style in Ada*. Cambridge: Cambridge University Press

Papadimitriou C. (1986). *Database Concurrency Control*. Rockville MD: Computer Science Press

Perrott R.H. (1987). *Parallel Programming*. Wokingham: Addison-Wesley

Peterson J. and Silberschatz A. (1983). *Operating System Concepts*. Reading MA: Addison-Wesley

Raynal M. (1986). *Algorithms for Mutual Exclusion*. Cambridge MA: MIT Press

Wirth N. (1985). *Programming in Modula-2*. New York NY: Springer

Chapter 3
Parallel Processes – Models

3.1 Introduction

Many phenomena which occur in everyday life are very complex in nature and in their structure. The drive to understand these phenomena has come from a desire to control them effectively as well as to analyse and make predictions about them. In order to do this, some significant aspects of the phenomenon are chosen and modelled by using certain premises; this is called 'model synthesis'. The premises are nothing but descriptive statements that encode the relevant information concerning the phenomenon. Ideally, therefore, one expects that the model is a true representation of reality. In such a case we say there exists a one-to-one correspondence or **isomorphism** between the model and the phenomenon. In practice, isomorphism is difficult to achieve and one synthesizes a model as close to reality as possible. The closer a model fits the phenomenon, the better would be the prediction that can be made by analysing the model.

3.2   Model theory and computer science

In computer science, the models are based on two-valued logics, that is on logics in which every statement is true or false. These models are called formal models, since they are meant for analysis by purely mechanistic means or algorithms. Such formal models use a well-defined language and notation defined by a syntax. To specify syntax we must specify the alphabet of symbols to be used in the language and how these symbols are to be put together to form legitimate expressions in the language. Such legitimate expressions or legal sentences are called well-formed formulas (wff). The specific branch of logic that deals with a study of the interconnection between legal sentences and their interpretations is known as 'model theory'. Therefore, model theory plays a fundamental role in formal computational models (Robinson, 1963; Mendelsohn, 1979).

3.2.1   First-order predicate calculus

Model theory uses a very important formal language known as the first-order predicate calculus. This language contains symbols corresponding to finite relations and finite operations on the mathematical objects under study. It also uses connectives ('and', 'or', 'not', 'if then') and quantifiers $\exists x$ (there exists an x such that . . .) and $\forall x$ (for all x such that . . .). Also, it uses variables ranging over the elements (or individuals) of the object under consideration. It is called the first-order predicate calculus because it does not contain other types of variables; for example, it has no variables ranging over subsets of the object under study. Many notions of algebra are first order. Examples of these are the axioms of groups, rings and fields.

However, some notions are not of first order, for instance the very frequently used Peano axioms for the natural numbers. This is because the induction axiom which states that 'for every set N, if $0 \in N$ and $n \in N$ implies $n + 1 \in N$, then every $n \in N$' contains a variable N ranging over sets. Thus, notions whose definition include variables ranging over natural numbers are generally not first order. The first-order calculus has the following properties.

3.2.1.1   Compactness property

A set of sentences is consistent if every finite subset is. (By consistent we mean that there exists some mathematical object in which every sentence is true.)

3.2.1.2   Skolem–Lowenheim property

A countable consistent set of sentences is valid (true) in some mathematical object which has only a countable set of elements.

3.2.1.3   Completeness property

The first-order predicate calculus is complete; that is, every true statement that can be expressed within the system can be proved within the system. (Note, however, that the second-order predicate calculus is incomplete.)

3.2.1.4   Interpretation of a wff (semantics)

When a wff is given one can assign a meaning to it by interpreting the various free variables and constant symbols contained within. By interpretation we mean that these variables and constants are given a real-world meaning. This is done by choosing a non-empty set of elements D called the domain of interpretation and assigning the constants and variables elements from D.

For example, in the domain of strings D, $f(x \cdot y)$ could mean computing a function f of the concatenated strings x and y. In the domain of natural numbers N it means computing the function f of the product of x and y.

By associating different interpretations with a given wff, we can obtain different statements where each statement is **true** or **false**.

If all the interpretations of the wff give the value **true** then we say the wff is **valid** (or universally true under any interpretation). A wff is non-valid or **invalid** iff there exists some interpretation for which the wff yields the value **false**; such an example is a counter example for the given wff and so called a **counter model** for the wff.

A wff is said to be **unsatisfiable** if it yields the value **false** for every possible interpretation. Thus a wff is **satisfiable** iff there exists some interpretation for which the wff is **true**. Such an interpretation is called a **model** of the wff. This means that a wff is **valid** iff its logical negation is unsatisfiable.

The notion of logically valid sentence extends the notion of tautology. In fact all the logically valid sentences constitute theorems in first-order predicate calculus. Similarly, the notion of unsatisfiable sentence extends the notion of a contradiction. For example:

- $\forall x(x = 0) \rightarrow (x = 0)$ is logically valid since all its instances are tautologies;
- $\forall x(x = 0)$ is logically invalid because it is not true in arithmetic; arithmetic is a counter model;

- $\forall x(x = 0)$ and (not $x = 0$) is unsatisfiable since all its interpretations are contradictions;
- $\forall x(x = x)$ is satisfiable since it is true in arithmetic; arithmetic is a model.

3.2.1.5   Decidability of wff

The truth table method can be used to determine the validity of wff in propositional calculus (that does not contain quantifiers and variables). One merely checks whether the wff is true for all possible valuations of the atomic formulas contained in the wff. In other words, there exists a decision procedure to decide the validity of a wff in the propositional calculus. However, in the case of first-order logic the validity cannot always be tested. This is because we cannot test all models of a hypothesis, since there may be infinitely many of them and testing the conclusion may involve considering an infinite number of instances. Thus there may not be a decision procedure for testing the validity of a wff in first-order predicate calculus.

The best we can do is to design a computer program that terminates only if the wff is valid. This is done by trying to show that the theory consisting of the hypothesis and the negation of the conclusion is unsatisfiable, that is it has no models. If the conclusion is not a logical consequence of the hypothesis then the model testing ends with a counter example, but it may go on forever inconclusively. Such programs which are guaranteed to terminate only if the argument is valid are called semidecision procedures. It was shown by Turing and Church that the validity problem of the first-order predicate calculus has only a semi-decision procedure. Hence this problem is called 'partially solvable or semidecidable'.

3.2.1.6   Uninterpreted wff

The different interpretations of a wff depend on the goals of the modelling. Sometimes one considers an uninterpreted wff without attaching any meanings. For example, the minimization of boolean functions can be carried out without assigning any meaning to them. The uninterpreted wff is useful for abstraction and analysis, while the interpreted wff is useful for description and synthesis. Also, the levels of interpretation of a wff can be varied.

For example, the axioms of group theory can be left uninterpreted and one can work with them purely algebraically. Also, one can associate with them real-world phenomena and models, for example permutation of objects.

3.2.2 Modelling power, decision power and complexity

From the above discussion it is seen that in synthesizing a model one must ensure that the model is a faithful representation of the situation. The deviation from the true situation is a measure of the deficiency in the 'modelling power'. Furthermore, the analysis of a model may lead to semidecidable or undecidable statements, thereby weakening the 'decision power' of a model. Usually the modelling power and decision power act in opposition – the greater the modelling power, the lesser the decision power, and conversely. We shall give examples of these later.

So far we have dealt with the question of the faithfulness as well as the decidability of the models used. In practice, however, we need to concern ourselves with the question of the 'efficiency' of analysis of a model. This is gauged by the amount of computer memory and time required for analysis. In particular, we want the time and memory requirements to be non-exponential in nature with respect to the input size of the problem under analysis. This requirement is essential if the model is to be useful for practical analysis and real-world applications. Thus for every model there should be an estimate of the complexity of analysis.

With this in mind we now look at the classical computational models, all of which are formulated using the language of sets and predicate calculus. The language of sets plays a fundamental role, since all computations can be expressed as either putting collections together or splitting them up or mapping one collection onto another collection.

3.3 Classical computational models

The classical computational models are classified under three categories (Tourlakis, 1983; Manna, 1974; Denning *et al.* 1978; Krishnamurthy, 1983).

(1)   Mechanistic or operational models: these deal with hypothetical operational models in which one can perform thought experiments. Models such as basic machines, finite state machines, push-down stack memory machines and Turing machines belong to this category.

(2)   Production or linguistic models: these deal with the notion of a grammar to construct strings of terminal symbols starting with a set of non-terminal symbols. For this purpose production rules which involve pattern matching of strings and substitution are defined. The Chomskian or phrase-structure languages, Post systems and Markov algorithms belong to this category.

(3) Functional models: these models are based on the concept of recursive functions introduced by Kleene, and the related lambda calculus of Church.

In this section we shall briefly summarize the results concerning these classical computational models, their modelling power and their interrelationships.

3.3.1 Basic or combinatorial machines

The basic machines are essentially combinations of switching devices. They map a finite set of elements, called the input alphabet I, to another finite set of elements called the output alphabet O.

Examples of these are logic gates (NOR, NAND, AND, NOT, EXCLUSIVE OR, combinational circuits), tree encoders–decoders and finite-size table-look-up devices.

The basic machines have no internal states and have no memory. In order to improve their capability, the finite state machine or sequential machine is introduced as a machine next in the hierarchy.

3.3.2 Finite state machines

The finite state machine (FSM) consists of a finite set of internal states S, a finite set of input symbols I (called the input alphabet) and a finite set of output symbols O (called the output alphabet). The FSM can be defined by a pair of functions called the machine function (MAF) and the state function (STF):

$$\text{MAF}: I \times S \rightarrow O$$
$$\text{STF}: I \times S \rightarrow S$$

where $\times$ denotes the cartesian product of sets, namely the set of ordered pairs $\{(i, s) | i \in I \text{ and } s \in S\}$, and $\rightarrow$ denotes mapping.

The behaviour of such a machine is completely determined provided that its initial state and input are known. We may also define a set of final states (possibly empty) from which the machine can never reach other states.

3.3.2.1 Transition graphs

The FSM can be represented by a directed graph, called the transition graph. Here the nodes are the states and the transitions between the states are the arcs. The input symbol to each state and the output symbol

Table 3.1 A finite state machine.

	s_0	s_1	s_2	s_3
s_0	0/0	1/0	–	–
s_1	–	–	0/0	1/0
s_2	–	–	1/1	0/1
s_3	–	–	–	–

$$I = \{0, 1\},\ S = \{s_0, s_1, s_2, s_3\},\ O = \{0, 1\}$$

$$\text{FSM} :: (I, O, S, \text{MAF}, \text{STF})$$

produced by each state are labelled along the arcs, as an ordered pair with a / as the punctuation symbol.

As an example consider the FSM described by Table 3.1. In this table the rows and columns are two succeeding states and the elements denote the input/output symbols for a given transition. For example, by inputting 1 to s_0 the transition from s_0 to s_1 is achieved, generating an output 0. The transition graph of Figure 3.1 is easily constructed from Table 3.1.

3.3.2.2 Acceptance, rejection, reachability

If we define s_0 as the initial state and s_3 as the final state, we find that all sequences beginning with any number (≥ 0) of 0s (denoted by 0*)

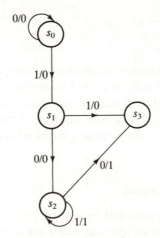

Figure 3.1 Transition graph.

followed by 11 or any number of 0s followed by 10 and any number ($\geqslant 0$) of 1s (denoted by 1*) and 0 will make the machine move from s_0 to s_3. The above sequences (0*11 or 0*101*0) are therefore called recognized or accepted words. The other words which are not accepted are called rejected words.

The subset of states to which an input word can lead a machine from an initial state is called the reachable set for that string. For example, in Figure 3.1 the string 010 has the reachable set $\{s_0, s_1, s_2\}$ and 011 has the reachable set. $\{s_0, s_1, s_3\}$. If a string has no reachable states then we say the null set $\varnothing$ is the reachable set. For example, in Figure 3.1 if we extend the alphabet set to $I = \{0, 1, 2\}$ then the string 200 has only $\varnothing$ as the reachable set.

It is sometimes convenient to define a string Λ called the null string or empty string with no symbols in it. This is helpful in defining a final state such as s_3 in Figure 3.1 from which there are no transitions.

3.3.2.3 Deterministic–non-deterministic FSM

The FSM as defined above is deterministic: there is a unique input symbol which takes each state to the next state. In other words, given a state s_i, the same input symbol cannot cause the FSM to move into more than one state.

If now we introduce an arc labelled 1/0 between s_0 and s_3 such a machine will be non-deterministic since, for the same input symbol 1, the moves s_0 to s_1 or s_0 to s_3 are possible. Thus a non-deterministic FSM permits more than one transition for the same input symbol.

The modelling power and the decision power are, surprisingly, the same for both the deterministic and the non-deterministic versions of the FSM. That is, their abilities to recognize sequences do not improve if non-determinism is introduced.

3.3.3 Production models and grammars

In the production model (due to Post, Thue and Markov), an algorithm is defined as a set of rules that transform a given initial string of symbols (called an axiom) from a given alphabet set into another string of symbols in another given alphabet. This concept of algorithm is remarkable from the point of view of the machine and language theory, and their interrelationship. Firstly, the formalism shows how a symbol manipulation system can do the same job as a machine. Secondly, it laid the foundation for a formal language theory by providing a mechanical scheme consisting of a set of rules of inference called production or rewrite rules, which involve pattern (string) matching and substitution operations.

One of the most significant applications of the production model is in modelling the grammar of a language. By a grammar is meant a set of formal rules for constructing the correct sentences in any language. Such sentences are called grammatical or well-formed sentences. The set of rules which we use to construct grammatical sentences is called the syntax. The syntax of a grammar helps us to construct strings of symbols in an alphabet of terminals, starting from a set of auxiliary symbols, called non-terminals. For example, in the English language, the non-terminals are the parts of speech (such as noun) and the terminals are the legal words (including the word 'noun' itself). Basically, non-terminals (such as parts of speech) do not appear in a generated sentence, but take part in the definition of the grammar and the construction of a sentence in a language.

For example, in an FSM the states correspond to the non-terminals, while the strings which cause state transitions correspond to the terminals. Thus all the accepted words are the terminal sentences. The non-terminals, however, play a memory role (that is remembering the past inputs) and help us to generate a correct terminal sentence.

With this as a prelude, we now proceed to study the relationship between the FSMs and their languages.

3.3.3.1 Finite state grammar

The FSMs recognize a language known as a 'type 3' or 'regular' or finite state language. This language is a subclass of a larger class of languages known as 'phrase structure languages' introduced by Chomsky in the 1950s. The phrase structure language is generated by a grammar called a phrase structure grammar G with the following property:

$$G \text{ is a quadruple, } G = (N, T, P, S)$$

where

N : a finite set of non-terminal symbols denoted by upper-case Latin letters $A, B, C, \ldots$

T : a finite set of terminal symbols denoted by lower-case Latin letters $a, b, c, \ldots$ and the null symbol Λ

with $N \cup T$ = the total vocabulary V and $N \cap T = \varnothing$ (null set) (in other words, there are no common elements between N and T), and

P : a finite set of ordered pairs of the form $\alpha \rightarrow \beta$ called **production rules**, α and β being the strings over V^* (the set of all words in V) and α containing at least one symbol from N

S : a symbol from N, called the starting symbol

In the phrase structure grammar described above, if in the production rule P we restrict the left-hand side α to be a non-terminal and the right-hand side β is restricted to contain at the most one non-terminal symbol (which is either the rightmost or the leftmost symbol), we say that the grammar is a regular (finite state or type 3) grammar.

When the non-terminal symbol occurs as the rightmost symbol as in the productions P

$$A \rightarrow cB, \quad A \rightarrow c, \quad A \rightarrow \Lambda \quad \text{(null string)}$$

the grammar is right linear. If, however, the productions P are of the form

$$A \rightarrow Bc, \quad A \rightarrow c, \quad A \rightarrow \Lambda \quad \text{(null string)}$$

the grammar is left linear. A grammar is regular if it is either right or left linear.

3.3.3.2   Relating grammatical and machine formalism

The above grammatical formalism and the transition graph (machine) formalism (Section 3.3.2.1) can be set in one-to-one correspondence thus:

set of states	$\equiv$	set of non-terminals
set of input/output symbols	$\equiv$	set of terminals
transitions	$\equiv$	set of production rules with the left-hand side as a given state and the right-hand side as the arc label followed by next state label
initial state	$\equiv$	start symbol
final state	$\equiv$	production leading to null symbol, indicating no transitions

As an example, the transition graph (Figure 3.1) is written in the production rule form with the left-hand side as the node label of a given state and the right-hand side as the arc label followed by the next state label:

$$s_0 \rightarrow 0/0 \, s_0$$
$$s_0 \rightarrow 1/0 \, s_1$$
$$s_1 \rightarrow 0/0 \, s_2$$

$$s_1 \rightarrow 1/0 \ s_3$$
$$s_2 \rightarrow 0/1 \ s_3$$
$$s_2 \rightarrow 1/1 \ s_2$$
$$s_3 \rightarrow \Lambda$$

3.3.3.3   Generation–analysis of strings

In the last subsection we showed how to represent a transition graph by production rules. This correspondence tells us that a production rule can be used in two ways:

(1)   as a method of generating all the strings of a language (synthesis);

(2)   as a means to analyse whether a given terminal string can be generated by the given grammar.

In the first case, the generated language corresponding to a node is made up of all the paths from the node to a final state. In the second case, a given string starting from the initial node should move the machine to the final accepting state. This is called parsing a string for grammatical recognition.

3.3.3.4   Regular expressions

We showed that, for any FSM, we can write a grammar that describes the language accepted by the FSM. We now describe another notation, which is algebraic in nature, to represent the behaviour of a FSM. This notation is called a **regular expression**. It is a compact means for expressing the same information contained in a transition graph. Also, it resembles an algebra in which operators and evaluation procedures are described; hence it is useful for algebraic manipulation.

A regular expression is formally defined over a finite alphabet set I thus:

(1)   Any terminal symbol and the symbol Λ (empty string) and ϕ (strings with reachability set $\varnothing$) are regular expressions.

(2)   If $a \in I$ then a is a regular expression.

(3)   If x and y are two regular expressions, then their set union denoted by $x + y$ is a regular expression; the string in $x + y$ is a string from a string x or from a string y.

(4)   The concatenation of two regular expressions x and y denoted by xy is a regular expression.

(5)   The iteration or arbitrary repetition (called Kleene closure) of a regular expression x denoted by x^* is a regular expression.

(6)   If x is a regular expression then so is the parenthesized version (x). (The parentheses are used for influencing the order of evaluation.)

(7)   There are no regular expressions other than those described in rules (1)–(6) and a finite number of applications of these rules.

A regular set is any set of strings which can be represented by a regular expression. Such a set is also generated by a regular grammar. We say two regular expressions are equivalent if they describe an identical set of strings.

3.3.3.5   Transition systems

The FSM and regular expressions serve as models for transition systems. In fact, the concept of path expressions (Section 2.6.5) is derived from that of regular expression. The path expression uses operators for selection, sequencing, repetition and concurrency which respectively correspond to union $(+)$, concatenation $(\cdot)$, closure $(*)$ and non-deterministic simultaneous transitions.

We now give a simple example of a transition system and introduce certain essential terms.

Consider the transition graph in Figure 3.2. This can be thought of as a transition system characterized by a set of possible states $\{A, B, C, D, E, F\}$. At any time the system may be in a particular state. The system may effect a transition from one state to another by executing an operation along the arc which is treated as a symbol from an alphabet set $\{0, 1, 2, 3, 4\}$.

Let A be the initial state. The sequences 02, 0243 and 13 have respectively the reachability sets $\{A, B, C\}$, $\{A, B, C, D, E\}$ and $\{A, D, E\}$. The sequence 021 has the reachability set $\{A, B, C, F\}$. If a transition system arrives in a non-final state that does not allow any further transition, we say it is a **deadlocked** state. For example, if F is not a final state the sequence 021 would deadlock. Also, we call a state active if and only if it allows further transition. We also define those transitions from states which are reachable from all other states and can be repeated forever, as key transitions.

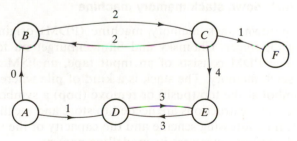

Figure 3.2   Transition system.

In the above example, the states $\{D, E\}$ are reachable from all the other states (except F). The transition 3 is called a key transition since it can be repeated forever reaching from other states. A system is called live if all its key transitions are active.

3.3.3.6   Modelling–decision power of FSMs

The modelling power of an FSM (and type 3 language) is limited, for example:

(1)   it cannot serve as a model for the generation of a product of two arbitrarily long numbers;

(2)   it cannot serve as a model for generating or recognizing an arbitrarily long sequence of well-formed left and right parentheses;

(3)   it cannot generate or recognize arbitrarily long palindromic words (words that read the same left to right or right to left).

However, the decision power of FSMs and the type 3 grammar is very high. All the properties concerning FSMs and type 3 grammar are decidable. In particular, we can decide whether a given sentence x belongs to the type 3 language; the equivalence of two regular languages can be decided; it can also be decided whether a type 3 grammar is ambiguous, that is whether there is more than one way a string can be generated.

On the other hand, the complexity of analysis required to prove the equivalence of two regular expressions or grammars is an exponential function of the size of the grammar.

The above limitations in the modelling power of the FSM arise from the lack of an unbounded memory device. Therefore, to increase the modelling power, other models such as the push-down stack machine, linearly bounded machine and Turing machine use auxiliary infinite memory devices.

3.3.4   Push-down stack memory machine

The push-down stack memory machine (PDM) originated from the works of Oettinger, Chomsky and Shutzenburger on formal language theory. The PDM consists of an input tape, an FSM and a one-way infinite stack memory. The stack is a kind of pile where we can push a stack symbol at the top (push) or remove (pop) a symbol from the top. Thus only two instructions are needed to store and recall data. Also, the stack has no addressing scheme and the capacity of the stack is infinite. The stack memory increases its modelling power.

First of all it can recognize a phrase structure language generated by a more complex type grammar, namely the type 2 grammar called context-free grammar. In this grammar the production rules P are of the form:

$$A \rightarrow \alpha \quad (A \in N, \alpha \in V^*)$$

In the right-hand side the starting symbol S can appear as in regular grammar; also, empty productions

$$A \rightarrow \Lambda \quad \text{(null string)}$$

are permitted as in regular grammar.

The context-free grammar properly contains the regular grammar. This means that there are context-free grammars which are not regular. A typical example is the grammar of well-formed parentheses sequences, given by:

$$G = (N, T, P, S)$$

where

$N = S$ = non-terminals
$T = \{ (,) \}$ = terminals
$P = \{ S \rightarrow SS, S \rightarrow (S), S \rightarrow ( ) \}$ = production rules
S = start symbol

This grammar can generate arbitrarily long well-formed parentheses sequences. It is known as a parentheses grammar.

3.3.4.1 Deterministic–non-deterministic PDM

For an FSM, the deterministic and non-deterministic models have the same power. This is not true for a PDM.

A deterministic PDM is one in which there is never a choice of move for any possible configuration of a state of FSM, an input symbol and a stack symbol. Such a PDM recognizes a subset of type 2 grammar, known as the deterministic context-free grammar. The parentheses grammar mentioned above belongs to this class.

A non-deterministic PDM permits several choices in moves for certain configurations of the state of the FSM, input symbol and stack symbol. A non-deterministic PDM can recognize a more general context-free grammar than a deterministic PDM.

As an example, the set of even palindromes WW^R (W = word, W^R = reverse of W) is accepted by a non-deterministic PDM but not by a deterministic PDM. However, WW^R can be generated by a deterministic PDM. Thus the generating power of the PDM remains the same, while the recognition power does not.

The higher modelling power of a non-deterministic PDM arises from the non-determinism embedded in the different choice moves that can be made.

3.3.4.2 Modelling power of PDM and modification

The increased modelling power of the PDM over the FSM no doubt enables the recognition of a more complex type 2 language. However, this results in a reduction in its decision power. The questions of equivalence and ambiguity of type 2 grammars are undecidable.

The modelling power can be further increased, if we add another infinite stack. This results in a computational power equivalent to that of a Turing machine.

Also, the modelling power of a PDM can be decreased by limiting the number of symbols in the stack alphabet to one. When the stack alphabet has two or more symbols the power of the PDM remains the same. However, when there is only one symbol for stack alphabet, the pop and push instructions have the effect of incrementing or decrementing an integer k. Hence this PDM is called a counting acceptor and it has a power between those of the FSM and PDM.

The counting acceptor can recognize the parentheses grammar whereas the FSM cannot. However, the counting acceptor cannot recognize a parentheses grammar with two or more different types of parentheses (such as [], (), {}).

3.3.5   Turing machines – deterministic and non-deterministic

The study of Turing machines (TMs) is a very large area in the foundations of logic and computer science. Therefore we shall discuss here only certain basic results that are essential to our topic.

The TM is the most powerful model of computation in the sense that no one has yet found a more powerful machine. Also, its high modelling power raises many basic undecidable questions in logic and computing.

A TM consists of an FSM, a read–write head and a two-way infinite tape memory marked off into square cells. The head can be positioned by moving left or right for reading or writing a symbol in the tape from a finite alphabet set I. The FSM has a finite set of states S.

Thus a TM has three functions called the machine function (MAF), state function (STF) and direction function (DIF):

MAF: $I \times S \rightarrow I$
STF : $I \times S \rightarrow S$
DIF : $I \times S \rightarrow \{L, R, N\} = D$
(where D is the direction of moves with L for left,
R for right and N for no move of the head)

A TM computation consists of initializing the tape at a square cell, and a given state, and then repeatedly executing the steps as dictated by the MAF, STF and DIF. Its action can be completely described by an ordered set of five elements (called a quintuple), for example (a, α, b, β, L) where $a \in I, \alpha \in S, b \in I, \beta \in S$ and $L \in D$. This quintuple has the following meaning:

If the head reads the symbol a, while the FSM is in the state α, the head writes the symbol b, and the FSM changes to a new state β and the head moves left by one square cell.

We can represent a TM by a transition matrix whose rows are labelled by each symbol in I and whose columns are labelled by each symbol in S and appropriately placing the remaining output triple drawn from $I \times S \rightarrow I, I \times S \rightarrow S, D$ in the matrix. It should be noted that this output triple is then deterministic, since it is unique to the input pair $(a, \alpha), a \in I, \alpha \in S$. However, if there is more than one triple for a given pair (a, α), then there is more than one choice of move. Such a TM is non-deterministic.

3.3.5.1 Grammar of the TM

The languages generated and accepted by both the deterministic TM and the non-deterministic TM, however, are identical. In other words the modelling power of the non-deterministic TM is identical to that of the deterministic TM.

The TM accepts and generates a phrase structure grammar of type 0 (unrestricted) where the production rule P is of the form:

$$\phi A \psi \rightarrow \phi \alpha \psi$$

This specifies that any non-terminal A found in the context $\phi A \psi$ may be replaced by a string α in the same context; here ϕ, ψ, and α may be any arbitrary string of terminals and non-terminals or empty strings.

The type 0 grammar raises many undecidable questions. For example, the questions of ambiguity and equivalence of type 0 grammar are both undecidable. These are equivalent to the well-known halting problem of the TM:

Given a TM M and an initial tape T, does M halt when started on tape T?

The halting problem is unsolvable in the sense it is beyond the capability of any TM.

3.3.5.2   Linearly bounded TM

We saw that the increased capability of the TM over the FSM is due to its infinite memory. In order to restrict the power of a TM we may restrict the use of its infinite memory. This results in what is known as a Linearly Bounded TM (LBTM)

In the LBTM the use of the memory tape is restricted as a linear function of the size of the input sequence. This results in a reduction in the power of the TM. The LBTM recognizes and generates a language known as a type 1 or context-sensitive or context-dependent language.

Type 1 production rules are like type 0 rules, except that the erasure of non-terminal symbols is not permitted. Thus the production rule is of the form:

$$\phi A \psi \rightarrow \phi \alpha \psi \quad (\alpha \neq \Lambda)$$

This type 1 grammar also raises many undecidable questions. For example, the questions of ambiguity and equivalence are still undecidable.

The additional power of the LBTM over the PDM arises from the fact that the LBTM has random access to its memory, while a PDM has access to only one end of its memory, organized as a stack with only push and pop operations.

3.3.6   Function models

The concept of the TM leads us to an understanding of computability. In order to characterize mathematically the computable functions, the concept of recursive functions was introduced by Gödel and Kleene. Historically, the concept of recursive functions evolved independently of the TM concept. The modelling of computer programs using the recursive function concept is known as a **function model**. The function model plays a very important role in understanding the meanings of programs via an important theorem called the fixed-point theorem.

The branches of mathematics relevant to the function model are logic, set theory and algebra. Therefore we introduce some essential concepts from these areas.

3.3.6.1   Relations, orderings and functions

Cartesian product   Let A and B be two sets. The cartesian product $A \times B$ is the set of ordered 2-tuples or pairs $\{(a, b) \mid a \in A, b \in B\}$. This can be generalized to a cartesian product of n sets giving rise to ordered n-tuples.

Relation, domain, codomain   A relation R between the sets A and B is any subset of $A \times B$:

$$R \subseteq A \times B$$

The domain of R is the set of first components of the pairs, while the range is the set of second components of pairs in R.

Partial order, total order   For a set A, a relation $R \subseteq A \times A$ is a partial ordering iff

(1)   for every $a \in A$: aRA (reflexive)

(2)   for every $a, b \in A$: $aRb \wedge bRa \rightarrow a = b$ (antisymmetrical)

(3)   for every $a, b, c \in A$: $aRb \wedge bRc \rightarrow aRc$ (transitive)

A partially ordered set is also called a **poset**. We also say that R is a total (or linear) order of A if, in addition

(4)   for every $a, b \in A$, at least one of aRb or bRa holds or every pair of elements is comparable. A totally ordered set is also called a chain.

Well-ordered set   A totally ordered set $(A, <)$ is well ordered if every non-empty subset of A has a least element.

For example, the set of natural numbers N is well ordered under $\leqslant$. However, the set of all positive rationals is not well ordered since it has no least element.

Induction   An important consequence of the well-orderedness of N is its induction property which states:

If $S \subseteq N$ is such that $0 \in S$ and $n \in S \rightarrow (n + 1) \in S$ then $S = N$

(In other words: any subset of N that contains 0 and n, as well as the successor of n, must be all of N.)

Well-founded set   A partially ordered set $(A, <)$ which contains no infinite decreasing sequences such as $a_0 > a_1 > a_2 \ldots > a_n$ of elements of

A is called a well-founded set. (Note that we use $a_0 > a_1$ for $a_1 < a_0$.) For example the set of rational numbers with the usual $<$ (less than) is partially ordered but not well founded since

$$\tfrac{1}{2} > \tfrac{1}{3} > \tfrac{1}{4} > \cdots$$

is infinitely decreasing.

The set of all integers under $<$ is again infinitely decreasing since

$$n > \cdots 4 > 3 > 2 > 1 > 0 > -1 > \cdots > -n \cdots$$

The set of natural numbers with the usual ordering $<$ is well founded. Also, if I is any alphabet then the set of all words over I with the substring relation $<$ (that is, $n < v$ iff n is a proper substring of v) is well founded.

The well-founded sets are useful in providing measures of program termination. A well-founded ordering $<$ on a set A gives rise to the transfinite induction principle:

> If, for some property P and any $a \in A$, a has property P can be proved under the assumption that property P holds for every $b < a$, then the property P holds for all $a \in A$.

Minimal element   In a partially ordered set A under the relation $<$, an element $a \in A$ is minimal iff there exists no $b \in A$ such that $b < a$.

Function   A relation $R \subseteq A \times B$ is a function f if it has the property

$(a, b) \in R$ and $(a, c) \in R$

implies $b = c$

We then write

$f : A \rightarrow B$

and say f maps A into B.

Domain, codomain   We have the following definitions of domain and range (codomain):

domain $f = \{a \in A \mid b = f(a)$ for some $b \in B\}$

range $f = \{b \in B \mid b = f(a)$ for some $a \in A\}$

A function, in contrast to an arbitrary relation, maps each element in its domain into at most one element of its range.

Onto, partial–total functions   If range $f \subseteq B$, we say the function f maps domain f **into** the set B. If range $f = B$, we say the function f maps domain f **onto** the set B. If domain $f \subseteq A$, we say f is a partial function; if domain $f = A$, we say f is total. If $a \in$ domain f we say f is defined at a; otherwise it is undefined at a.

1–1, one-to-one correspondence   We say a function is 1–1 iff the inverse mapping $f^{-1}(b)$ contains at most one element in A for each $b \in B$.

   If $f: A \rightarrow B$ is total, onto and 1–1 then f is said to be in one-to-one correspondence.

Remark

In computer science the term codomain is replaced by domain since there is no need to distinguish between arguments and a function applied to arguments, for the latter can again become arguments for another function.

3.3.6.2   Partial and total *n*-variable functions

Partial function   Let $X_1, X_2, \ldots X_n$ and Y be certain sets and

$$X = X_1 \times X_2 \times \ldots \times X_n$$

that is, X is the cartesian product of $X_1, X_2, \ldots X_n$. Then a partial function from X to Y is defined to be a subset f of $X \times Y$ such that for each choice of x_1 in X_1, x_2 in X_2, $\ldots$, x_n in X_n there is at the most one element y in Y for which $(x_1, x_2, \ldots, x_n, y)$ belongs to f.

Total function   A total function from X to Y is defined to be a subset of $X \times Y$ such that for each choice of x_1 in X_1, x_2 in $X_2, \ldots$, x_n in X_n there is exactly one element y in Y for which $(x_1, x_2, \ldots, x_n, y)$ belongs to f.

n-ary functions, domain, codomain   Since X is the cartesian product of n sets, a partial or total function from X to Y is called an *n*-variable or *n*-ary function. We denote this by

$$f: X \rightarrow Y$$

   The domain of f is the set of all *n*-tuples, called arguments $(x_1, x_2, \ldots, x_n)$, for which there exists an element y, called a value, in Y such that $(x_1, x_2, \ldots, x_n, y)$ belongs to f.

   The codomain or range of f is the set of those elements y (values) in Y for which there exists some choice of elements $x_1, x_2, \ldots, x_n$ (arguments) such that $(x_1, x_2, \ldots, x_n, y)$ belongs to f.

If f is a function from X to Y and if $(x_1, x_2, \ldots, x_n) \in$ domain f, we say that f is defined for the combination of the arguments $x_1, x_2, \ldots, x_n$; if $(x_1, x_2, \ldots, x_n) \notin$ domain f, we say that f is undefined for the arguments $x_1, x_2, \ldots, x_n$.

Therefore a function is total iff its value is defined for all n-tuple argument values.

3.3.6.3 Composition

The combination of two functions such that the values of one become the arguments of the other is called composition.

If h is an m-variable partial function and $g_1, g_2, \ldots, g_m$ are n-variable partial functions then the composition of h with $g_1, g_2, \ldots, g_m$ is the n-variable function f so defined that $(x_1, x_2, \ldots, x_n, z) \in f$ iff there exist elements $y_1, y_2, \ldots, y_m$ such that

$$(x_1, x_2, \ldots, x_n, y_1) \in g_1$$
$$(x_1, x_2, \ldots, x_n, y_2) \in g_2$$
$$\vdots$$
$$(x_1, x_2, \ldots, x_n, y_m) \in g_m$$
$$(y_1, y_2, \ldots, y_m, z) \in h$$

The composite function f is written as

$$f = h \circ (g_1, g_2, \ldots, g_m)$$

If $h, g_1, g_2, \ldots, g_m$ are all total then f is total. If $h, g_1, \ldots, g_m$ are not all total then f is undefined for combinations of argument values for which $g_1, \ldots, g_m$ is undefined or for which the values of $g_1, g_2, \ldots, g_m$ are defined but the resulting value of h is not defined.

3.3.6.4 Primitive recursive functions

Functions f which map the n-tuples of natural numbers N into natural numbers N are called number-theoretic functions. We denote this by

$$f: N^n \to N, n \geq 1$$

The primitive recursive functions are a class of number-theoretic functions that can be constructed from the following base functions F and the set S of strategies to be described below (Yasuhara, 1971; Manna, 1974; Tourlakis, 1983; Manna and Waldinger, 1985).

Base functions F

(1)   Zero function:

$$ZERO(x) = (0)$$

(2)   Successor function:

$$SUCC(x) = x + 1$$

(3)   Projection function:

$$I_k(x_1, x_2, \ldots, x_n) = x_k$$

This selects the kth argument among n ordered arguments. All these functions are total.

Strategy set S

Composition   If f is an n-ary function and $g_1, g_2, \ldots, g_n$ are k-ary functions then $f \circ (g_1, \ldots, g_n)$ is a k-ary function where

$$f(g_1, \ldots, g_n)(x_1, x_2, \ldots, x_k)$$
$$= f(g_1(x_1, \ldots, x_k), \ldots, g_n(x_1, \ldots, x_k))$$

In other words, the inputs to g_i are the k arguments $x_1, x_2, \ldots, x_k$ and the n outputs g_1, g_2, g_n become the inputs to the function f to produce the result. This is called the composition of functions. Informally, therefore, composition overlaps or feeds the output of a previous computation as the input to a succeeding computation.

Primitive recursion   Given any n-ary total function g and an $(n + 2)$-ary total function h, the $(n + 1)$-ary total function f defined by primitive recursion is

$$f(0, x_n, x_{n-1}, \ldots, x_1) = g(x_n, x_{n-1}, \ldots, x_1)$$
$$f(m + 1, x_n, x_{n-1}, \ldots, x_1)$$
$$= h(m, f(m, x_n, x_{n-1}, \ldots, x_1), x_n, x_{n-1}, \ldots, x_1)$$

where h is a composite function involving simpler arguments (a typical recursion!) and m is an integer inductive variable.

Informally, therefore, primitive recursion is a repetitive composition in which the input to a succeeding computation is the output from a preceding computation carried out for a simpler set of the same arguments.

Some examples of the primitive recursive functions are as follows.

(1)   Sum:

$$\text{SUM}(x, y) = x + y; \text{ this is defined by}$$
$$\text{SUM}(0, y) = I_2(0, y)$$
$$\text{SUM}(x + 1, y) = \text{SUCC}[I_2(x, \text{SUM}(x, y), y)]$$

(2)   Product:

$$\text{PROD}(x, y) = x \cdot y; \text{ this is defined by}$$
$$\text{PROD}(0, y) = \text{ZERO}(y)$$
$$\text{PROD}(x + 1, y) = \text{SUM}[I_2(x, \text{PROD}(x, y), y),$$
$$I_3(x, \text{PROD}(x, y), y)]$$

(3)   Proper subtraction:

$$\text{PROSUB}(x, y) = x \doteq y; \text{ this is defined by}$$
$$\text{PROSUB}(x, y) = \begin{cases} x - y \text{ if } x \geq y \\ 0 \text{ otherwise} \end{cases}$$

(4)   Division (lower integral part of quotient of x/y where $y \neq 0$):

$$\text{DIV}(x, y) = \begin{cases} 0 \text{ if } x < y \\ \text{SUM}(\text{DIV}(x - y, y), 1) \text{ otherwise} \end{cases}$$

Note that the evaluation of a primitive recursive function for a given set of arguments as in

$$\begin{aligned} \text{PROD}(2, 3) &= \text{SUM}(I_2(1, \text{PROD}(1, 3), 3), I_3(1, \text{PROD}(1, 3), 3)) \\ &= \text{PROD}(1, 3) + 3 \\ &= \text{SUM}(I_2(0, \text{PROD}(0, 3), 3), \\ &\quad I_3(0, \text{PROD}(0, 3), 3)) + 3 \\ &= 3 + 3 \\ &= 6 \end{aligned}$$

is a finitely terminating computation. Such an evaluation can be represented by a finitely branching tree.

The primitive recursive functions are the smallest class of functions on N that are closed under composition and recursion. Also, such functions are described by a finite system of equations. From the programming viewpoint, the primitive recursive functions are those that can be produced only using 'for' or 'count' loops.

3.3.6.5   Partial recursive functions

We now enlarge the class of primitive recursive functions to a larger class called partial recursive functions. This class of functions properly contains the primitive recursive functions. However, such functions are not necessarily described by finite evaluation schemes. Therefore the solution of such equations may never be computable.

To construct partial recursive functions, we introduce yet another operation in the strategy set S. This operation is known as the **minimalization operation**. This arises because there are many problems in which we need to evaluate the smallest value of a variable for which a specified condition holds. For example, in computing the integral part of the square root of a positive integer x we need to find the least y such that

$$(y + 1)^2 - x \geqslant 0$$

For this purpose we define the minimization operation thus:

Let

$$g : N^{n+1} \to N$$

be a total function, not necessarily primitive recursive. Define

$$f : N^n \to N \text{ so that}$$
$$f(x_1, x_2, \ldots, x_n) = \mu y[g(x_1, x_2, \ldots, x_n, y) = 0]$$

is the least integer $y \geqslant 0$ for which $g(x_1, x_2, \ldots, y) = 0$. Then we say that f is obtained from g by bounded minimalization.

The function f can be evaluated for a given argument a by evaluating $g(a, y)$ for $y = 0, 1, 2, \ldots$, or by sequential computation

$$g(a, 0), g(a, 1), \ldots$$

If y_0 is the first value of y for which $g(a, y) = 0$, we assign $f(a) = y_0$. Since for some choices of a, there may be no value of y such that $g(a, y) = 0$, it is possible that the computations may never terminate; hence f need not be total. If g is computable, the evaluation of f terminates if f is defined for that argument.

For example, the function

maximum$(x, y) = y + (x \dot{-} y) = \text{MAX}(x, y)$ where $\dot{-}$ is proper subtraction

can be expressed by

$$\text{MAX}(x, y) = \mu z[(x \dot{-} z) + (y \dot{-} z) = 0]$$

The function

$$g(x, y, z) = (x \dot{-} z) + (y \dot{-} z) = 0$$

only if $z = \text{MAX}(x, y)$.

This is illustrated by the following example in which $\text{MAX}(x, y) = $ least z such that $g(x, y, z) = 0$. This is obtained by evaluating $g(x, y, z)$ for $z = 0, 1, 2, \dots$. For $x = 3$, $y = 5$, we have

$$g(3, 5, 0) = 8$$
$$g(3, 5, 1) = 6$$
$$g(3, 5, 2) = 4$$
$$g(3, 5, 3) = 2$$
$$g(3, 5, 4) = 1$$
$$g(3, 5, 5) = 0$$

That is, $\text{MAX}(3, 5) = 5$.

The class of primitive recursive functions is not closed under minimalization. When g is not a total function, we may never be able to obtain a bound on y. This leads to partial or general recursive functions for which the minimalization operation is unbounded.

The class of partial recursive functions and functions computed by a TM are identical; that is, the TM has the same modelling and decision power.

From the programming point of view, the partial recursive functions are those generated by a while loop. This class contains the for loop functions (primitive recursive functions). Note that a while loop may never terminate when the partial recursive function associated with it is undefined.

3.3.6.6   Simultaneous recursion

The notion of recursion can be generalized to more than one variable in a function definition. This is called simultaneous or mutual or multiple recursive definition. These definitions lead to continuously performing computations.

Here we are given two or more recursive definitions of the form

$$f = F(f, g)$$
$$g = G(f, g)$$

where F and G are both total. The solutions here then occur as ordered pairs.

In general, for n-variable mutual recursion there will be a set (finite or infinite) of vectors with n components as a family of solutions.

EXAMPLE 3.1

Consider

$$
\begin{aligned}
f(n) &= f(n - 1) + g(n) + h(n) \\
g(n) &= f(n - 1) + g(n - 1) + h(n) \\
h(n) &= f(n - 1) + g(n - 1) + h(n - 1)
\end{aligned}
$$
with $f(0) = g(0) = 1$ and $h(0) = 0$

This can be written in the matrix form

$$
\begin{bmatrix} f(n) \\ g(n) \\ h(n) \end{bmatrix} = \begin{bmatrix} 4 & 3 & 2 \\ 2 & 2 & 1 \\ 1 & 1 & 1 \end{bmatrix} \begin{bmatrix} f(n - 1) \\ g(n - 1) \\ h(n - 1) \end{bmatrix}
$$

Thus we have an equation of the form

$$
\mathbf{H}(n) = \mathbf{A}\mathbf{H}(n - 1), \quad \text{where } \mathbf{H}(n) = \begin{bmatrix} f(n) \\ g(n) \\ h(n) \end{bmatrix}
$$

and obtain the simultaneous solution values

$$
\mathbf{H}(0) = \begin{bmatrix} 1 \\ 1 \\ 0 \end{bmatrix} \quad \mathbf{H}(1) = \begin{bmatrix} 7 \\ 4 \\ 2 \end{bmatrix} \quad \mathbf{H}(2) = \begin{bmatrix} 44 \\ 24 \\ 13 \end{bmatrix}
$$

satisfying the matrix recursive equation

$$
\mathbf{H}(n) - \mathbf{A}\mathbf{H}(n - 1) = \mathbf{0}
$$

Note that the above mutually recursive program does not halt after a finite number of steps. It performs continuously and yet exhibits a behaviour pattern which is stationary and orderly. Also, each element in it is generated by using only a finite number of well-defined operations. Hence the function computed is total.

The above continuous behaviour pattern generating an infinite set of solutions is not to be confused with and is to be distinguished from the non-terminating computations arising from undefined functions.

EXAMPLE 3.2

Consider

$$f(n + 1) = g(n); f(0) = 0$$
$$g(n + 1) = f(n); g(0) = f(1)$$

This results in

$$f(2n) = 0 \quad (n \text{ any integer})$$
$$f(2n + 1) \text{ is undefined}$$

Thus mutual recursions at times can lead to partial recursive computations and need not necessarily define primitive recursive functions.

In Example 3.1, no doubt, the conventional notion of termination fails. However, there is a behaviour pattern which we may call completeness; this generalizes the notion of termination in single recursion. The term completeness means that the function is computed without any holes or gaps and cannot be completed any further. In other words, the functions yield a complete result when given a complete set of arguments; hence the resulting functions are total.

In Example 3.2, the solution contains incomplete objects or holes which can never be filled or completed. In this sense they behave like functions with singularities (hence we call them incomplete or partial functions).

To understand these aspects it is necessary to study the algebraic and analytic properties of the recursive functions. In the following sections we therefore introduce the notions of complete partial order, lattices, monotonicity, continuity and a key theorem called the Knaster–Tarski fixed-point theorem. Some simple applications of these results are also given.

3.3.6.7 Complete posets, lattices

lub   Let $(A, \leqslant)$ be a poset and $\varnothing \neq B \subset A$. Then $a \in A$ is an upper bound of B iff $(\forall x) \; x \in B \to x \leqslant a$.

a is called a least upper bound (lub) of B iff a is an upper bound of B and, for any upper bound c of B, $a \leqslant c$.

glb   Similarly we define $a \in A$ as a lower bound of B iff

$$(\forall x) \; x \in B \to a \leqslant x$$

a is called a greatest lower bound (glb) of B iff a is a lower bound of B and, for any lower bound c of B, $c \leqslant a$.

Chains   A chain in a poset $(A, \leqslant)$ is an infinite sequence of elements

$$\{a_0, a_1, a_2, \dots\}$$

such that

$$a_i \leqslant a_{i+1} \text{ for all } i$$

Intuitively $a_i \leqslant a_{i+1}$ means that a_{i+1} represents all the information contained in a_i and possibly some more.

A chain is in fact a set of objects with increasing information; hence the existence of least upper bounds for chains guarantees the ability to collect all the information presented by an increasing sequence of objects. Therefore it is a very useful concept from the point of view of information processing, information transfer and computation.

cpo   A complete partially ordered set (cpo) is a partially ordered set $(A, \leqslant)$ such that

(1) A contains a least element a (i.e. for $\forall x \in A : a \leqslant x$).

(2) A is closed under a least upper bound of chains (i.e. if $a_0 \leqslant a_1 \leqslant a_2$ ... then $\cup_i a_i \in A$).

Lattice   A lattice is a partially ordered set in which every pair of elements has a least upper bound and a greatest lower bound. As an example, the set of every pair of integers under the relation 'divides' forms a lattice in which the glb is the greatest common divisor and the lub is the least common multiple.

Complete lattice   A lattice is called complete iff every subset has both a lub and a glb.

3.3.6.8   Monotonicity, continuity and fixed-point theorem

Let $f: A \to B$ be a function and (A, R_1) and (B, R_2) be partially ordered sets under the relations R_1 and R_2.

Then f is monotone (or order preserving) iff

$$f(x) R_2 f(y)$$

whenever

$xR_1 y$

We say f is continuous iff for any chain $X \subset A$ whenever lub(X) exists then so does lub($f(X)$) and lub($f(X)$) = f lub(X).

Informally the above equation means that our information about a function value is proportional to our information about the arguments of the function.

Fixed point   Let $f: A \to A$ be a monotone and continuous mapping. Then $a \in A$ such that $f(a) = a$ is called a fixed point of f.

Least fixed point a is called a least fixed point of f if

(1)   it is a fixed point of f and
(2)   for any $b \in A$, if $f(b) = b$ then $a \leqslant b$.

Knaster–Tarski theorem   Let $(A, \leqslant)$ be a poset with a minimum element m in which every chain has an lub.

Let $f: A \to A$ be monotone and continuous. Then there is an $a \in A$ such that $f(a) = a$ or a is a fixed point of f.

3.3.6.9   Application of the fixed-point theorem

The fixed-point theorem plays a vital role in proving the properties of recursive programs. This may be seen as follows. Every program can be thought of as a partial recursive function. At the initial step the program begins with a crude approximation to the final result and, as the recursion proceeds, it computes better and better approximations to the result over a complete partially ordered set. To determine whether a program terminates therefore amounts to finding or proving inductively on the level of recursion the existence of fixed points. This is the fundamental principle used in Scott's theory of denotational semantics; see Stoy (1977), McGettrick (1980) and Schmidt (1988).

Scott's semantics is also known as continuous semantics. Here, each expression is assigned a value in some domain. The values assigned are intended to represent the available information about the meaning of the expression, and hence this is called **semantic valuation**. Continuity means that our information about a function value is proportional to our information about the arguments of the function (as explained in Section 3.3.6.8). Domains are partially ordered according to the information content. Sometimes it is useful to choose a well-founded set to assign semantic valuation to expressions as will be illustrated in the following example.

Consider the ASORDER function which orders a sequence of positive integers in ascending order:

ASORDER(4, 2, 1, 3) = (1, 2, 3, 4)

This function has a fixed point (1, 2, 3, 4) since

ASORDER(1, 2, 3, 4) = (1, 2, 3, 4)

Thus any algorithm or program starting with a permutated input set (a_1, a_2, a_3, a_4) will eventually produce the set in ascending order if the program has a specification to do so and it does it correctly.

In particular, consider the program given by the repetitive guarded commands (see Section 2.7.2.2)

ASORDER :: *[**If** $a_1 > a_2 \rightarrow (a_1, a_2) := (a_2, a_1)$
[] $a_2 > a_3 \rightarrow (a_2, a_3) := (a_3, a_2)$
[] $a_3 > a_4 \rightarrow (a_3, a_4) := (a_4, a_3)$
fi]

Starting from the input sequence (4, 2, 1, 3) this program will proceed through the sequences (non-deterministically)

(4, 2, 1, 3) → (2, 4, 1, 3) → (2, 1, 4, 3) → (2, 1, 3, 4) → (1, 2, 3, 4)

or

(4, 2, 1, 3) → (4, 1, 2, 3) → (1, 4, 2, 3) → (1, 2, 4, 3) → (1, 2, 3, 4)

By choosing a well-founded, partially ordered set, we can create a non-negative numeric measure of the distance of the approximations from the result. This tells us how this distance decreases as the result marches towards its fixed point, where $f(a) - a = 0$.

For the above example, we choose a measure of disorder D defined by:

$$D(a_1, a_2, a_3, a_4) = \sum_{i=1}^{4} d_i$$

where d_i is the distance of a_i from its rightful place in the final specified result. (Note that for a $(2n + 1)$-member sequence $0 \leqslant D \leqslant 2n(n + 1)$ and for a $2n$-member sequence $0 \leqslant D \leqslant 2n^2$; see Exercise 3.11 (Gries, 1981).)

For the above example $0 \leqslant D \leqslant 8$ and the two computations shown go through a non-increasing disorder measure:

6 → 6 → 4 → 2 → 0

Note that the ordering scheme is a monotone and continuous transformation. The well-founded ordering measure is not infinitely decreasing, since the choice is based on natural numbers under the usual order $<$.

It is also clear from the above example that, if we are unable to find a suitable measure under which the successive computations are monotone and continuous, then proving that the program terminates is not easy.

A precautionary note is in order at this point: from the above sorting example, one should not infer that proving the termination and finding fixed points are easy; not at all. In practice these may be extremely difficult and may well be impossible in some cases. For instance, there is no way to prove that the following program terminates:

```
while x ≠ 1 do
    If 2 divides x then x := x/2 else x := 3x + 1
```

Finding the fixed points and proving termination are therefore still not in the hands of practitioners (Lassez *et al.*, 1982; Allison, 1987; Manna, 1974).

3.3.6.10   Church's thesis and universal machines

The famous logician Alonzo Church recognized that all three formalisms, that is the machine formalism, the production formalism and the recursive function formalism, yield the same class of computable functions called **effectively computable functions**.

The effectively computable functions can be computed in a universal machine with the following instructions:

(1)   Add 1 to an integer variable x and go to the next instruction.

(2)   If $x \neq 0$, then subtract one from x and go to the instruction with a definite label; otherwise go to the next instruction.

(3)   Stop and print x.

In other words, every problem having an algorithmic solution can be solved by this machine. This is a restatement of 'Church's thesis'. Thus, using names of variables and instruction labels, we can program this machine using the three instructions:

(1)   <variable> = <variable> + 1

(2)   <variable> = <variable> − 1

(3)   to <label> if <variable> = 0

The last instruction is called 'zero testing' and is a fundamental operation for a model to have the same power as a TM.

3.3.7   The lambda calculus model

The lambda (λ) calculus model was invented by the logician Alonzo Church in the 1930s. It is a mathematical operational counterpart of the Turing machine and is analogous to the concept of recursive functions (see Barendregt (1984), Hindley and Seldin (1986), Stoy (1977), Allison (1987), Glaser *et al.* (1984) and Revesz (1988)).

The primary aim for developing this model is one of communication between different parts in the sequential functional derivation. Certainly, communication can be achieved only by using names for objects so that they can often be referred to or substituted in certain contexts without changing the meaning. The λ-calculus achieves this in two parts:

(1)   providing the λ-notation;
(2)   providing a computational methodology or calculus, namely rules for evaluation and substitution.

3.3.7.1 λ-notation and prefix names

In popular mathematics we give naive prefix names to objects and functions. Examples are sin, log and mod. These are essentially assigned names, where the meaning of the function or its computational procedure is not built in. What Church attempted was to develop a uniform method for constructing prefix names which are unambiguous and have an associated computational procedure. Therefore Church's prefix names may be called deducible or derived names (with a meaning).

Usually in mathematics we use the symbol $f(x)$ in three different ways:

(i) f is a function of variable x;
(ii) f is to be applied to x to get the image of x;
(iii)   substitution for x results in the value of $f(x)$ – in other words, x is simply a device which gives the functional value for an unspecified argument.

In practice, it is necessary to distinguish the three different ways. Church's notation clarifies and distinguishes these three ways in the context of free and bound variables.

In mathematics and logic, when we use a variable, we either link it with some previously defined concepts or leave it unlinked (free). Typically in calculus consider

$$I = \int x \, dx \, y$$

Here x is a linked variable to the integral symbol and also to the following dx whereas y is unlinked. In logic

$$(\exists x) \text{ or } (\forall x)$$

links the variable x to the quantifier $\exists$ or $\forall$.

We call 'linked' variables **bounded** and 'unlinked' variables **free**. For example, in

$$x < y \wedge \exists x \cdot y = 4x$$

the leftmost x and the two y are free, while the rightmost two x are bound. The scope of a link is that part of the expression controlled by the link symbol. To define it unambiguously, one has to use parentheses or precedence rules.

For example, in $(\exists x)(P(x, a) \supset (\forall y)Q(x, y))$ the scope of $\exists x$ is $(P(x, a) \supset (\forall y) Q(x, y))$ whereas the scope of $\forall y$ is $Q(x, y)$. Here both x and y are bound variables. In $(\exists x) (P(x, y) \supset (\forall y) Q(x, y))$ the scope of $\exists x$ is $P(x, y)$; here y is free, x is bound. For $\forall y$, the scope is $Q(x, y)$; here x is free, y is bound.

A similar notation is used in λ-calculus. Church chose λ as the link symbol. For example, consider an expression

$$E = x + 2y$$

This can be thought of as defining a function f of x or a function g of y thus:

$$f : x \rightarrow x + 2y$$
$$g : y \rightarrow x + 2y$$

Obviously f and g are different. λ-notation expresses this difference clearly:

$$f = \lambda x \cdot x + 2y = \lambda x \cdot E$$
$$g = \lambda y \cdot x + 2y = \lambda y \cdot E$$

It indicates that in f the variable x is bound in E, while in g the variable y is bound in E. The expression E is called the body or base and the dot is a delimiter. Also, we call λ<variable>·<expression>

an abstraction and this represents the prefix name of the function.

The above notation facilitates substitution of a value to a specific variable and evaluates the function.

For instance, we can now apply the prefix name to an argument; this is called application. When we apply an abstraction to some argument, the bound variables are replaced by substitution. This permits the evaluation of a function or finding the value of a function for a specified argument.

For example, substitution of x = 0 results in

$$(\lambda x \cdot x + 2y)(0) = +2y$$

and substitution of y = 1 results in

$$(\lambda y \cdot x + 2y)(1) = x + 2$$

3.3.7.2   Syntax and currying

The λ-calculus expressions are defined by the syntax:

<expression> ::=   <variable>|<expression> <expression>|
                   λ<variable>·<expression>|(<expression>)

As already mentioned, <expression><expression> is an application while λ<variable>·<expression> is an abstraction.

In addition to the above rules we remove ambiguity by using the following two precedence rules:

(1)   Association occurs to the left.

(2)   When an abstraction $\lambda x \cdot E$ occurs, the E is taken as extending as far as possible to the right, to the first unmatched right parenthesis or to the end of the expression, whichever occurs first. This is called the scope of the occurrence of λ on the left.

As examples, we have:

(1) $\lambda x \cdot PQ \equiv (\lambda x \cdot (PQ))$

(2) $MNPQ \equiv (((MN)P)Q)$

(3)   In $(\lambda y \cdot yx(\lambda x \cdot y(\lambda y \cdot z)x)vw)$ the scope of the leftmost λ is $yx(\lambda x \cdot y(\lambda y \cdot z)x)$ while that of the middle λ is $y(\lambda y \cdot z)x$ and that of the rightmost λ is z.

When extending the λ-notation to several variables, we do not need a special notation. What we need is to use functions whose values are not numbers but other functions.

For example, if we define

$$f(x, y) = x + 2y$$

and

$$f^* = \lambda x \cdot (\lambda y \cdot x + 2y)$$

then f^* is a one variable function. That is,

$$f^*(1) = \lambda x \cdot (\lambda y \cdot x + 2y)(1)$$
$$= \lambda y \cdot 1 + 2y$$

and

$$(f^*(1))(2) = (\lambda y \cdot 1 + 2y)(2) = 1 + 2 \times 2 = 5$$
$$= f(1, 2)$$

Thus if x and y are of type N (natural numbers) then the type of f is $N \times N \to N$ while that of f^* is $N \to (N \to N)$. In other words,

$$\text{curry} : [(A \times B) \to C] \simeq [A \to (B \to C)] \quad (\simeq \text{ means isomorphic})$$

If $f : A \times B \to C$ and $(a, b) \in A \times B$ then

$$\text{curry} : \quad (f)(a)(b) = f(a, b)$$

We can thus convert a function of two or more arguments into an equivalent function which takes one argument at a time in an isomorphic domain. This conversion operation is called **currying** (after the logician Curry).

We can in fact think of both abstraction and application as curried operations which are essentially sequential.

3.3.7.3   Free–bound variables, substitution and simplification

Free–bound variables   Since a function is defined as an abstraction, the λ-expression defines a procedure to compute a function. For example,

$$\text{ABS}(x) = (\text{If } x \geqslant 0 \text{ then } x \text{ else } -x)$$

has the abstraction

ABS $= \lambda x \cdot ($If $x \geqslant 0$ then x else $-x)$

We can say that λ-expressions of two identical computational procedures will be equal if we have a means of performing syntactic operations on the λ-expressions and compare them for equality. This leads us to the λ-calculus.

In the following treatment we use upper-case Latin letters for arbitrary terms and lower-case letters to stand for variables.

An occurrence of a variable x in a term P is bound iff it is in a part of P with the form $\lambda x \cdot M$; otherwise, it is free. If x has at least one free occurrence in P it is called a free variable of P; the set of all such variables is called $FV(P)$. A closed term is a term without any free variables. For example in

$$P \equiv (\lambda y \cdot yx(\lambda x \cdot y(\lambda y \cdot z)x)vw)$$

all four y are bound, the leftmost x is free, while the other x are bound and z, v, w are free. Thus $FV(P) = \{x, z, v, w\}$.

We can formalize the definitions of free and bound variables thus:

- Free variables

    (1) x occurs free in x (but not in any other variable);
    (2) x occurs free in XY iff it occurs free in X or Y (or both);
    (3) x occurs free in $\lambda y \cdot X$ if x and y are different variables and x occurs free in X;
    (4) x occurs free in (X) iff x occurs free in X.

- Bound variables:

    (1)   no variable occurs bound in y for any variable y;
    (2) x occurs bound in XY iff it occurs bound in X or Y (or both);
    (3) x occurs bound in $\lambda y \cdot X$ if x and y are the same variable or if x occurs bound in X;
    (4) x occurs bound in (X) iff x occurs bound in X.

We now introduce the formal syntactic conversion rules of λ-calculus.

Substitution   For any M, N, x we define $[N/x]M$ to be the result of substituting N for every free occurrence of x in M. The substitution rule is given in Figure 3.3, in the form of a tree where M can have three possible choices: a variable, a compound expression or a λ-expression. The appropriate substitution rules are indicated in the leaves of the tree. These rules were formulated by the famous logician H.B. Curry; hence we call Figure 3.3 the Curry tree. In Figure 3.3, the rightmost branch

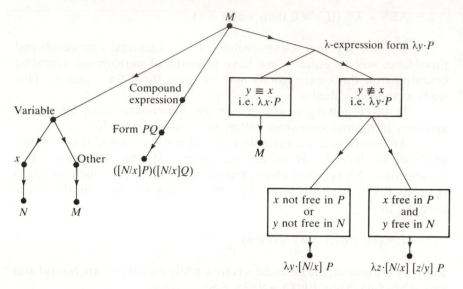

Figure 3.3 λ-substitution rule.

requires explanation. Here essentially we carry out 'renaming' to avoid collision of variable names. The necessity for such a renaming is seen from the following example.

Consider $[a/b](\lambda c \cdot b)$; $(\lambda c \cdot b)$ here is a constant function whose value is b; thus we have

$$[a/b](\lambda c \cdot b) \equiv (\lambda c \cdot a)$$

by the rule of the Curry tree. Suppose we change c to a; now $a \neq b$, and the term $\lambda a \cdot b$ represents the constant function whose value is b. However, if now we take $[a/b](\lambda a \cdot b)$ and use the rule of the Curry tree, we obtain $\lambda a \cdot a$ which is the identity function and not a constant function. This absurdity has arisen because of name collision. Therefore we use the rule of renaming as given in the rightmost branch; thus

$$\begin{aligned}[a/b](\lambda a \cdot b) &\equiv \lambda z \cdot [a/b][z/a]b \\ &\equiv \lambda z \cdot [a/b]b \\ &\equiv \lambda z \cdot a\end{aligned}$$

which stands for the same constant function $\lambda c \cdot a$.

In other words, the renaming rule rescues us from a disaster that will result when we substitute N for x in P when $y \neq x$ but y is a free variable in N and b is a free variable in P. The rescue attempt goes through a renaming process in which we choose a new variable z not occurring free in N or P.

Simplification rules   We can now devise conversion rules for transformation and simplification of λ-expressions.

We use the notation X conv Y to denote that either one of X or Y may be replaced by the other whenever either occurs in an expression or as a subexpression in a larger expression.

α-rule (renaming)   If y is not free in X then $\lambda x \cdot X$ conv $\lambda y \cdot [y/x]X$. This is called the α-rule of inference. It is essentially a renaming rule allowing a bound variable to be renamed without collision.

β-*rule (substitution)*

$$(\lambda x \cdot M)N \text{ conv } [N/x]M$$

This rule permits the parameter of a λ-abstraction to be substituted for its bound variable and the λ to be dropped.

η-*rule (eliminating redundancy)*

If x is not free in M then
$\lambda x \cdot Mx$ conv M

This rule eliminates redundant parameters and gives an equivalent function.

Redex and normal forms   When used in the left-to-right direction the β- and η-rules both replace an expression with some other (often simpler) expression. Hence we call it a reduction and the expression replaced is called a **redex**, that is $(\lambda x \cdot M)N$ is a β-redex and $\lambda x \cdot (Mx)$ is an η-redex, if x is not free in M.

The symbol Red is used to indicate a reduction instead of conv. Thus A Red B asserts that A may be transformed to B by one or more reduction steps and possibly some α conversions.

An expression containing no redexes is said to be in **normal form**.

3.3.7.4   Examples

(1) $(\lambda a \cdot a)b$ Red b

(2) $(\lambda a \cdot b)c$ Red b

(3) $(\lambda x \cdot xa)(\lambda y \cdot y)$ Red $(\lambda y \cdot y)a$ Red a

(4) $(\lambda x \cdot \lambda y \cdot y)ab$ Red $(\lambda y \cdot y)b$ Red b

(5) $(\lambda x \cdot \lambda y \cdot yx)ab$ Red $(\lambda y \cdot ya)b$ Red ba

(6) $(\lambda x \cdot \lambda y \cdot yx)yw$; here, since y is to be substituted for x, we need to rename y so that there is no confusion. Thus we have

$$(\lambda z \cdot [y/x]([z/y] yx))w$$
$$\text{Red } (\lambda z \cdot [y/x](zx))w$$
$$\text{Red } (\lambda z \cdot (zy))w$$
$$\text{Red } (wy)$$

(7) $(\lambda x \cdot xx) (\lambda x \cdot xx) \text{ Red } (\lambda x \cdot xx) (\lambda x \cdot xx)$
This has no normal form and evaluation does not terminate; hence it is called **irreducible**.

(8) $(\lambda x \cdot \lambda y \cdot y)((\lambda x \cdot xx)(\lambda x \cdot xx)) \text{ Red } \lambda y \cdot y$ if we choose the leftmost β-redex. However, if we choose the other β-redex, evaluation never terminates.

The last two examples raise two important questions:

(1) Is it possible that two different reduction sequences might terminate with different results?

(2) Is there an order of evaluation which is guaranteed to terminate whenever a particular expression is reducible to normal forms?

These two questions are answered by the Church–Rosser theorems.

3.3.7.5 Church–Rosser theorems and orders of reduction

The two important theorems of Church–Rosser are:

(1) **Theorem 1**
If X conv Y then there exists an expression Z such that X Red Z and Y Red Z.
As a corollary we see that no expression can be converted to two distinct normal forms (that is, normal forms which are not convertible using the α-rule). Thus no two orders of evaluation can reduce to different normal forms, although some may not terminate at all. In other words, there is at most one normal form for any λ-expression.

(2) **Theorem 2**
If A Red B, and B is in the normal form, then there exists a normal order reduction from A to B where normal order reduction is that which at each stage reduces the leftmost redex in the expression. Here no argument is evaluated unless needed and the evaluation proceeds from the outside in.

Normal order reduction is guaranteed to terminate with a normal form if any order of evaluation does. As an example:

$$(\lambda x \cdot \lambda y \cdot y)((\lambda x \cdot xx)(\lambda x \cdot xx))b$$
$$\text{Red } (\lambda y \cdot y)b$$
$$\text{Red } b$$

Another order of reduction is called **applicative order** where the function and argument of an application are separately evaluated to normal form before the function is actually applied to the argument. While the first Church–Rosser theorem guarantees that whenever this order of evaluation terminates it will give the same result as the normal order, it is possible that the applicative order does not terminate.

However, an advantage of the applicative order is that when it does terminate it is often faster than normal order since it evaluates the arguments only once, before they are substituted into the body of the function. In contrast, normal order must evaluate an argument as many times as its corresponding binder occurs in the body of the function after the substitution. This is the source of the extra power it has over the applicative and other orders of evaluation.

Normal order is also known as the 'call by name' or 'evaluate last' or 'leftmost' rule. Applicative order is also known as the 'call by value' or 'evaluate first' or 'leftmost innermost' rule.

3.3.7.6   Representation of functions

We indicate briefly how λ-calculus can define some basic functions and recursive functions.

Boolean functions   We represent T (true) and F (false) by:

$$T \equiv \lambda x \cdot \lambda y \cdot x$$
$$F \equiv \lambda x \cdot \lambda y \cdot y$$

Thus

$$Tab \equiv (\lambda x \cdot \lambda y \cdot x)ab \text{ Red } (\lambda y \cdot a)b \text{ Red } a$$
$$Fab \equiv (\lambda x \cdot \lambda y \cdot y)ab \text{ Red } (\lambda y \cdot y)b \text{ Red } b$$

Also

$$\text{Not} \equiv \lambda u \cdot uFT$$

Thus

$$\text{Not } T \equiv (\lambda u \cdot uFT)T \text{ Red } TFT \text{ Red } F$$

$$\text{Not } F \equiv (\lambda u \cdot uFT)F \text{ Red } FFT \text{ Red } T$$

We have also

> And $\equiv \lambda u \cdot \lambda v \cdot uvF$
> Or $\equiv \lambda u \cdot \lambda v \cdot uTv$
> Equivalence $\equiv \lambda u \cdot \lambda v \cdot uv(vFT)$
> Implication $\equiv \lambda u \cdot \lambda v \cdot uv \cdot T$

Integers   The non-negative integers $0, 1, 2, \ldots, n$ can be represented by

> $0 \equiv \lambda f \cdot \lambda x \cdot x$
> $1 \equiv \lambda f \cdot \lambda x \cdot fx$
> $\vdots$
> $n \equiv \lambda f \cdot \lambda x \cdot f^n x$

where $f^n = f \ldots f(n$ times$)$. Thus

> $nAB = (\lambda f \cdot \lambda x \cdot f^n x)AB$
> $\qquad$ Red $(\lambda x \cdot A^n x)B$
> $\qquad$ Red $(A^n B)$

or n is the abstraction that applies its first argument n times to its second.

Successor (succ)

> succ $\equiv \lambda k \cdot \lambda f \cdot \lambda x \cdot f(kfx)$

Thus

> succ $n \equiv (\lambda k \cdot \lambda f \cdot \lambda x \cdot f(kfx))(\lambda f \cdot \lambda x \cdot f^n n)$
> $\qquad$ Red $\lambda f \cdot \lambda x \cdot f((\lambda f \cdot \lambda x \cdot f^n n)fx)$
> $\qquad$ Red $\lambda f \cdot \lambda x \cdot f(f^n x)$
> $\quad \equiv \lambda f \cdot \lambda x \cdot f^{n+1} x$
> $\quad = (n + 1)$

Addition

> sum $\equiv \lambda m \cdot \lambda n \cdot m$ succ n

Thus

> sum $ij \equiv (\lambda m \cdot \lambda n \cdot m$ succ $n)ij$
> $\qquad$ Red i succ j
> $\qquad$ Red succ$^i j$
> $\qquad$ Red $i + j$

Zero test

$$\text{Is zero} = \lambda k \cdot k(TF)T$$

Thus

$$
\begin{aligned}
\text{Is zero } 0 &\equiv \lambda k \cdot k(TF)T(\lambda f \cdot \lambda x \cdot x)\\
&\quad \text{Red } (\lambda f \cdot \lambda x \cdot x)(TF)T\\
&\quad \text{Red } (\lambda x \cdot x)T\\
&\quad \text{Red } T\\
\text{Is zero } n &\equiv (\lambda k \cdot k(TF)T)(\lambda f \cdot \lambda x \cdot f^{\,n}x)\\
&\quad \text{Red } (\lambda f \cdot \lambda x \cdot f^{\,n}x)(TF)T\\
&\quad \text{Red } (TF)^{n}T\\
&\equiv TF((TF)(\ldots((TF)T)\ldots))\\
&\quad \text{Red } F
\end{aligned}
$$

Multiplication

$$\text{product} \equiv \lambda m \cdot \lambda n \cdot m(n \text{ succ})0$$

$$
\begin{aligned}
\text{product } ab &\equiv (\lambda m \cdot \lambda n \cdot m(n \text{ succ})0)ab\\
&\quad \text{Red } a(b \text{ succ})0\\
&\quad \text{Red } (b \text{ succ})^{a}0\\
&\quad \text{Red } (b \text{ succ})^{a-1}b\\
&\quad \text{Red } (b \text{ succ})^{a-2}(b+b)\\
&\qquad \vdots\\
&\quad \text{Red } (b+b+\ldots+b) \; (a \text{ times}).
\end{aligned}
$$

In other words, this algorithm adds a copies of b.

Conditional expression
The conditional expressions take the form

$$\lambda x \cdot (Px)(Ax)(Bx)$$

where P is an expression which when applied to suitable operands evaluates to T or F.

$$
(\lambda x \cdot (Px)(Ax)(Bx))z \text{ Red } (Pz)(Az)(Bz)
$$
$$
\text{Red } \begin{cases} Az \text{ if } Pz \text{ Red } T\\ Bz \text{ if } Pz \text{ Red } F \end{cases}
$$

Recursion and fixed point
In Section 3.3.6.8 we mentioned that, for a monotone and continuous mapping $f : A \rightarrow A$, a is called a fixed point if

$$f(a) = a = fa$$

In order to express this equation as a λ-expression, we need to find a suitable operator Y which converts to a when applied to Y. Such a Y is given by

$$Y = \lambda h \cdot (\lambda x \cdot h(xx)) (\lambda x \cdot h(xx))$$

If we now apply f to Y

$$
\begin{aligned}
Yf &= (\lambda h \cdot (\lambda x \cdot h(xx)) (\lambda x h(xx)))f \\
&= (\lambda x \cdot f(xx)) (\lambda x \cdot f(xx)) \\
&= f(\lambda x \cdot f(xx)) (\lambda x \cdot f(xx)) \\
&= fYf
\end{aligned}
$$

The operator Y is the fixed-point operator.

3.3.7.7 Call by need

We described earlier in Section 3.3.7.5 the two different types of reduction, namely call by value and call by name.

In call by value each argument of a function is evaluated before the function body is evaluated. The body is then evaluated with the value of the actual parameter bound to the formal parameter.

In call by name a parameter is not evaluated until a reference to it is encountered in the execution; further, each time a formal parameter is encountered in the execution of the procedure body, the corresponding actual parameter is re-evaluated.

In order to avoid the wasteful computation encountered in call by name a hybrid procedure **call by need** is useful. In call by need the actual parameters whose values are not required (or demanded) are not evaluated; however, those parameters which are required are evaluated only once and subsequently used. This is also called 'lazy evaluation' (Henderson, 1980).

3.3.7.8 Advantages of λ-calculus

We now briefly recall what is achieved by using λ-calculus.

(1) The λ-calculus provides a name localization mechanism. The definition of a function is unique in a given program.

(2) The λ-calculus suggests various orders of evaluation and provides a theory for termination/non-termination.

(3) The λ-calculus provides a basis for several other calculi for parallel computation, i.e. Milner's calculus, CSP and other related models.

3.4   Parallel computational models – approaches

During the last 20 years, two major approaches have been taken for developing models of asynchronous parallel computing systems:

(1)   The first approach, taken by the theoreticians, aims at 'abstraction and formalization'. This helps in understanding computational power and analysing correctness and complexity.

(2)   The second approach, taken by practitioners, aims at 'pragmatics and design'. This is meant for the description of large systems and is operational in nature, incorporating both the control and the dataflow.

The first approach is analogous to the classical formalisms such as TMs and recursive functions. The second approach is analogous to the use of practical tools such as flowcharts and programming language primitives. Of course, these two approaches are not unrelated. Their interrelationships have been studied and are well understood.

In this book, we essentially emphasize the second approach, although we include some elements from the first approach later in this chapter.

Among the models in the second approach, Petri nets and related graph models have been studied extensively and used by practitioners. Therefore we first describe Petri nets and related models, their applications and limitations.

3.5   Petri net and related models

The Petri net model was first proposed by Carl Adam Petri in 1962 (Peterson, 1981; Reisig, 1985). Since then it has been one of the most popular models for asynchronous, non-deterministic concurrent systems. The Petri net model is an extension of the concept of transition graphs used in FSM. In the transition graph, we only model the transitions between states. In the Petri net model, it is possible to model the more complex condition–event systems that permit both the control and dataflow. Accordingly, the Petri net can model process synchronization and mutual exclusion. Also, it can be used to detect deadlocks and safety of boundedness in the use of resources.

There are several limitations, however. Its higher modelling power over FSM reduces the decision power; as a result several undecidable and intractable problems arise. Also, the classical Petri net model cannot test for zero; this limits its ability to compute even the primitive recursive functions. However, if an instruction equivalent to **zero testing** is added to the model, it is equivalent to a TM. Then undecidable questions arise concerning liveness and safety of boundedness in the use of resources.

Like any grammatical or axiomatic or well-formed structure, a Petri net structure can be given several different interpretations, depending on the applications to which it is put. If a Petri net structure is left uninterpreted, then it is useful for abstraction and analysis. If, however, a Petri net structure is interpreted, it is useful for simulation, description, data dependence and correctness questions. If both descriptive and analytical power are needed, we need to balance the levels of interpretation of the Petri net structure. For instance, a totally interpreted structure is useful to describe a multiprogrammed operating system, and an uninterpreted structure is adequate to study the absence of deadlock.

We can relate the Petri net formalism to formal language theory. It turns out that every regular language is a Petri net language. However, there exist context-free languages which are not Petri net languages; in fact a Petri net cannot simulate a PDM. Also, surprisingly, the Petri net can generate a context-sensitive language. The Petri net languages are, however, properly contained within the context-sensitive languages (Gischer, 1981). If, however, an instruction for zero testing is included the Petri net language is as powerful as the type 0 (or unrestricted) phrase structure language.

3.5.1 Basic concepts

A Petri net is a bipartite, weighted directed graph with two different types of nodes called **places** and **transitions**. This graph is called bipartite because no two transitions or no two places can be adjacent (or directly linked by a directed arc).

It is called weighted since each place is assigned a non-negative integral weight. It is customary to represent the integral weight as an equivalent number of tokens residing within a place.

The places are connected to transitions by directed (arrowhead) arcs, each arc having a specified strength which is a positive integer. Similarly, the transitions are connected to places by directed arcs of specified integral strength.

Note that places can have zero tokens, but all the arcs have a non-zero strength.

Places from which arcs enter into a transition are called its **sources**; and places into which arcs enter from a transition are called its **sinks**.

In a modelling situation, places represent conditions, while transitions represent events. From a computing point of view, therefore, places correspond to memory devices and transitions correspond to switching devices.

A transition adjacent to one or more sources is fireable or enabled if the number of tokens in each one of its sources is greater than or equal to the strength of the arc that connects each source to that transition. In other words, the primitive recursive predicate 'Has each source got a number of tokens greater than or equal to the strength of the corresponding linking arc?' acts as a **guard** to the occurrence of an event.

When an enabled transition fires, it carries out the following two operations:

(1)   It removes (or subtracts) from each source an amount of tokens equal to the strength of the corresponding arc.

(2)   It delivers (or adds) to each sink an amount of tokens equal to the strength of the corresponding arc.

To remember these operational rules we use the analogy of a chemical reaction (Figure 3.4):

$$3As_2S_3 + 4H_2O + 28HNO_3 \rightarrow 28NO + 6H_3AsO_4 + 9H_2SO_4$$

We can model this reaction by putting the three reactants in three places and the three products in three places; the transition is the chemical reaction. The strengths of the input arcs to the transition are the weights required for triggering a reaction. The strengths of the output arcs from the transition are the weights of products. (The analogy ends here, since in conventional Petri nets the tokens in different places are indistinguishable, that is not coloured.)

From this analogy we see that, when each place is initially filled with a certain (non-negative) number of tokens, the transitions are enabled if the guards are true. The firing of a transition results in a new distribution of the number of tokens. We call the initial assignment of tokens **initial marking** of places and the new distribution arising from a

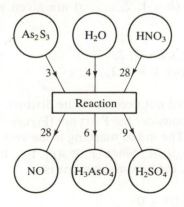

Figure 3.4   Chemical reaction analogy.

fired transition the **new marking**. Note that the markings are non-negative integral vectors with m components, where m is the number of places.

A transition behaves like a distributor (with no memory), between a source (or producer) and a sink (or consumer). The successive firings of transitions result in the generation of a sequence of new number-theoretic m-ary vectors from an initial vector.

Starting from an initial vector, if we eventually reach a new vector and halt, we say the new vector is reachable from the initial vector by the sequence of transition firings. If there exists no sequence of firings that can take an initial vector to a given vector, we say the given vector is not reachable from that initial vector.

3.5.2   Pictorial representation

A Petri net is pictorially represented by indicating its places by circles and its transitions by rectangles. The places are labelled p_i ($i = 1, 2, \ldots, m$) and transitions are labelled t_j ($j = 1, 2, \ldots, n$). The number of tokens or weight of a place p_i is denoted by P_i (i.e. the corresponding italics letter) and its value is indicated within the circle; the strength of each directed arc (p_i, t_j) or (t_j, p_i) is denoted respectively by $s(p_i, t_j)$ or $s(t_j, p_i)$ and marked on the arc; if the strength is unity we may omit this marking.

With this notation the condition for enabling any transition t_j whose sources are p_i ($i = 1, 2, \ldots, r$) and sinks are p_k ($k = 1, 2, \ldots, s$) is given by the primitive recursive predicate:

$$\text{if } P_i \geqslant s(p_i, t_j) \text{ for all } i = 1, 2, \ldots, r \text{ then } t_j \text{ is enabled}$$

When a transition t_j fires, then each of its r sources p_i ($i = 1, 2, \ldots, r$) and each of its s sinks p_k ($k = 1, 2, \ldots, s$) are given new assignments as follows:

$$P_i := P_i - s(p_i, t_j), i = 1, 2, \ldots, r$$
$$P_k := P_k + s(t_j, p_k), k = 1, 2, \ldots, s$$

Note that P_i and P_k need not necessarily be distinct.

As an example consider the Petri net (Figure 3.5) with four places and three transitions. The initial marking is the vector (ordered 4-tuple) $(P_1, P_2, P_3, P_4) = (1, 1, 0, 0)$. Since $P_2 \geqslant s(p_2, t_2)$, the transition t_2 is enabled. When t_2 fires, the new assignment is:

$$P_2 := P_2 - s(p_2, t_2) = 0$$
$$P_1 := P_1 + s(t_2, p_1) = 2$$

$$P_3 := P_3 = 0$$
$$P_4 := P_4 + s(t_2, p_4) = 1$$

which corresponds to $(2, 0, 0, 1) = (P_1, P_2, P_3, P_4)$. Note that t_2 can no longer fire; also, with the new marking, t_1 now is enabled. When t_1 fires the new assignment is $(1, 0, 1, 0)$. Now t_3 is enabled; when t_3 fires we obtain the new marking $(2, 0, 0, 1)$.

3.5.3 Matrix representation

Any m-place, n-transition Petri net can be represented by an $n \times m$ matrix $\mathbf{A} = ((a_{ij}))$ called an incidence matrix whose row index $i = 1, 2, \ldots, n$ is the transition label t_i and column index $j = 1, 2, \ldots, m$ is the place label p_j.

The elements a_{ij} are defined thus:

(1)   If p_i is a source adjacent to t_j, then $a_{ij} = -s(p_i, t_j)$.

(2)   If t_j has a sink p_i adjacent to it, then $a_{ij} = s(t_j, p_i)$.

(3)   If t_j and p_i are not adjacent then $a_{ij} = 0$.

For the Petri net shown in Figure 3.5, the incidence matrix is given by

$$\mathbf{A} = \begin{array}{c|cccc}
 & p_1 & p_2 & p_3 & p_4 \\
\hline
t_1 & -1 & 0 & 1 & -1 \\
t_2 & 1 & -1 & 0 & 1 \\
t_3 & 1 & 0 & -1 & 1
\end{array}$$

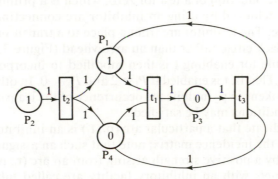

Figure 3.5   A Petri net model.

Remark

If p_i is both a source and a sink of t_j then it is called a self-loop. Then

$$a_{ij} = s(t_j, p_i) - s(p_i, t_j)$$

For example, if we add a self-loop between p_2 and t_2 in Figure 3.5 the new incidence matrix becomes

	p_1	p_2	p_3	p_4
t_1	-1	0	1	-1
$A = t_2$	1	0	0	1
t_3	1	0	-1	1

Note that $a_{22} = 0$ or there is a loss of information. To obviate this, we should leave the entries unevaluated. For example, in this case we should leave $a_{22} = -1 + 1$, rather than evaluate it to zero. In our treatment, we shall use this convention.

In Chapter 4 we show how the matrix representation is useful for analysing a Petri net model.

3.5.4   Inhibitory Petri net

In the basic definition of a Petri net, a transition is enabled only if a source has a weight greater than or equal to the arc strength, which is at least 1. Therefore, there is no provision to determine whether a particular place is empty or has a zero weight. The absence of this provision reduces the modelling power of a Petri net compared with that of TM, since the design of a universal machine (Section 3.3.6.10) needs the three basic instructions: add 1, subtract 1, and test for zero.

The introduction of a test for zero, which is a primitive recursive predicate, is achieved by using an inhibitor arc connecting a transition from a source. The inhibitor arc from a place to a transition is indicated by a small black circle rather than an arrowhead (Figure 3.6).

The rule for enabling t is then modified to incorporate the zero testing of p_2. That is, t is enabled if $P_1 \geqslant 2$ and $P_2 = 0$. In other words, the presence of tokens in p_2 inhibits the occurrence of the transition although the other conditions may be satisfied.

To indicate that a particular arc (p_i, t_j) is an inhibitory arc we set $a_{ij} = -\infty$ in the incidence matrix; note that such an assignment will not be annulled by a positive strength arising from an arc (t_j, p_i), if any.

Petri nets with an inhibitory facility are called inhibitory Petri

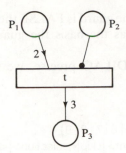

Figure 3.6   Inhibitory Petri net.

nets. They are also called 'extended Petri nets' as the inhibitory facility extends the power of a Petri net to that of a TM.

Any primitive recursive and partial recursive functions may be computed if inhibitory Petri nets are used. We shall illustrate these in a later section.

3.5.5   Dijkstra's language of guarded commands

In Section 2.7.2 we briefly introduced Dijkstra's language of guarded commands (DILAG). Here we use DILAG as a language to describe Petri nets. This is possible since DILAG is as powerful as a TM and properly contains the language of Petri nets and is as powerful as the inhibitory Petri net.

DILAG is chosen here for the following reasons:

(1)   It is a very basic building block for non-deterministic concurrent programs.

(2)   It is clear and concise and hence is a good notational aid.

(3)   The syntax and semantics of DILAG are well defined; hence standard programming theory can be applied to Petri net problems.

(4)   It eliminates the need for drawing cumbersome Petri net pictures.

(5)   The incidence matrix representation for a Petri net is easily obtained from the DILAG description by a simple algorithm.

3.5.5.1   Syntax of DILAG

In its simplest form a guarded command consists of two expressions. The first, the guard, is a boolean expression. If its value is TRUE, we say the guard is enabled and the value of the guarded command is the value of the second expression. If the guard is FALSE the guarded command has a NULL value. Using this as the basis the guarded command language (DILAG) is developed.

In order to make DILAG precise, we specify its syntax in the Backus–Naur form (BNF):

```
<integer> ::= {<digit>} *
<digit> ::= {0|1|2|3|4|5|6|7|8|9}
<statement> ::= <assignment>|skip|<selection>|<repetition>|<composition>
<composition> ::= <statement>; <statement>
<assignment> ::= <variable>:= <expression>
<selection> ::= [<boolean-expression> → <statement>]|
               [{   [ ]<integer>:
                    <boolean-expression> → <statement>}*
               ]
<repetition> ::= *<selection>
```

Remarks

(i)   We no longer use the terms **If**, **fi**, **do**, **od** in this syntax.

(ii)   In <integer> and <selection> the * in the right-hand side is a syntactic repetition.

(iii)   In <repetition> the * preceding <selection> means repeated <selection> , or the **do ... od** construction.

3.5.5.2   Semantics of DILAG

Skip   Does nothing; the final state of a program is the same as its initial state.

Assignment   a := b assigns the value b to a.

Selection   When the guards are all mutually exclusive there will be at most one selection and so we call it a deterministic selection.

If no guards are true then there is a failure. However, if the guards are not mutually exclusive, several of them may evaluate to be true. In this case, non-determinism emerges as to which command is to be selected. Then three distinct methods are possible for selection:

(1)   Select an arbitrary command for execution (called **committed choice non-determinism**).

(2)   Impose an order on the evaluation of guards to obtain a deterministic selection; for example, Petri net computations do this by

restricting the number of tokens and using inhibitor arcs (called **forced determinism**).

(3) Permit multiple choices of execution, provided that common variables do not occur (called exploratory or AND–OR parallelism).

The non-deterministic selection and its repetition play a crucial role in concurrent computing and logic programming.

Repetition   Here the inner part of the operation is a selection. The selection procedure is therefore executed repeatedly until all the guards fail. Then the execution terminates and the control is transferred to a succeeding statement. Note that multiple choices can occur and these are dealt with as in selection.

Composition   The meaning of E;F is executing E first, and on termination executing F. If E does not terminate then composition does not terminate. When E contains multiple choices, we can permit composition only when these multiple choices do not interact (or conflict) or modify common variables. Also, since non-determinism is involved, E may be executed in several ways and hence the composition may not be unique. This leads to AND–OR parallelism.

3.5.5.3   AND–OR parallelism

We mentioned that the language of guarded commands permits multiple choices of execution. The different ways in which the exploratory parallelism should proceed constitute a very large area of study in parallel logic programming. Usually, two kinds of parallelism are used: OR parallelism and AND parallelism.

In OR parallelism alternative clauses of the same goal are executed in parallel. The alternative clauses have identical initial states and do not interfere with each other, except for possible concurrent initialization attempts of a goal variable by multiple clauses.

In AND parallelism the conjunctive goals of a clause body are executed in parallel. In general, the goals may share variables and thus can interfere with each other when the shared variables are accessed concurrently.

A variety of techniques have been developed for taking care of the shared variable contention in the context of non-deterministic multiple choices. These techniques include supplying multiple copies of variables, communication and synchronization among the processes; see IEEE (1988), Tick (1988), Woods (1985) and Campbell (1984).

3.5.6 Some Petri nets

In this section, we will give examples of computation by Petri nets, their description in DILAG and their conversion to the incidence matrix representation.

3.5.6.1 Adder

The Petri net adder is shown in Figure 3.7. It computes $SUM(z + y)$ where z and y are positive integers (stored as tokens in p_z and p_y respectively). This is a primitive recursive function and is computed by accumulation of tokens to place p_z and simultaneously reducing the tokens from the place p_y storing y. The net is initiated by a token at p_0. The algorithm used here is:

```
{ (y > 0) ∧ (z > 0) }
begin
    Py := y; Pz := z
    while Py ≠ 0 do
        begin
            Py := Py – 1; Pz := Pz + 1;
        end;
end.
{ SUM = Pz }
```

There are four places and three transitions in this net and an inhibitory arc for t_3 that tests $y = 0$. If this arc is absent, conflict arises and the token

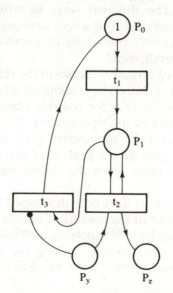

Figure 3.7 A Petri net adder.

at p_1 may activate either t_2 or t_3 non-deterministically (see Remarks below). In the absence of fairness, the token may more often fire t_3 and the SUM function can have a result between z and $z + y$. (We then say that the net performs weak addition.) The presence of the inhibitory arc grants priority to addition, before putting the token back to p_0 by testing $y = 0$.

Remarks

If all the time t_3 is chosen, the goal of addition is not achieved; hence we call such an undesirable choice a 'demonic non-deterministic choice', leading to bad luck.

If all the time t_2 is chosen, the goal of addition is achieved; hence we call such a favourable choice an 'angelic non-deterministic choice', leading to good luck.

If t_3 or t_2 is erratically fired we call it an 'erratic non-deterministic choice'.

If probabilities are associated with the choice of t_3 or t_2, we say it is a 'probabilistic non-deterministic choice'. If the choice of t_3 or t_2 is not under our control we call it an 'oracle non-deterministic choice'.

DILAG description   Using DILAG we can represent this adder as a repetitive composition of two programs E (enabling transitions) and F (firing transitions) thus:

$$\text{ADDER} ::= \ *[E;F], (P_0, P_1, P_y, P_z) := (1, 0, y, z)$$

where

$$
\begin{aligned}
E ::= \ & [\ [] \ 1: P_0 \geqslant 1 \rightarrow t_1 \\
& \ [] \ 2: P_1 \geqslant 1 \wedge P_y \geqslant 1 \rightarrow t_2 \\
& \ [] \ 3: P_1 \geqslant 1 \wedge P_y = 0 \rightarrow t_3 \\
&] \\
F ::= \ & [\ [] \ 1: t_1 \rightarrow P_1 := P_1 + 1; P_0 := P_0 - 1 \\
& \ [] \ 2: t_2 \rightarrow P_1 := P_1 - 1; P_1 := P_1 + 1; \\
& \qquad\qquad P_y := P_y - 1; P_z := P_z + 1 \\
& \ [] \ 3: t_3 \rightarrow P_0 := P_0 + 1; P_1 := P_1 - 1 \\
&]
\end{aligned}
$$

Incidence matrix from DILAG description   The incidence matrix can be obtained easily from the E and F programs, since they contain the required information of the strengths $s(p_i, t_j)$ and $s(t_j, p_i)$:

(1)   In the E program $s(p_i, t_j)$ for each P_i is the positive integer following the symbol $\geqslant$ and preceding the $\rightarrow$ or logical symbol, if any, for a t_j. Hence $a_{ij} = -s(p_i, t_j)$.

(2)   In the F program $s(t_j, p_i)$ for each t_j is the positive increment assigned to a given P_i. Hence $a_{ij} = s(t_j, p_i)$.

The incidence matrix is obtained from these rules. Conversely, the E and F programs can be obtained from the incidence matrix. In this matrix, as mentioned earlier, we use the symbol $-\infty$ for the entry corresponding to the inhibitory arc from p_y to t_3. Also, we leave the entries unevaluated to prevent any possible cancellation of the strengths, which can result in a loss of information.

For Figure 3.7, we thus obtain:

$$
A = \begin{array}{c|cccc}
 & p_0 & p_1 & p_y & p_z \\
\hline
t_1 & -1 & 1 & 0 & 0 \\
t_2 & 0 & (-1+1) & -1 & 1 \\
t_3 & 1 & -1 & -\infty & 0
\end{array}
$$

It is easy to obtain the pictorial representation from the matrix A, given the DILAG description of a Petri net.

Markings and reachability   The Petri net of Figure 3.7 has the following sequence of markings (this can easily be verified):

P_0	P_1	P_y	P_z	
(1,	0,	y,	z)	: Initial
(0,	1,	$y-1$,	$z+1$)	
(0,	1,	$y-2$,	$z+2$)	
$\vdots$	$\vdots$	$\vdots$	$\vdots$	
(0,	1,	$y-y$,	$z+y$)	
(1,	0,	0,	$z+y$)	: Final

Continuous behaviour   When $P_y = 0$, the inhibitory arc fires t_3, sending a token to p_0. After this the token loops, firing t_1 and t_3 successively, exhibiting a continuous behaviour (responsiveness) and waiting for further inputs to p_y. If further input is available it proceeds. Thus the adder works on the availability of the input data.

Composition   The Petri net adder allows parallel composition. For instance, if the places p_y and p_z are the output places of some other Petri nets which compute say $y := a + b, z := c + d$, we can compose them to obtain $(a + b) + (c + d)$. Such computations are carried out on the basis of data tokens available in these places and hence the Petri net can model data-driven computations (Section 1.5).

3.5.6.2   Proper subtraction–modulus

This example is chosen to illustrate non-determinism arising in a concurrent program or a Petri net.

The primitive recursive operation proper subtraction $(\dot{-})$ is defined by (Section 3.3.6.4)

$$z \dot{-} y = \begin{cases} z - y & \text{if } z \geq y \\ 0 & \text{otherwise} \end{cases}$$

The modulus function $|z - y| = \text{MOD}(z, y)$ is defined (using a simultaneous computation of $\dot{-}$) by the primitive recursive relation

$$\text{MOD}(z, y) = \text{SUM}((z \dot{-} y), (y \dot{-} z))$$

The inhibitory Petri net (Figure 3.8) computes $\text{MOD}(z, y)$ using the algorithm:

```
{ (y > 0) and (z > 0) }
begin
    Py := y; Pz := z
    while Py ≠ 0 or Pz ≠ 0 do
        begin
            Py := Py – 1; Pz := Pz – 1
        end;
end.
{ MOD = Py + Pz }
```

Its DILAG description is given below

$$\text{MODULUS} : := * [E; F], (P_0, P_1, P_y, P_z) := (1, 0, y, z)$$

where

```
E ::= [ [ ] 1: P0 = 1 → t1
        [ ] 2: P1 = 1 ∧ Py = 0 → t2
        [ ] 3: P1 = 1 ∧ Pz = 0 → t3
        [ ] 4: Py ≥ 1 ∧ Pz ≥ 1 ∧ P1 ≥ 1 → t4
      ]
F ::= [ [ ] 1: t1 → P1 := P1 + 1; P0 := P0 – 1
        [ ] 2: t2 → P0 := P0 + 1; P1 := P1 – 1
        [ ] 3: t3 → P0 := P0 + 1; P1 := P1 – 1
        [ ] 4: t4 → P1 := P1 – 1; P1 := P1 + 1;
                    Py := Py – 1; Pz := Pz – 1
      ]
```

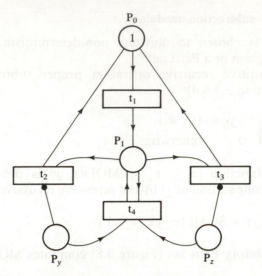

Figure 3.8   Modulus Petri net.

Here non-determinism arises since we do not know *a priori* whether $y \geq z$ or $z \geq y$. If $y \geq z$, P_y is the result, and, if $z \geq y$, P_z is the result; then a token is returned to the place p_0. When $z = y$ only one of t_2 or t_3 can fire non-deterministically leaving a token 1 in p_0. This is achieved by the inhibitor arcs in t_2 (from p_y) and in t_3 (from p_z) and restricting the number of tokens in p_1 to be unity.

Markings and reachability   The above program MODULUS has the following sequence of markings and effects.

(P_0, P_1, P_y, P_z)	Effect	(P_0, P_1, P_y, P_z)	Effect
(1, 0, 3, 4)	Fires t_1	(1, 0, 4, 3)	Fires t_1
(0, 1, 2, 3)	Fires t_4	(0, 1, 3, 2)	Fires t_4
(0, 1, 1, 2)	Fires t_4	(0, 1, 2, 1)	Fires t_4
(0, 1, 0, 1)	Fires t_2	(0, 1, 1, 0)	Fires t_3
(1, 0, 0, 1)	Fires t_1	(1, 0, 1, 0)	Fires t_1
(0, 1, 0, 1)	Fires t_2	(0, 1, 1, 0)	Fires t_3
(1, 0, 0, 1)	Loops	(1, 0, 1, 0)	Loops

Continuous behaviour–composition   Note that this program also exhibits continuous behaviour in the sense that if a stream of tokens is arriving in p_y and p_z it can continue computing the modulus.

Also, note that the output of this machine can be made as input to the adder so that we can find SUM ($(y \cdot z), (z \cdot y)$); this gives the composition of the primitive recursive functions $(y \cdot z)$ and $(z \cdot y)$.

Comparison with adder   A comparison of Figures 3.7 and 3.8 reveals that the modulus net requires one extra transition and an inhibitory arc. Also, the modulus turns out to be a symmetric operation in which the answer can be available non-deterministically in one or the other outputs. Thus finally a selection operation or an addition operation is needed to pick up the answer.

Repetition of modulus function   The modulus generator can be repeatedly used to find the greatest common divisor of y and z using the algorithm below:

```
GCD ::= * [   [ ] 1: y > z → y := y - z
              [ ] 2: z > y → skip
              [ ] 3: y > z → skip
              [ ] 4: z > y → z := z - y
          ]
```

This is left as an exercise.

3.5.6.3   Multiplier

The FSM cannot multiply two arbitrarily large numbers. This is due to its inability to store the intermediate products. Also, the Petri net without inhibitory arcs cannot multiply two numbers since the primitive recursion (Section 3.3.6.4) involves a test for zero:

$$PROD(x, y) = SUM(PROD(x - 1, y), y)$$
$$PROD(0, y) = ZERO(y) = 0$$

The Petri net in Figure 3.9 realizes the multiplication of two positive integers x and y by adding x copies of y. The multiplier x and the multiplicand y are represented by the number of tokens in p_x and p_y; that is we use the unary notation. The product comes out in p_z as a token count. We use the following algorithm:

```
{ (x > 0) ∧ (y > 0)}
begin
    Px := x; Py := y; Pz := 0; Pstore := 0
    while Px ≠ 0 do
      begin
        while Py ≠ 0 do
          begin
            Py := Py - 1; Pz := Pz + 1; Pstore := Pstore + 1
          end;
            Px := Px - 1; Py := Pstore ; Pstore := 0
      end;
end.
{ PROD = Pz }
```

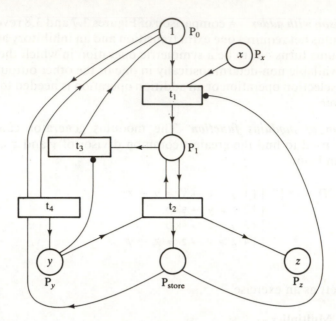

Figure 3.9   Petri net multiplier.

In this process y is lost from p_y after each iteration. Therefore, it is necessary to store y in p_{store} and to retrieve it again for the next step of accumulation. The transition t_2 pumps y into P_z, while the transition t_4 retrieves y after each iteration.

Action and computation   The net computes by firing t_1 first and removing one token from p_x. Then t_2 fires successively, pumping y into p_z and p_{store} simultaneously, until $y = 0$. Then t_3 fires, taking the token back to p_0. Now p_{store} is full and inhibits the firing of t_1; therefore t_4 fires repeatedly, retrieving the y back to p_y from p_{store}. When p_{store} is empty t_1 fires to restart decrementing p_x and to proceed for the next accumulation of y in p_z. This repetition continues until $x = 0$.

Here p_0 and p_1 play the role of control mechanisms while p_x, p_y, p_{store}, p_z play the role of data mechanisms. Transitions t_1 and t_3 act as closed valves as long as p_{store} and p_y respectively are not empty.

Note also that the net can be reactivated by sending a stream of tokens to x, to continue finding the product $x \cdot y$ for a new value of x and the same value of y.

Role of inhibitory arcs and non-determinism   If the inhibitory arc (p_y, t_3) is removed, then conflict results between firing t_2 and t_3. Either of these can fire non-deterministically, interfering with the accumulation of the product xy in p_z, resulting in a value between 0 and xy (similar to the Petri net adder); we then say that the net performs **weak multiplication**. Also, if the inhibitory arc (p_{store}, t_1) is absent, the firing of t_1 and t_4 will be in conflict, resulting in improper pumping back of y to p_y. If there is non-deterministic firing, there will be confusion in this case.

Further, comparing the Petri net adder and multiplier, we see that the latter is an extension, with additional hardware for t_4, p_x and p_{store}. By setting $P_x = 1$, we can convert the multiplier to adder provided that we place z in p_z, so that we get $z + xy$. This fact is easily seen from a comparison of the two algorithms; the inner **while** loop in the multiplier does the addition operation.

3.5.6.4   Divider

Let us first invoke (Section 3.3.6.4) the following conditional expressions for the product and the quotient:

$$PROD(x, y) = [x = 0 \rightarrow 0, SUM(PROD(x - 1, y), y)]$$

and the lower integral part of the quotient of x divided by y is given by

$$DIV(x, y) = [x < y \rightarrow 0, SUM(DIV(x - y, y), 1]$$

The similarity of the conditional expressions of $DIV(x, y)$ and $PROD(x, y)$ helps us to design a divider.

In the PROD operation the multiplicand y is lost during the accumulation and we store it. In a similar manner, here in DIV, the divisor y is lost by substraction and we need to store it and to retrieve it or pump it back from the store.

The construction of a Petri net divider is left as an exercise.

3.5.7   Petri nets and Markov algorithms

We shall now briefly explain the relationship between Petri nets, production systems and Markov algorithms.

A production system consists of a set of alphabet T (terminals), a set of axioms A (initial strings over T) and a set of rules P, called production rules, to derive new strings (theorems) from the strings produced earlier. Usually, another set of alphabet N called non-terminals (or an auxiliary alphabet) which plays the memory or variable role is used to write the production rules.

It is easily seen that the Petri net transitions correspond to production rules with the initial marking as the axiom. Each time a transition fires, new strings are derived.

A production system is, in general, non-deterministic. To force determinism, Markov introduced the following constraints:

(1)   The production rules are indexed and ordered.

(2)   There is a production rule for 'halt'.

(3)   If more than one production is applicable to a given string, choose that production with the least index.

(4)   If a production is applicable to a word on more than one of its segments (that is, if there is a conflict) then the leftmost segment is to be chosen.

The Petri net implements the above constraints by ordering the transitions and using inhibitors as explained in Sections 3.5.6.1 and 3.5.6.3.

3.5.8   Petri-net-related models

3.5.8.1   Marked graphs

A marked graph is a subclass of Petri nets in which each place is an input for exactly one transition and an output of exactly one transition. Therefore firing of a transition cannot result in conflict.

The marked graph can model synchronization and concurrency but not conflicts. It has a modelling power less than that of ordinary Petri nets.

The marked graphs have an important property called the 'cyclic conservation property' which means that the number of tokens on a cycle does not change as a result of transition firings.

3.5.8.2   Computation graphs

The computation graph is one of the earliest parallel computational models and was proposed by Karp and Miller (1966). It has a power greater than that of marked graphs but less than that of an ordinary Petri net and semaphore systems.

A computation graph $G = (N, A)$ is a directed graph with the node set $N = \{1, 2, \ldots, n\}$ representing processors and the arc set $A = \{a_1, a_2, \ldots, a_m\}$ representing data transfer, where each arc a_k directed from node i to node j is denoted by the ordered pair (i, j).

Associated with each arc (i, j) is a 4-tuple $\{ Q_{ij}, D_{ij}, R_{ij}, S_{ij} \}$ which has the following meaning:

Q_{ij} = initial number of items or tokens in the queue from i to j

D_{ij} = number of tokens delivered by i along the arc (i, j) when i is executed

R_{ij} = number of tokens removed from the arc (i, j) when j is executed

S_{ij} = minimum number of tokens (strength) needed in the arc (i, j) to enable j to execute

Therefore, when j is enabled it removes R_{ij} tokens from arc (i, j) and delivers D_{jr} tokens to k other nodes $(r = 1, 2, \ldots, k)$ adjacent to j and directed away from j.

A computation graph can be modelled by a Petri net, although not conversely, because of the higher power of the latter. To model a computation graph as a Petri net we set up a one-to-one correspondence thus:

set of arcs (i, j) = place p_{ij}

set of nodes i = transition t_i

Hence there will be now m places and n transitions.

Figure 3.10 illustrates this correspondence together with the 4-tuples and their interpretation. The initial marking of place p_{ij} is Q_{ij}, the strength of arc (t_i, p_{ij}) is D_{ij}, the strength of arc (p_{ij}, t_j) is S_{ij}, and the strength of arc (t_j, p_{ij}) is $S_{ij} - R_{ij}$. Thus when t_j fires it removes S_{ij} tokens and puts back $S_{ij} - R_{ij}$ tokens into place p_{ij}; or, in other words, t_j removes R_{ij} tokens where $R_{ij} \leqslant S_{ij}$.

Thus we have the following enabling and firing programs:

$$E ::= \quad [\,[\,] \ 1: Q_{ri} \geqslant S_{ri} \rightarrow t_i \ (r = 1, 2, \ldots, p)$$
$$[\,] \ 2: Q_{ij} \geqslant S_{ij} \rightarrow t_j$$
$$]$$

and

$$F ::= \quad [\,[\,] \ 1: t_i \rightarrow Q_{ij} := Q_{ij} + D_{ij}$$
$$[\,] \ 2: t_j \rightarrow Q_{ij} := Q_{ij} - R_{ij}$$
$$Q_{jr} := Q_{jr} + D_{jr}$$
$$(r = 1, 2, \ldots, k)$$
$$]$$

If $R_{ij} = S_{ij}$, then we note that the returning arc from t_j to p_{ij} is absent and each place has a single input and a single output. This is a marked graph.

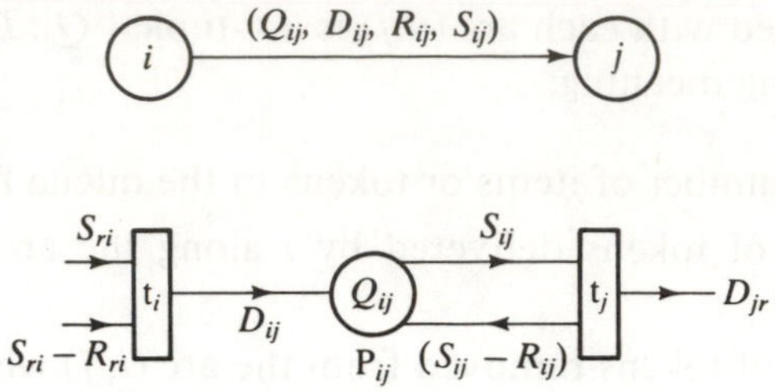

Figure 3.10   Computational graph.

3.5.8.3   P–V systems

In Section 2.6.2, we described in detail the semaphore devices for synchronization and mutual exclusion. These devices are also called P–V systems and they carry out the following operations:

P(S):   **while** S $\leq$ 0 **do** skip;
         S := S – 1
V(S):   S := S + 1

The semaphore system is more powerful than the computation graphs, but less powerful than an ordinary Petri net. Hence a P–V system can model a computation graph and can be modelled by a Petri net.

Modelling computation graphs   Each arc (i, j) in a computation graph is associated with a semaphore σ_{ij}. Its value will be Q_{ij} initially. For a node j, we execute S_{ij} type P operations on σ_{ij} for all arcs (i, j) directed into j; we also execute ($S_{ij} - R_{ij}$) type V operations on σ_{ij} to restore the value of σ_{ij}. Then, for each node j, we need to execute D_{jr} type V operations to deliver the tokens to the adjacent k nodes ($k = 1, 2, \ldots, r$) directed away from j.

Petri net model for P–V systems   To model a semaphore by a Petri net we set a shared place q_s with Q_s tokens as the value of the semaphore.
     The P and V operations are then carried out by two transitions t_p and t_v respectively. The region between t_p and t_v is the critical section. The place q_s is the input to t_p and output from t_v. There is an input place p_0 and output place p_1 and a place p_c in the critical section. The following Petri net PETRISEM models a semaphore (Figure 3.11):

PETRISEM ::= *[E;F], (P$_0$, P$_c$, P$_1$, Q$_s$) := (1, 0, 0, 1)

where

$$E ::= \quad [\,[\,]\,1: P_0 \geq 1 \wedge Q_s \geq 1 \rightarrow t_p$$
$$[\,]\,2: P_c \geq 1 \rightarrow t_v$$
$$]$$
$$F ::= \quad [\,[\,]\,1: t_p \rightarrow Q_s := Q_s - 1;$$
$$P_0 := P_0 - 1;$$
$$P_c := P_c + 1$$
$$[\,]\,2: t_v \rightarrow Q_s := Q_s + 1;$$
$$P_c := P_c - 1;$$
$$P_1 := P_1 + 1$$
$$]$$

3.5.9 Vector calculus

Karp and Miller (1966) proposed a vector calculus for analysing parallel processes. This system is equivalent to a Petri net and has the same modelling power.

The vector calculus system consists of:

(1)   a starting vector S with m non-negative integral components;

(2)   a set B of basis vectors b_j ($j = 1, 2, \ldots, n$) each with m integral components;

(3)   a binary operation $+$ of vectors;

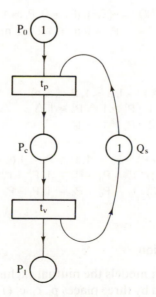

Figure 3.11 Petri net semaphore.

(4)   a generative rule that recursively defines a set V called the reachability set:

- $S \in V$
- If $x \in V$ and $(x + b_j) \geq 0$ then $(x + b_j) \in V$

The correspondence between the Petri nets and vector calculus is established by identifying S as the initial marking in the m places and b_j as the removal or addition of tokens due to the firing of the transitions (Pratt and Stockmeyer, 1976).

3.6.   Modelling concurrent systems with Petri nets

In the last section, we saw how to model the sequential programming constructs such as **while–do**, **for** and **if–then–else**. In this section, we give examples where Petri nets can be used for modelling concurrent systems.

3.6.1   PARBEGIN/PAREND

The following Petri net models n independent branching processes beginning and ending together. Each branching process is modelled by places p_i, p_i^1 and transition t_i; the initial place is p_0 and all p_i branch from the initial transition t_0; all p_i^1 join at t_0^1; t_0^1 is connected back to p_0:

$$\text{PARBEGIN/PAREND} ::= *[E;F], (P_0 := 0, P_i := 1 \ (i = 1,2,\ldots, n),$$
$$P_i^1 := 0 \ (i = 1,2,\ldots, n))$$

where

$$
\begin{aligned}
E ::= \quad & [\ [\ ] \ i : P_i \geq 1 \rightarrow t_i \ (i = 1, 2, \ldots, n) \\
& [\ ] \ (n + 1) : P_1^1 \geq 1 \wedge P_2^1 \geq 1 \wedge \ldots \wedge P_n^1 \geq 1 \rightarrow t_0^1 \\
& [\ ] \ (n + 2) : P_0 \geq 1 \rightarrow t_0 \\
&] \\
F ::= \quad & [\ [\ ] \ i : t_i \rightarrow P_i^1 := P_i^1 + 1; P_i := P_i - 1 \ (i = 1, 2, \ldots, n) \\
& [\ ] \ (n + 1) : t_0^1 \rightarrow P_0 := P_0 + 1; P_i^1 := P_i^1 - 1 \ (i = 1, 2, \ldots, n) \\
& [\ ] \ (n + 2) : t_0 \rightarrow P_0 := P_0 - 1; P_i := P_i + 1 \ (i = 1, 2, \ldots, n) \\
&]
\end{aligned}
$$

3.6.2   Mutual exclusion

The following Petri net models the mutual exclusion of n processes. Each process i is represented by three places p_i, c_i, c_i^1 ($i = 1, 2, \ldots, n$) and three transitions r_i, s_i, t_i ($i = 1, 2, \ldots, n$). They share a common place m which controls the access to each critical region beginning in r_i and ending in t_i:

$$\text{PETRI–MUTEX} ::= *[\text{E;F}], (P_i := 1 \ (i = 1, 2, \ldots, n), C_i := 0 \ (i = 1, 2, \ldots, n),$$
$$C_i^1 := 0 \ (i = 1, 2, \ldots, n), M := 1)$$

where

$$
\begin{aligned}
\text{E} ::= \quad &[\ [\ ] \ i : P_i \geqslant 1 \wedge M \geqslant 1 \rightarrow r_i \ (i = 1, 2, \ldots, n) \\
&[\ ] \ j : C_i \geqslant 1 \rightarrow s_i \ (i = 1, 2, \ldots, n) \text{ and } (j = n + 1, \ldots, 2n) \\
&[\ ] \ k : C_i^1 \geqslant 1 \rightarrow t_i \ (i = 1, 2, \ldots, n) \text{ and } (k = 2n + 1, \ldots, 3n) \\
&]
\end{aligned}
$$

$$
\begin{aligned}
\text{F} ::= \quad &[\ [\ ] \ i : r_i \rightarrow P_i := P_i - 1; M := M - 1; C_i := C_i + 1 \ (i = 1, 2, \ldots, n) \\
&[\ ] \ j : s_i \rightarrow C_i := C_i - 1; C_i^1 := C_i^1 + 1; (i = 1, 2, \ldots, n) \ (j = n + \\
&\quad 1, \ldots, 2n) \\
&[\ ] \ k : t_i \rightarrow M := M + 1, C_i^1 := C_i^1 - 1; (k = 2n + 1, \ldots, 3n)(i = 1, \\
&\quad 2, \ldots, n) \\
&]
\end{aligned}
$$

The correspondence to the use of semaphores (Section 2.6.2.1) is clearly seen in the above program. Also, note the non-determinacy in the choice of a process that can enter into its critical region. If there is no fairness some processes may starve.

3.6.3 Priority in mutual exclusion

Consider the case of two processes ($n = 2$) in the above example (Section 3.6.2). Suppose we require that, in addition to mutual exclusion, process 1 requires priority over process 2. If there are incoming tokens to p_1, then we can permit r_2 to fire only when p_1 is empty. This is done by introducing an inhibitory arc from p_1 to r_2. That is, the instruction [ ] 2 in the E program will now read

$$[\ ] \ 2 : P_2 \geqslant 1 \wedge M \geqslant 1 \wedge P_1 = 0 \rightarrow r_2$$

As an illustration we now show how the Ada construct 'select' implements the mutual exclusion with priority (Section 2.7.2.4):

```
loop
  select
    accept request for r₁ do
    r₁ ;                          (fire r₁)
    end request for r₁ ;
  or
    when P₁ = 0
```

```
        accept request for r₂ do
          r₂ ;                                    (fire r₂)
          end request for r₂ ;
        end select ;
      end loop ;
```

3.6.4 Modelling rendezvous in Ada

Two concurrent processes A and B may need to synchronize or communicate with each other. We can represent synchronization and communication using Petri nets.

Let process A be represented by places (p_1, p_2, p_3, p_4) and transitions (t_1, t_2), and process B be represented by places (p_1^1, p_2^1, p_3^1, p_4^1) and transitions (t_1^1, t_2^1). Also, let us assume that B does not want to activate its transition t_1^1 until process A has fired its transition t_1 and that A does not want to fire its transition t_2 until B has fired its t_2^1. This is **synchronization**.

If process B reaches its point p_1^1 before process A has fired its t_1, process B waits in p_1^1. Then process B detects the firing of t_1 by the now filled place p_3^1. Also, process A waits in its place p_2 until it detects a token in its place p_3, when it fires t_2 to proceed further to p_4.

This above situation is a **rendezvous**. The following program models rendezvous (Section 2.7.2.4):

$$RENDEZVOUS ::= *[E;F], (P_1, P_2, P_3, P_4, P_1^1, P_2^1, P_3^1, P_4^1) := (1, 0, 0, 0, 1, 0, 0, 0)$$

where

$$
\begin{aligned}
E ::= \quad & [\, [\,] \, 1 : P_1 \geq 1 \rightarrow t_1 \\
& [\,] \, 2 : P_2 \geq 1 \wedge P_3 \geq 1 \rightarrow t_2 \\
& [\,] \, 3 : P_1^1 \geq 1 \wedge P_3^1 \geq 1 \rightarrow t_1^1 \\
& [\,] \, 4 : P_2^1 \geq 1 \rightarrow t_2^1 \\
&]
\end{aligned}
$$

$$
\begin{aligned}
F ::= \quad & [\, [\,] \, 1 : t_1 \rightarrow P_1 := P_1 - 1; P_3^1 := P_3^1 + 1; P_2 := P_2 + 1 \\
& [\,] \, 2 : t_1^1 \rightarrow P_1^1 := P_1^1 - 1; P_3^1 := P_3^1 - 1; P_2^1 := P_2^1 + 1 \\
& [\,] \, 3 : t_2^1 \rightarrow P_2^1 := P_2^1 - 1; P_3 := P_3 + 1; P_4^1 := P_4^1 + 1 \\
& [\,] \, 4 : t_2 \rightarrow P_2 := P_2 - 1; P_3 := P_3 - 1; P_4 := P_4 + 1 \\
&]
\end{aligned}
$$

In RENDEZVOUS, the deterministic transitions fire in the following sequence: t_1, t_1^1, t_2^1, t_2 when p_1 and p_1^1 are filled.

3.6.5   Producer–buffer–consumer system

We now illustrate how a Petri net can model the producer–buffer–consumer system (see Sections 2.6.2.3 and 2.7.2.3).

We assume that the following conditions are to be met:

(1)   The buffer is bounded; that is, it can hold at most n objects.

(2)   The production rate and consumption rate are non-deterministic; hence a constant or steady flow of objects may not be possible.

(3)   If the buffer is full, it must only release the objects to the consumer and cannot accept the objects from the producer.

(4)   If the buffer is empty, it must ask the producer to send items and tell the consumer to wait.

(5)   If the buffer is neither empty nor full it must serve the waiting process (consumer or producer) in a fair manner.

To model this system we need an extended Petri net.

Here we use two places (p_1, p_2) and two transitions (t_1, t_2) for the producer, two places (b_1, b_2) for the buffer and the buffer vacancy count respectively, and two places (c_1, c_2) and two transitions (s_1, s_2) for the consumer.

The following Petri net PETROCON models the above situation:

$$\text{PETROCON} ::= \ast[\text{E};\text{F}], (P_1, P_2, B_1, B_2, C_1, C_2) := (1, 0, 0, n, 1, 0)$$

where

$$
\begin{aligned}
E ::= \ &[\,[\,] 1 : P_1 \geqslant 1 \to t_1 \\
&[\,] 2 : P_2 \geqslant 1 \wedge B_2 \geqslant 1 \to t_2 \\
&[\,] 3 : B_1 \geqslant 1 \wedge C_1 \geqslant 1 \to s_1 \\
&[\,] 4 : C_2 \geqslant 1 \to s_2 \\
&]
\end{aligned}
$$

$$
\begin{aligned}
F ::= \ &[\,[\,] 1 : t_1 \to P_1 := P_1 - 1; P_2 := P_2 + 1 \text{ (produce)} \\
&[\,] 2 : t_2 \to P_1 := P_1 + 1; P_2 := P_2 - 1; B_1 := B_1 + 1; \\
&\qquad\quad B_2 := B_2 - 1 \text{ (put in buffer)} \\
&[\,] 3 : s_1 \to C_1 := C_1 - 1; C_2 := C_2 + 1; B_1 := B_1 - 1; \\
&\qquad\quad B_2 := B_2 + 1 \text{ (removal from buffer)} \\
&[\,] 4 : s_2 \to C_1 := C_1 + 1; C_2 := C_2 - 1 \text{ (consume)} \\
&]
\end{aligned}
$$

Note that if b_2 is disconnected (that is, the literal B_2 is removed together with the conditions and assignments) we obtain the unbounded producer–buffer–consumer system.

The Petri net described above is not an ordinary Petri net but an extended Petri net. An ordinary Petri net cannot model the above problem. In the above net, note that we have $B_1 + B_2 = n$; thus the test $B_2 \geq 1$ essentially permits a last object to get into B_1 and then deactivates t_2. This is equivalent to zero testing.

It is possible to extend the above Petri net for multiple consumer–single buffer–multiple producer systems. This is left as an exercise.

3.6.6   Readers–writers' problem

We recall the readers–writers' problem mentioned in Section 2.6.2.4. Here we have a total of n readers and writers sharing a common file. The constraints are:

(1)   Several reader processes can access the shared file concurrently, assuming that their number is bounded and known.

(2)   When a process is writing, it is mutually exclusive to the other writer and reader processes.

(3)   A waiting reader gets a priority over a waiting writer.

(4)   When all the readers finish, a waiting writer is given access.

We assume that there are n processes (both reader and writer) and represent this in a common place c.

The Petri net model for this problem is structurally similar to the one described for mutual exclusion with priority (Section 3.6.3). The main differences, however, are in the strength of the arcs that connect the writer processes to the mutual exclusion place and the presence of a counter to limit the number of interacting processes to n.

The net is shown in Figure 3.12. Here the writer processes have places w_1, w_2 and transitions t_1, t_2, t_3 while the reader processes have places r_1, r_2 and transitions s_1, s_2, s_3. The common exclusion place is e with n tokens. The counter c keeps the total count of the processes. The mutual exclusion is taken care of by place e; when the number of tokens in e is equal to n, the transition t_2 fires, leaving e empty and permitting one token in w_2. This allows only one writer to access. Note, however, that there is no provision for fairness.

The translation to an E;F program is very straightforward from Figure 3.12.

Remark

If n is not bounded, we cannot use this model since there is no way to test for emptiness of the place e.

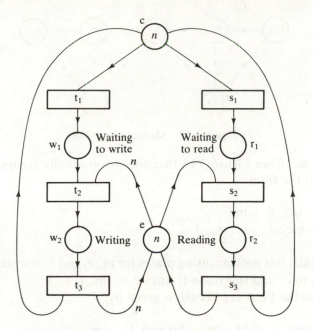

Figure 3.12   Readers–writers' problem.

3.6.7 The dining philosophers' problem

We dealt with the dining philosophers' problem in Sections 2.6.3.2 and 2.6.3.3. We now indicate how this problem is modelled by an extended Petri net.

We assume that each philosopher's label is P_i ($i = 0, 1, \ldots, n-1$), where the corresponding left fork label is f_i ($i = 0, 1, \ldots, n-1$) and right fork label is $f_{(i-1)(\bmod n)}$ ($i = 0, 1, \ldots, n-1$). The states of P_i are m_i (meditating) or e_i (eating).

We can easily see the two mutually interacting recurrent processes:

(1) P_i in state m_i picks up f_i, picks up f_{i-1}, goes to state e_i, leaves f_i, leaves f_{i-1}, goes to state m_i;

(2) f_i picked up by P_i in state m_i or f_i picked up by P_{i+1} in state m_{i+1}; or f_i left by P_i after state e_i or f_i left by P_{i+1} after state e_{i+1}.

The above interaction of two mutually recursive processes is shown in Figure 3.13.

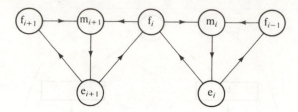

Figure 3.13   Mutual recursion.

We see from Figure 3.13 that the two mutually recursive definitions are of the form:

$$e_i = \psi(f_i, f_{i-1}, m_i)$$
$$f_i = \phi(e_i, e_{i+1}, m_i, m_{i+1})$$

We can model this problem using places for m_i, e_i and f_i; transition t_i links (m_i, f_i, f_{i-1}) to e_i; and transition t_i^1 links e_i to (m_i, f_i, f_{i-1}).

Thus the Petri net DINPHIL is given by:

DINPHIL :: = [E;F], $(M_i := 1 \ (i = 0, 1, \ldots, n - 1),$
$E_i := 0 \ (i = 0, 1, \ldots, n - 1),$
$F_i := 1 \ (i = 0, 1, \ldots, n - 1))$

(suffix i arithmetic operations are in modulo n) with

E ::=   [[ ] 1: $M_i = 1 \wedge F_i = 1 \wedge F_{i-1} = 1 \rightarrow t_i$
          [ ] 2: $E_i = 1 \rightarrow t_i^1$
       ]

F ::=   [[ ] 1: $t_i \rightarrow E_i := E_i + 1; M_i := M_i - 1;$
              $F_i := F_i - 1; F_{i-1} := F_{i-1} - 1;$
          [ ] 2: $t_i^1 \rightarrow F_i := F_i + 1; M_i := M_i - 1$
              $F_{i-1} := F_{i-1} + 1; E_i := E_i - 1;$
       ]

3.6.8   Bibliography

The study of Petri nets is a vast research area. For recent advances in this area interested readers should consult the following Springer-Verlag *Lecture Notes in Computer Science*: Brauer (1979); Pagnoni and Rozenberg (1983); Brauer *et al.* (1986a, 1986b); Rozenberg (1986); Brookes *et al.* (1984). In Rozenberg (1987) there is an extensive bibliography of over 2000 papers on Petri nets. For Petri net modelling of multiprocessor performance, see Ajmone Marsan *et al.* (1986).

3.7 Milner's calculus

A very important algebraic model of concurrency is due to Robin Milner (Milner, 1980). This model is known as calculus of communicating systems (CCS). This calculus describes algebraically the behaviour of concurrent systems, provides specifications, serves as a programming language and is well suited for proving the correctness of programs. CCS has its origin in regular expressions, λ-calculus and Milner's earlier work on flow graphs and flow algebras. (For related models, see Hennessy (1988).)

It is not possible for us to describe the entire CCS theory here. We shall give only a glimpse of CCS; for a detailed treatment Milner's original work is to be referred to.

CCS is based on two central ideas:

(1) establishing behavioural equivalence–congruence under observation;

(2) synchronized communication.

The first idea is concerned with establishing various kinds of behavioural equivalence of programs from the strong identity relation to weakly congruent relations. Depending on the nature of the chosen behavioural equivalence, different algebraic rules can be formulated. This approach is very similar to the use of arithmetic with equalities or arithmetic with congruences (or residue number system) which have different formal rules for manipulation.

The second idea is concerned with parallel composition, synchronization and non-determinism.

CCS, as already mentioned, derives its ideas from both the regular expressions that describe an FSM operation and the more powerful λ-calculus that describes a Turing-computable function. As in regular expressions, it uses a set of combinators; also as in λ-calculus, it uses concepts such as binding of variables, name localization, substitution, evaluation, passing values, establishing equivalences, recursion and fixed points. Thus, CCS is both an operational and a functional model. The additional power over an FSM arises from its ability to have parallel composition, non-deterministic choice and a mutual coupling operator for internal synchronization between interacting actions.

3.7.1 CCS – principles

The CCS consists of two sets of objects:

(i) a set of basic computing agents performing actions;

(ii)   a set of operators, both dynamic and static, for structuring and
building a combination of agents.

The basic computing agents can perform certain named actions.
The names are chosen from a denumerable set of labels $\Delta = \{\alpha, \beta, \gamma, \ldots\}$.
Also corresponding to each action in Δ, there is a coaction, whose names
are chosen from another denumerable set of labels $\overline{\Delta}$ called **conames**: $\overline{\Delta} =$
$\{\overline{\alpha}, \overline{\beta}, \overline{\gamma}, \ldots\}$, where $\overline{\Delta}$ is disjoint from and in bijection with Δ so that

$$\alpha\ (\in \Delta) \rightarrow \overline{\alpha}\ (\in \overline{\Delta})$$

The labels in Δ and $\overline{\Delta}$ are called complementary. Note that $\overline{\overline{\alpha}} = \alpha$.

We define also that each action α can only synchronize with its
coaction $\overline{\alpha}$ (called a **partner**). When they synchronize, there is an
interaction which produces a silent coupling action denoted by τ. We
thus have

$$L = \Delta \cup \overline{\Delta} \cup \{\tau\}$$

as the set of names.

When coupling takes place, the two synchronized actions α and $\overline{\alpha}$
are neither visible nor available as external input or output. This
situation is described by a restriction on the use of α and $\overline{\alpha}$ denoted by $\backslash\alpha$

3.7.2   CCS operators and their algebra

We first introduce the basic operators.

3.7.2.1   No action

This is represented by NIL.

3.7.2.2   Sequential composition and recursion

An action α followed by another action β is denoted by $\alpha \cdot \beta$. This is a non-
commutative but associative operation (like concatenation).

A process P exhibiting a continuous behaviour of actions α
followed by β repetitively is denoted by

$$P = \alpha \cdot \beta \cdot P$$

or

$$P = (\alpha \cdot \beta)^+$$

where $^+$ denotes one or more repetitions.

It is convenient to visualize that each action α is occurring in a system designated by ports, which are message carriers (both input and output). There is no loss in generality in naming each port by the observed action in it, namely α, since each port is identified with a unique action.

3.7.2.3 Summation (+)

This is a non-deterministic choice. Here a process Q that consists of either an action α or an action β, followed by γ repetitively, is represented by $Q = \alpha \cdot \gamma \cdot Q + \beta \cdot \gamma \cdot Q$. This operation + is commutative and associative; we use = to represent equality. NIL is a nullity for + ; that is, $Q + \text{NIL} = Q$.

3.7.2.4 Parallel composition (|)

We mentioned in Section 2.2.2 that parallelism is treated as a non-deterministic interleaving. Almost all models introduce this notion by using different operators (Gischer, 1981). (See also Section 8.4.)

Parallel composition (|) in CCS introduces non-deterministic choice (+) as well as coupling (τ) as byproducts. It is commutative and associative.

If we have two processes $P = \alpha \cdot P$ and $Q = \beta \cdot Q$ then their parallel composition is

$$(\alpha \cdot P) \,|\, (\beta \cdot Q) = \alpha \cdot (P \,|\, \beta \cdot Q) + \beta \,(\,(\alpha \cdot P) \,|\, Q)$$

Also, if P and Q are synchronized at ports α and $\bar{\alpha}$, then

$$(\alpha \cdot P) \,|\, (\bar{\alpha} \cdot Q) = \alpha \cdot (P \,|\, \bar{\alpha} \cdot Q) + \bar{\alpha} \cdot (\,(\alpha \cdot P) \,|\, Q) + \tau \cdot (P \,|\, Q)$$

where τ is the internal synchronization operator.

Thus the operator | makes a composition that either does α and then does $(P \,|\, \beta \cdot Q)$ or does β and then does $(\alpha \cdot P \,|\, Q)$.

Coupling can occur only between two processes with action and coaction. If more than two processes are ready, then the choice as to which pair will couple is non-deterministic. For example,

$$(\,(\,(\alpha \cdot P) \,|\, (\alpha \cdot Q) \,) \,|\, (\bar{\alpha} \cdot R) \,)$$
$$= \alpha \cdot (P \,|\, (\alpha \cdot Q) \,|\, (\bar{\alpha} \cdot R) \,)$$
$$+ \ \alpha \cdot (\,(\alpha \cdot P) \,|\, Q \,|\, (\bar{\alpha} \cdot R) \,)$$
$$+ \ \bar{\alpha} \cdot (\,(\alpha \cdot P) \,|\, (\alpha \cdot Q) \,|\, R)$$
$$+ \ \tau \ \cdot (P \,|\, (\alpha \cdot Q) \,|\, R)$$
$$+ \ \tau \ \cdot (\,(\alpha \cdot P) \,|\, Q \,|\, R)$$

3.7.2.5 Restriction (\)

This operator when followed by a name α (or $\bar{\alpha}$) hides both α and $\bar{\alpha}$. In other words, it eliminates the occurrence of certain specified actions and their coactions. Thus

(1) $\alpha \cdot P \backslash \alpha = \bar{\alpha} \cdot P \backslash \alpha = \text{NIL}$

(2) $(P + Q) \backslash \alpha = (P \backslash \alpha) + (Q \backslash \alpha)$

(3) $((\alpha \cdot P) | (\bar{\alpha} \cdot Q)) \backslash \alpha = \tau \cdot (P | Q) \backslash \alpha$

(4) $((\alpha \cdot P | \alpha \cdot Q) | (\bar{\alpha} \cdot R)) \backslash \alpha = \tau \cdot ((P | (\alpha \cdot Q) | R) \backslash \alpha) + \tau \cdot (((\alpha \cdot P) | Q | R) \backslash \alpha)$

(5) $P \backslash \alpha \backslash \beta = P \backslash \beta \backslash \alpha$

(6) $P \backslash \alpha = P$ (if $\alpha, \bar{\alpha} \notin L$)

3.7.2.6 Relabelling ([ ])

This operator permits relabelling of actions or ports. When an action α is to be renamed as β, we write $[\beta/\alpha]$. This relabels α to β and simultaneously $\bar{\alpha}$ to $\bar{\beta}$.

Since the composition ($|$) requires coupling with only complementary labels, it is necessary to relabel some actions to make interconnections and to retain the bijection property. Hence it plays a vital role in the calculus. This notion of relabelling is the same as in λ-calculus to provide a local name (free of clashes) which is autonomous and independent so that a communication process can access each port uniquely.

The following rules are applicable for relabelling:

(1) $P/\gamma = P[\beta \backslash \gamma] \backslash \beta$;

(2) $P[\,] = P$ (identity label);

(3) $P[R][S] = P[S \cdot R]$; that is, two successive labellings constitute a functional composition ($\cdot$) of labellings;

(4) $P \backslash \alpha [R] = P[R \cup \lambda/\alpha] \backslash \beta$, where $\alpha \in L$, name $(\lambda) = \beta \notin$ range of names in R.

Remarks

(i)   Of the above operations, $+$, NIL and actions are dynamic while $\backslash$, $|$ and [ ] are static.

(ii)   In CCS algebraic manipulation, rules are derived using the above operators for specific equivalences.

3.7.3 Semaphore in CCS

This example is an illustration of the use of CCS and its manipulative complexity. A binary semaphore S can be represented by the two repetitive actions α_P (P type) and α_V (V type) thus:

$$S = \alpha_P \cdot \alpha_V \cdot S$$

Suppose we have two processes X and Y seeking mutual exclusion; let each have ports α_P and α_V which are linked to S in $\bar{\alpha}_P$ and $\bar{\alpha}_V$. Further, assume that (β_X, γ_X) and (β_Y, γ_Y) are the critical sections of process X and process Y respectively. Then

$$X = \alpha_P \cdot \beta_X \cdot \gamma_X \cdot \alpha_V \cdot X$$
$$Y = \alpha_P \cdot \beta_Y \cdot \gamma_Y \cdot \alpha_V Y|$$

Also, the composite process Z can be described in CCS thus:

$$Z = (X \mid Y \mid S) \setminus \alpha_P \setminus \alpha_V$$

We must remember now that

$$S = \bar{\alpha}_P \cdot \bar{\alpha}_V \cdot S$$

Using this,

$$Z = (\alpha_P \cdot \beta_X \cdot \gamma_X \cdot \alpha_V \cdot X | \alpha_P \cdot \beta_Y \cdot \gamma_Y \cdot \alpha_V \cdot Y | \bar{\alpha}_P \cdot \bar{\alpha}_V \cdot S) \setminus \alpha_P \setminus \alpha_V$$

The algebra in CCS reduces this to

$$Z = \tau \cdot \beta_X \cdot \gamma_X \cdot \tau \cdot Z + \tau \cdot \beta_Y \cdot \gamma_Y \cdot \tau \cdot Z$$
$$= \tau \cdot (\beta_X \cdot \gamma_X + \beta_Y \cdot \gamma_Y) \cdot \tau \cdot Z$$

(This equation reminds us of the classical RST – flipflop equation.) The recursive form in Z is to be noted; this guarantees the continuous behaviour; the other terms correspond to synchronization and mutual exclusion. Obviously the fixed point or solution to the recursive equation in Z in an infinite set consisting of operations either in X or in Y in a mutually exclusive, non-deterministic fashion (see Sections 3.3.6.6 and 3.3.7.6).

3.7.4 Value communication

It is possible to have value communication embedded in CCS. This is a generalization of the notion of bound variables in λ-calculus. CCS uses many different binders such as $\alpha, \beta, \gamma \ldots$ rather than one binder, namely λ.

For example, a process P such as the Petri net multiplier (Section 3.5.6.3) can be expressed by

$$P = \alpha x \cdot \beta y \cdot \bar{\gamma} \cdot (z + x \cdot y) \cdot P$$

which means that the ports α and β receive the values of x and y respectively and the port $\bar{\gamma}$ outputs the result. For instance, if we substitute $x = 4$, $y = 3$ and $z = 1$:

$$P = \xrightarrow{\alpha 4} \beta y \cdot \bar{\gamma}(z + 4y) \, P \xrightarrow{\beta 3} \bar{\gamma}(z + 4 \cdot 3) \xrightarrow{\bar{\gamma} 1} (1 + 4 \cdot 3)$$

Thus it is possible to use localization of names for communicating values and evaluating the result. This permits the language to have both control and dataflow features.

3.7.5 Programming in CCS and proving correctness

Many concurrent algorithms can be expressed in CCS with clarity. Attempts have been made to use CCS as a programming language. However, other later developments such as Ada and CSP have been found to be practically more useful in program design and implementation.

Recently a language called COSY has been developed based on CCS for concurrent programming (Best, 1986); also, proof methods based on CCS have been developed for systolic systems by Hennessy (1986).

3.8 Hoare's CSP and TCSP

In Section 2.7.2.1 we introduced the basic constructs of CSP (communicating sequential processes) due to Hoare. Here we introduce the mathematical model of TCSP, a more recent version of CSP (Olderog, 1986; Hoare, 1985).

First, we summarize some details of CSP.

In CSP parallel composition is an n-ary operator denoted by

$$[P_1 :: S_1 \| P_2 :: S_2 \| \ldots \| P_n :: S_n]$$

where each $P_i :: S_i$ ($i = 1, 2, \ldots, n$) is a sequential program consisting of a unique process name P_i and a sequential statement S_i that uses all the operators of DILAG. The statements S_i have disjoint sets of local variables.

The communication between different processes is established via communication commands

$P_i ? x$ and $P_j ! y$

inside each sequential process. The command $P_i ? x$ expresses an input request from the process name P_i; $P_j ! y$ is an output request for the value of expression y to P_j. These requests are granted only if simultaneously P_i is ready for $P_j ! y$ and P_j is ready for $P_i ? x$. The effect of simultaneous execution is equivalent to $x := y$; that is the assignment of P_i's value of y to the local variable x in P_j. This is known as handshake synchronization between P_i and P_j.

To model disjunctive waiting, communication commands may also appear in the guards of the alternative and repetitive commands. For example, in

P_1 :: do B_1 ; $P_i ? x \rightarrow S_1$
      [ ] B_2 ; $P_j ? y \rightarrow S_2$
      od

if both B_1 and B_2 are true, P_1 waits for a handshake with either P_i or P_j. If P_i comes first the value is assigned to the variable x and S_1 is executed; if P_j comes first the value is assigned to y and S_2 is executed. If P_i and P_j are both ready, then a non-deterministic choice is made. After completion of S_1 or S_2 the do–od command is repeated. The repetitive command terminates successfully under the following conditions: (i) if both B_1 and B_2 evaluate to false or (ii) if B_1 and/or B_2 evaluate(s) true but the processes P_i and/or P_j addressed in the subsequent commands $P_i ? x$ and/or $P_j ? y$ have already terminated.

3.8.1   Comparison or TCSP and CCS

TCSP differs from CCS in the following essential points.

3.8.1.1   Non-determinism

Two kinds of non-determinism are introduced. The internal non-determinism performs a selection between two processes *P* or *Q*, without the knowledge of external environment (denoted by $P \Pi Q$).

The external non-determinism is that for which the environment can control which of *P* and *Q* will be selected. This operator is indicated by [ ].

Both of these operators are commutative, idempotent and associative. Also, the operator [ ] distributes over Π. Thus

$$P [] (Q \sqcap R) = (P [] Q) \sqcap (P [] R)$$
$$P \sqcap (Q [] R) = (P \sqcap Q) [] (P \sqcap R)$$

3.8.1.2   Parallelism

The combinator || for parallelism in TCSP is simpler than | in CCS. || only introduces synchronization and concurrency whereas | introduces non-determinism and hiding as side effects.

3.8.1.3   Synchronization

In CCS when two processes run concurrently, synchronization can occur only in pairs (name–coname ports). Their joint participation is hidden by the τ operator. In addition, we need a restriction operator \ to conceal the ports (Section 3.7.2.5).

In CSP there is a concealment operator \ which restricts the occurrence of certain events and, in addition, a hide operator for hiding a single symbol.

3.8.1.4   Recursion

In CCS there are no rules for unguarded recursion, whereas in TCSP there is a notion of divergence of a process whose recursion is unguarded. This results in non-termination when non-total functions arise. The recognition of recursive divergence is vital to understanding the functional meaning of a program.

3.8.1.5   Communication

In CSP the communication takes place as an event that is described by a pair $c \cdot v$ where c is the channel name and v is the value of the message passed.

3.8.1.6   Equivalence

In TCSP the approach to abstraction is different from that of CCS. Two processes in TCSP are identified if we cannot discover a difference in their divergence-free histories and deadlocks.

In CCS processes are identified only if every possible observable behaviour of one process can be simulated by the other process, and vice versa. In CCS this is called observational equivalence. Proving observational equivalence is difficult since the behaviour of a process cannot be studied without an environment. To obviate this difficulty, TCSP uses the concept of a refusal set for processes.

A refusal set is a family of sets of symbols for which a process refuses to engage in action even though the environment is ready for it.

In fact non-determinism and determinism are distinguished in TCSP using the notion of a refusal set. A process is called deterministic if it can never refuse any event in which it can engage, whereas a non-deterministic process may refuse at sometime some event in which it can engage.

3.8.1.7 Semantic model

A model known as a refusal set or failure set model can be used to give semantics to CSP. This model has as its only primitives the set of atomic communications between processes. Communications are events when the participating processes agree to execute them. Input and output are modelled at a higher level by varying the set of possible communications of processes.

It is also assumed that each process communicates with its environment, which could be other processes, users or observers, using symbols from a set Σ.

A process is then modelled as a pair (F, D). The first component F is the relation between possible traces of the process (the elements of Σ^* which are the possible sequences of communications of the process) and the sets of symbols which the process can refuse to respond to after the traces (refusals). In other words F consists of a set of ordered pairs (s, x) where the process can refuse to communicate when offered the set x by its environment after the trace s.

For example, in the transition system of Figure 3.2 (Section 3.3.3.5), $\Sigma = \{0, 1, 2, 3, 4\}$; the trace 021 takes it to F and then the machine refuses to respond and becomes deadlocked.

The second component D is the set of traces for which the process may diverge, that is engage in an infinite unbroken sequence of internal actions. When a process diverges it does not communicate with its environment again and the environment can never detect that this is so.

If a process deadlocks or diverges chaos results. It is possible to give denotational semantics for chaos in a compound process in terms of chaos in component processes.

The conventional method of specifying correctness is based on positive information, namely specifying which traces are allowable, thereby dealing with safety or partial correctness. The failure set model, in contrast, uses negative information which enables us to specify liveness and total correctness (see Section 1.8.2). These two are complementary ways of studying the behaviour of large systems – one dealing with conditions for success and the other dealing with conditions for failures.

3.8.2   CSP as a programming tool

We shall briefly introduce some simple constructs of CSP to illustrate its application to programming. The syntax of CSP (here we include additional IO (input–output) commands over DILAG) is as follows.

(1)   P is a CSP program iff P is a terminal string of the grammar

$$P ::= P_1 :: C_1 \| P_2 :: C_2 \| \ldots \| P_n :: C_n$$

Here P_i is a unique identifier for each sequential component C_i.

(2)   Cs are defined thus:

C ::= Skip | V := EXPR (assignment) | C_1; C_2 (sequence) | IO
    (input–output command) |
      If $G_1 \rightarrow C_1$
      [ ] $G_2 \rightarrow C_2$
      [ ] $G_n \rightarrow C_n$
      fi (choice) | do $G_1 \rightarrow C_1$ [ ] $\ldots$ [ ] $G_n \rightarrow C_n$ od (loop)
      for $n \geqslant 1$;
IO ::= P_j ! V (receive V from P_j – input) |
      P_j EXPR (send EXPR to P_j – output$^\backslash$
G :: = B (simple guard) |
      B; IO (guard with communication)

where V, EXPR, B are respectively a variable, an expression and a boolean expression.

(3)   Two IO commands P_j ? V and P_i ! EXPR are said to be partners iff the former occurs in P_i and the latter occurs in P_j.

$$P = P_1 \| P_2 \| \ldots \| P_n \text{ is such that:}$$

- each P_i contains only local variables;
- if P_i contains an IO command addressing P_j then $i \neq j$ and P_j must contain at least one partner IO command addressing P_i.

     A pair of partner IO commands can be executed jointly (and has the effect of an assignment V := EXPR) iff the two commands are executable individually. If one of them (or both) is preceded by a boolean expression in the context B; IO $\rightarrow$ C then the joint execution can take place only if all involved boolean expressions are true. IO commands occurring in the guards of an alternative command indicate selective communication; if one of the alternatives cannot be entered (whether because a boolean expression is false or a communication partner is not ready), others may. If P_j is addressed in the guard of a loop then the distributed termination convention of CSP requires the termination of P_j to imply the termination of the loop.

3.8.3 Example

We now give an example of the use of CSP to find the minimum of n distinct positive integers, using n processors in a ring.

For this purpose, we assume that there is a ring of processes P_i each with an associated buffer B_i ($i = 1, 2, \ldots, n$) and processes can communicate with their neighbours with higher index i modulo n. We assume also that each process P_i has a unique identity $ID(i)$ which is the positive integer contained in it.

Each process P_{i-1} passes its ID number to its buffer B_{i-1}; then B_{i-1} sends the number $ID(i - 1)$ to P_i. Then P_i acts as follows: if the number received is smaller then $ID(i)$, P_i sends it to B_i; if the number received is bigger than $ID(i)$ it does nothing; if the number received is equal to $ID(i)$ it sends it out. Thus larger numbers are dropped and the lowest is sent out.

The CSP program is:

$$P = P_1 \parallel B_1 \ldots P_n \parallel B_n$$
$$B_1 :: \text{do } P_i ? Z_i \rightarrow P_{i+1} ! Z_i \text{ od}$$
$$P_1 :: B_i ! ID(i) ; \text{ do } B_{i-1} ? x_i \rightarrow \text{ If } x_i > ID(i) \rightarrow \text{Skip}$$
$$[\,] \; x_i < ID(i) \rightarrow B_i ! x_i$$
$$[\,] \; x_i = ID(i) \rightarrow \text{OUT} ! x_i$$
$$\text{fi}$$
$$\text{od}$$

3.9 Dataflow and related multiset models

Several other models have been recently proposed for concurrent computation. These models derive their basic concepts from CCS, CSP and functional models. In all these models concurrent processes are treated as networks, where each process communicates with other processes solely by the asynchronous transmission of messages through input–output ports. This form of computation is also known as dataflow, since processes can function concurrently as long as data is available; there is no control flow.

These models have the following features.

(1) Input–output behaviour:
The computation is described solely as a function with a specified input–output behaviour; the internal states are hidden.

(2) Ability to deal with non-determinism:
In deterministic computations, the input–output behaviour is determinate. This means that for a given input sequence (called a history vector) the output history vector is unique and completely

defined. A non-deterministic system is one which exhibits different behaviours for the same input history. In other words, unlike deterministic computations, non-deterministic computations are not repeatable; they exhibit multiple possible output histories. As a result, the computation proceeds along two dimensions: choice and approximation. The former deals with selection among alternatives during a computation and the latter produces better and better approximations of the intended result. Thus any model needs to address these two aspects.

(3)   Denotational semantics:
       The Petri net model gives operational semantics which expresses the behaviour in terms of possible sequences of transition firings during a computation. It is useful for specifying implementations but not sufficiently abstract to be of great use for understanding the behaviour (such as the correctness of large programs). It is therefore preferable to use a model that gives denotational semantics; here, the objective is to abstract away from details of program representation and a compound process is described in terms of its components. In other words, any syntactic operation for combining processes has a corresponding natural operation in the semantic domain for combining the meanings.

(4)   Computational procedure:
       The model should provide a method for computing the behaviour of a compound network in terms of its components by a successive approximation or substitution technique that converges or has a least fixed point.

3.9.1 Kahn's model

One of the earliest models for determinate networks is due to Kahn (1974). Here a process is viewed as a function from n-tuples of histories to histories. Each connection or channel of the net is associated with such a history. A network of processes is then characterized as a system of recursive equations. Its behaviour for a given input sequence can then be obtained and approximations to its behaviour can be computed by the fixed-point method. A typical example of such a network is shown in Figure 3.14.

Here the problem is, given functions F_1, F_2, F_3, how to express the function represented by the entire network which takes input sequences x and y and yields the output sequence z. We can see that

$$w = F_2(x, F_1(w, y))$$

and

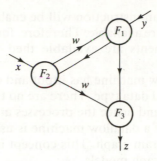

Figure 3.14   Kahn's model.

$$z = F_3(w, F_1(w, y))$$

which are mutually recursive.

Although this analysis looks simple, it has very serious limitations:

(1)   if the nodes of the network are non-deterministic or not fully described as a function, there is no easy way to describe the network;

(2)   there is no ordering imposed on the arrival of the inputs, and hence an inadequate description is produced;

(3)   realization of the model needs unbounded memory.

To remove these limitations Brock and Ackermann (1981) introduced a model known as a 'scenario model'. This model takes into account the ordering of events and multiplicity of events. The Brock–Ackermann model uses the theory of partially ordered multisets. A multiset (also known as a bag) is a generalization of the set concept. Unlike a set, which can have only distinct elements (with no multiplicity), a multiset may contain repeated elements with known multiplicities.

Brock and Ackermann showed that history relations among components do not completely specify the behaviour of non-deterministic networks. Therefore, other approaches were needed. One such approach is due to Pratt (1985, 1986) who proposed a partially ordered multiset model (pomset model) which formalizes the Brock–Ackermann model.

3.9.2   Dennis–Rumbaugh dataflow model

In Section 1.5 we briefly introduced the concept of the dataflow computing model (Sharp, 1985; Dennis, 1984). An important rule of dataflow computing is that an instruction will be enabled for execution only when all its arguments are available. Therefore, for several instructions if all the required arguments are available then they can be executed simultaneously.

A typical dataflow machine has input and output ports with each port having a designated data type. There are no timings associated with the events at the ports and hence the processes are asynchronous.

The behaviour of a dataflow machine is usually abstracted in the form of a dataflow program graph. This concept is very much similar to Petri nets and related graph models.

Each node represents an instruction or operation and two nodes are linked by an arc which represents data dependences. The flow of data along the arcs is represented by tokens. Each token can represent one data or control value. The control values are boolean data values.

It is assumed that only one token may reside upon an arc at any one time. Nodes are said to be enabled when there is a token present on all their input arcs (except in the special case of a merge node) and there are no tokens on their output arcs. These constraints help to clear old tokens before new tokens are produced, thereby avoiding collisions. When nodes are enabled they absorb the incoming tokens and emit appropriate tokens on the output arcs.

Synchronization is achieved by having all the inputs present before execution. However, other modifications have also been introduced for partial input execution.

3.9.2.1 Fundamental operators

The following fundamental operators are introduced.

(1)   Primitive application:
Applies function f to the inputs and generates the output.

(2)   Duplicator:
Provides the appropriate number of copies of a token.

(3)   Value generator:
Inserts literal values (including integers, booleans and other data types).

In addition to the above three operators two other fundamental control operators are introduced. These are called 'switch' and 'merge'. These are shown in Figures 3.15(a) and 3.15(b). Note that the switch resembles the fork operation and the merge resembles the join operation.

(4)   The switch:
This node has two inputs and two outputs. One of the inputs

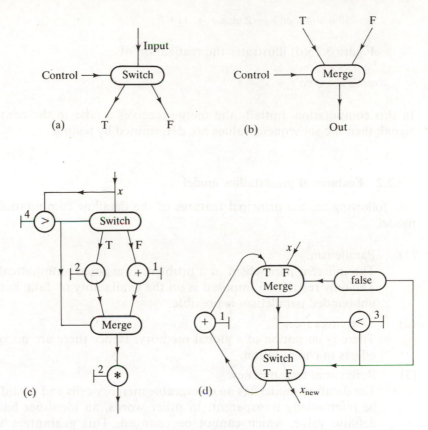

Figure 3.15 (a) Switch operator; (b) merge operator; (c) realization of 'if . . . then
. . . else'; (d) realization of 'while . . . do'.

carries an input data token and the other a boolean control token.
The two output arcs are labelled true (T) and false (F). If the
control outputs true then the input data value is switched to
output T; otherwise, to output F. This node is also called a
distributor.

(5)   The merge:
This node has three inputs, that is a boolean control, data T and
data F, and an output. If the control signal is true, data T is
selected as output; otherwise, data F is selected as output. This
node is also called a **selector**.

Using the switch and merge sequentially, conditionals can be
realized; also, using the merge first and switch next, iterative constructs
can be realized. These are illustrated in Figures 3.15(c) and 3.15(d).
Figure 3.15(c) illustrates the realization of:

y := [If x > 4 then x − 2 else x + 1] * 2

Figure 3.15(d) illustrates the realization of

while x < 3 do x := x + 1

In this computation, initially the merge receives a false in the control signal; then the subsequent values are determined by testing.

3.9.2.2   Features of the dataflow model

The following are the principal features of the dataflow computational model.

(1)   Parallelism:
       The inherent parallelism in a problem is exposed automatically. The only restriction imposed is on the availability of data; hence unbounded parallelism is possible.

(2)   Side effect free:
       There is no notion of a global memory. Hence there are no side effects in computation.

(3)   Referential transparency:
       The dataflow model has no changeable memory cells and is said to be referentially transparent. In other words, an identifier has a definite value, which cannot be changed. This guarantees the absence of aliasing and side effects. Hence a dataflow program will always produce the same result, within a given context.

(4)   Single semantic assignment rule:
       We cannot alter the definition of an identifier that has already been defined in the environment. Thus assignments take the form of equalities in the conventional mathematical sense.

(5)   Locality of effect:
       Data produced at one node does not produce a long-term effect elsewhere, but is used immediately afterwards. Features (2)–(5) support modularity and functional processing.

(6)   Non-determinism:
       This can be expressed using the merge operator. For example, if there are two sequences or streams of elements S1 and S2, then merge produces a stream that contains all the elements from S1 and S2 such that ordering of elements within S1 and S2 is preserved; however, the order in which an element from either S1 and S2 occurs is arbitrary. Thus we are able to obtain interleaving.

3.9.2.3 Deadlock issues

If two operations are dependent on the outputs of each other then deadlock results. It is impossible to perform either operation, assuming that all inputs must be present before evaluation takes place. In order to prevent such constructions, where it is impossible to define a partial ordering on the operations, the following rule is used:

> No operations may be combined in such a manner as to cause an operation to be dependent, either directly or indirectly, upon its own output or outputs.

The above rule then forbids the construction of loops or cyclic graphs and requires only acyclic graphs. This means that conventional iteration is not supported and successive iterations are to be performed on copies. Various modifications to this type of processing have been introduced.

For further studies on non-deterministic dataflow programs, their fixed points and correctness proofs, see Staples and Nguyen (1985) and Broy (1986).

3.9.3 Probabilistic model

The asynchronous execution behaviour of several concurrent processes which use randomization has also been studied by Hart *et al.* (1983). Here each process is viewed as a discrete Markov chain over the set of common execution states.

Based on this, Hart *et al.* present a decision procedure of almost sure termination of concurrent probabilistic programs having a finite state space.

Hart *et al.* also deal with the power of probabilistic synchronization schemes. They show that if n processes participate in a synchronization protocol using a shared variable V on which indivisible test-and-set operations are allowed, at least $\sqrt{2n}$ values of V are needed to ensure mutual exclusion and freedom from lock out. Also, they show that if each process has only a single state while in its idle section then at least $(n + 1)/2$ values of V are required.

3.10 Models for synchronous computers

So far we have been concerned with asynchronous, non-deterministic models for parallel computing. We now introduce some basic models for synchronous deterministic parallel computing. In view of their simplicity they are more easily understood than asynchronous non-deterministic machines.

As already mentioned in Section 1.9.2, synchronous computers are also known as 'systolic processors' owing to their rhythmic act of performance in pumping data in and out, analogously to the functioning of the heart.

Two important properties of the systolic automata are:

(1)   The inputs are rhythmically pumped into and out of the system at regular, consecutive and specified instants of time (hence deterministic).

(2)   The flow of information in the system is unidirectional to ensure that an input will never get mixed up with previous inputs.

The modelling power and decision power of a systolic automaton depends very much on the nature of the interconnections. The simplest model is that of systolic tree automata (STA). A more complex model is that of systolic lattice or mesh (or trellis) automata (SMA). The former accepts languages that are strictly contained in the family of languages accepted by the latter.

3.10.1   Systolic tree automata (STA)

This model has an underlying abstract graph structure that is a rooted binary tree. It is assumed that the input information is a word from an alphabet set and is pumped up from a suitable level at the bottom of the tree; the acceptance of the word is decided at the root of the tree; hence we call this **bottom-up parsing**. The processors are located at the various nodes of the tree. A typical systolic binary tree is shown in Figure 3.16.

In Figure 3.16 every node has two sons except the leaf nodes. The given input word is to be presented at a least level k such that $2^k \geq n$, where n is the word length of the input word. If $2^k > n$ then $2^k - n$ positions are filled with the symbol #.

From the point of view of systolic processing, it is convenient to define three sets of alphabets:

- Σ_P: the alphabet that acts as names of the processors;
- Σ_O: the operational alphabet;
- Σ_I: the input alphabet.

We assume that the letter # is present in both Σ_O and Σ_I and $\Sigma_I - \{\#\}$ and $\Sigma_O - \{\#\}$ are not empty.

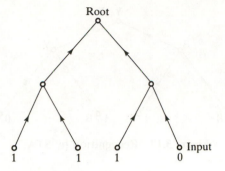

Root

1   1   1   0   Input

Figure 3.16 Systolic tree.

The function of the systolic processor can now be mathematically described using two functions:

$$G : \Sigma_I \to \Sigma_O$$

and

$$F : \Sigma_O \times \Sigma_O \to \Sigma_O$$

for every letter in Σ_O.

The function G maps an input letter to an operational letter and F maps an input pair of operational letters to another operational letter. In addition, we specify a subset of Σ_O as the set of accepting letters.

In Figure 3.16 let us assume

$$\Sigma_P = \{x\}, \Sigma_O = \{A, B, Y, \#\}, \Sigma_I = \{0, 1, \#\}$$

and define

$$G(0) = A, G(1) = B, G(\#) = \#$$
$$F(B, B) = B, F(A, A) = A, F(B, A) = Y,$$
$$F(B, Y) = Y, \text{ and } F(\alpha, \beta) = \# \text{ for all other cases}$$

Here we use Y to denote acceptance. The above systolic tree recognizes the string 1110 as shown in Figure 3.17.

The above principle can be generalized to a binary tree with k levels in which 2^k elements exist at level k.

3.10.1.1 Languages accepted

The family of languages accepted by the STA contains all regular languages and is closed under boolean operations. Some non-context-free

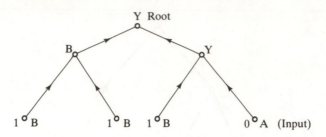

Figure 3.17   Recognition by STA.

languages are also accepted by STA. However, no characterization, as yet, is available.

The STA has the same decision power whether it is deterministic or non-deterministic.

3.10.1.2   Homogeneous and stable STA

An STA is said to be **homogeneous** if the alphabet Σ_P contains only one letter; that is, the processors are indistinguishable from each other in their behaviour.

An STA is **stable** if the accepted language is invariant even though the input is fed into different levels of the tree.

It is possible to construct a stable STA that is equivalent to a given STA.

3.10.2   Systolic mesh automata (SMA)

Here the underlying graph is a mesh or lattice as shown in Figure 3.18. Unlike the STA, here, at every level, the number of processors is one more than at the next higher level. Also, the leftmost and rightmost nodes have only one father node while the innermost nodes have two father nodes.

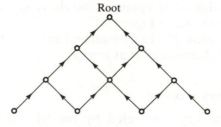

Figure 3.18   Systolic mesh.

The input word is presented at a level that can take the entire given input word. In this case, since every possible length is available it is not necessary to fill the empty spaces with #.

3.10.2.1 SMA for parentheses grammar

We now give an example of recognizing the well-formedness of a set of left and right parentheses (see Section 3.3.4). For this purpose, we consider the following three alphabet sets:

$$\Sigma_P = \{ i, R, L, t \}$$

where the symbols i, R, L and t respectively are the labels of inner, rightmost, leftmost and topmost (root) processors,

$$\Sigma_I = \{ (,) \}$$

and

$$\Sigma_O = \{ (,), Y, N \}$$

where Y (yes) and N (no) denote acceptance and rejection respectively. We have now

$$G(( ) = ($$
$$G( )) =)$$

Let us now define the functions F_L, F_R, F_i and F_t for recognizing the parentheses grammar (note that the following production rules define the parentheses grammar (Section 3.3.4):

(1) $S \rightarrow SS$
(2) $S \rightarrow (S)$
(3) $S \rightarrow ( )$

F_t	(	)	Y	N
(	N	Y	N	N
)	N	N	N	N
Y	N	N	Y	N
N	N	N	N	N

F_i	(	)	Y	N
(	(	Y	(	N
)	Y	)	Y	N
Y	Y	)	Y	N
N	N	N	N	N

F_L	(	)	Y	N
(	(	Y	(	N
)	N	N	N	N
Y	Y	)	Y	N
N	N	N	N	N

F_R	(	)	Y	N
(	N	Y	N	N
)	N	)	Y	N
Y	N	)	Y	N
N	N	N	N	N

This SMA transmits the left parentheses along the L processors and the right parentheses along the R processors until they match (indicated by Y) or mismatch (indicated by N) at the top processor. Matching and mismatching are shown in Figure 3.19.

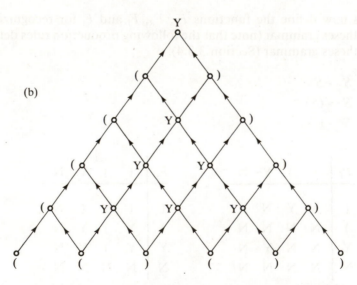

Figure 3.19   (a) Mismatch in SMA; (b) match in SMA.

3.10.2.2   Language accepted

The mesh automaton (SMA) is more powerful than the tree automaton (STA). Note that an STA cannot recognize a parentheses grammar which is not regular (see Section 3.3.4.2).

The non-deterministic SMA is more powerful than the deterministic SMA. Some restricted TM models can be considered equivalent to these automata. These are useful for complexity studies (for a detailed study refer to Gruska (1984) and Salomaa (1985)).

3.10.3   Cellular array automata

A closely related topic to SMA is that of cellular and array automata. Research in this area is rapidly growing (Legendi *et al.*, 1986): in particular, for applications to parallel and distributed computing.

3.11   Alternating Turing machine model

We will now briefly summarize an important model known as the alternating TM model (ATM) based on an extension of the TM concept. This model is more abstract and is useful for complexity studies.

The ATM was introduced by Chandra *et al.* (1981). It is a generalization of the notion of a non-deterministic TM (NDTM) (Section 3.3.5).

In the case of an NDTM, the transition rules allow a single machine configuration α to reach several configurations $\beta_1, \beta_2, \ldots, \beta_n$ in one step; by definition, the configuration α leads to acceptance iff there exists at least one successor β_i which leads to acceptance; we may call it an 'or acceptance'. In addition to these 'existential branches', an ATM can make 'universal branches' and 'negating moves'.

In a universal branch, a configuration α can reach several configurations $\beta_1, \ldots, \beta_n$ as in an NDTM, but now there is a difference; α leads to acceptance iff all the successors $\beta_1, \ldots, \beta_n$ lead to acceptance. Thus here we want an 'and acceptance'.

In a negating move, a configuration α has only one successor β, and α leads to acceptance iff β leads to a rejection.

A formalization of these notions leads to the ATM. These notions can be applied to PDMs. It turns out that alternating PDMs are strictly more powerful than a non-deterministic PDM. It can also be shown that ATMs have the same power as a TM. It also turns out that alternation does not add power to the FSMs (Hromkovic, 1984).

An alternating machine can also be viewed as a machine with unbounded parallelism in which processes communicate only with their parent or offspring. When in a configuration α with several successors β_1, ..., β_n the machine spawns n independent offspring which run to completion, report acceptance or rejection back to their parent α and then die. The parent α then combines the answers by 'or', if α is existential; if α is universal, the answers are combined by 'and'. The resulting answer is then passed on to α's parent and so on.

A study of a variety of parallel machine models leads to the parallel computation thesis which states that 'time on a parallel machine is polynomially related to space on a sequential TM'. Chandra *et al.* prove that alternating time and deterministic space are polynomially related. This leads to the result that an ATM is, to within a polynomial, among the most powerful types of parallel machines.

Shapiro (1984) has studied the relationship between ATM and logic programming. His study has revealed a relationship between the structural complexity and computational complexity of logic programs. The ATM serves as an important analytical tool for parallel logic programming.

SUMMARY

This chapter dealt with the various models of computational processes. After a brief introduction to model theory, we described the classical computational models – mechanistic or operational models, such as finite state machines, push-down stack machines, Turing machines, and the relationship to linguistic models, namely chomskian languages, and to function models, namely recursive functions and the λ-calculus.

We then introduced the algebraic and analytic properties of recursive functions – partial orders, lattices, monotonicity, continuity and the Knaster–Tarski fixed-point theorem.

We then took up the approaches to parallel computational models. Here the Petri net model was studied in great detail; we introduced the matrix description as well as the DILAG (Dijkstra's language of guarded commands) description of Petri nets; also, we made a comparative study of the related models such as the vector addition system, marked graphs and computation graphs.

Then we described the more recent models – Milner's CCS, Hoare's CSP–TCSP and the dataflow models.

The systolic approach to computation is an important step in synchronous, deterministic, parallel computing. Two important models – systolic tree automata and systolic mesh automata – and their properties were then introduced.

Finally, we introduced the more abstract model called the alternating Turing machine and its relationship to parallel logic programming.

EXERCISES

3.1 Examine the axioms of groups in algebra. How should these axioms be written precisely using the first-order predicate calculus?

3.2 Learn about the fundamentals of model theory and its impact on programming language design.

3.3 What are the limitations of models used in physics? Are they subject to the same undecidability questions?

3.4 Show why a finite state machine cannot recognize a set of well-formed parentheses.

3.5 Show that a deterministic push-down machine can recognize both single and double parentheses grammar.

3.6 Show why an even palindrome cannot be recognized by a deterministic push-down machine but can be recognized by a non-deterministic push-down machine.

3.7 Convert the binary addition operation into a production system. What type of grammar does it belong to?

3.8 Show that a finite state machine can model the axioms of a semigroup.

3.9 Show that the addition operation modulo 2 is a model for the group axioms.

3.10 Show that an uninterpreted flowchart for computing the factorial of an integer n and that for reversing a string are isomorphic.

3.11 Let the disorder function be defined by

$$D(a_1, a_2, \ldots, a_m) = \sum_{i=1}^{m} d_i$$

where $(a_1, a_2, \ldots, a_m)$ is a permutation of the m-tuple $(1, 2, \ldots, m)$ and d_i is the distance of a_i measured from its rightful place.

Show that the maximum value of D is $2n^2$ for m even (= $2n$) and $2n^2 + 2n$ for m odd (= $2n+1$).

3.12 Find a well-founded set measure to prove the termination of a program for computing the greatest common divisor by the euclidean algorithm.

3.13 Draw a Petri net to compute the quotient $[x/y]$ where x and y are integers and $[\,]$ stands for the lower integral part (Section 3.5.6.4).

3.14 Draw a Petri net for finding the lower integral part of the positive square root of a positive integer.

3.15 Study a composite Petri net by simulation.

3.16 Write a program in Pascal or Modula to convert the incidence matrix representation of a Petri net to DILAG and conversely.

3.17 Examine the 'select' construct in Ada and study its uses.

3.18 Use Milner's CCS to describe a Petri net that non-deterministically computes the maximum of two positive integers.

3.19 Describe the computation of the greatest common divisor of two positive integers using CCS.

3.20 Study the two types of non-determinism used in CSP. Give a few practical cases where such types of non-determinism arise.

3.21 Write a CSP program to find the greatest common divisor of n positive integers.

3.22 Express the 16 two-variable boolean functions using the λ-notation.

3.23 Study the properties of multisets and partially ordered multisets.

3.24 Study the properties of semirings. How are they used in modelling concurrent processes? (See Pratt, 1985.)

3.25 Construct a systolic mesh automaton that accepts well-formed sequences of words from two pairs of parentheses: (,) and [,].

3.26 Simulate the alternate Turing machine model using PROLOG.

References

Ajmone Marsan M., Babbo G. and Conte G. (1986). *Performance Models of Multiprocessor Systems*. Cambridge MA: MIT Press

Allison L. (1987). *A Practical Introduction to Denotational Semantics*. London: Cambridge University Press

Barendregt H.P. (1984). *The Lambda Calculus*. Amsterdam: North-Holland

Best E. (1986). Cosy – its relation to nets and CSP. *Lecture Notes in Computer Science*, **255**, 416–41

Brauer W. (1979). Net theory and applications. *Lecture Notes in Computer Science*, **84**

Brauer W., Reisig W. and Rozenberg G. (1986a). Petri nets: central models and their properties. *Lecture Notes in Computer Science*, **254**

Brauer W., Reisig W. and Rozenberg G. (1986b). Petri nets, applications and relationship to other models of concurrency. *Lecture Notes in Computer Science*, **255**

Brock J.B. and Ackermann W.B. (1981). Scenarios: a model of nondeterminate computation. In *Formalization of Programming Concepts* (Diaz J. and Ramos I., eds.). *Lecture Notes in Computer Science*, **107**, 252–9

Brookes S.D., Roscoe A.W. and Winskel G. (1984). Seminar on concurrency. *Lecture Notes in Computer Science*, **197**

Broy M. (1986). A theory for nondeterminism, parallelism, communication and concurrency. *Theoretical Computer Science*, **45**, 1–61

Campbell J.A. (1984). *Implementations of Prolog*. Chichester: Ellis Horwood

Chandra A.K., Kozen D.C. and Stockmeyer L.J. (1981). Alternation. *J. ACM*, **28**, 114–33

Denning P.J., Dennis J.B. and Qualitz J.E. (1978) *Machines, Languages and Computation*. Englewood Cliffs NJ: Prentice-Hall

Dennis J.B. (1984). Control flow and dataflow: concepts of distributed programming. In *Int. Summer School, Ser. F* (Broy M., ed.), Vol. 14, pp. 345–99. New York: Springer

Gischer J. (1981). Shuffle languages, Petri nets and context-sensitive grammar. *Comm. ACM*, **24**, 597–605

Glaser H., Hankin C. and Till D. (1984). *Principles of Functional Programming*. Englewood Cliffs NJ: Prentice-Hall

Gries D. (1981). *The Science of Programming*. New York: Springer

Gruska J. (1984). Systolic automata – power, characterization, non-homogoneity. *Lecture Notes in Computer Science*, **176**, 32–49

Hart S., Sharir M. and Pnueli A. (1983). Termination of probabilistic concurrent programs. *ACM Trans. Programming Languages and Systems*, **5**, 356–81

Henderson P. (1980). *Functional Programming*. Englewood Cliffs NJ: Prentice-Hall

Hennessy M. (1986). Proving systolic systems correct. *ACM Trans. Programming Languages and Systems*, **8**, 344–87

Hennessy M. (1988). *Algebraic Theory of Processes*. Cambridge MA: MIT Press

Hindley J.R. and Seldin J.P. (1986). *Introduction to Combinators and λ-calculus*. Cambridge: Cambridge University Press

Hoare C.A.R. (1985). *Communicating Sequential Processes*. Englewood Cliffs NJ: Prentice-Hall

Hromkovic J. (1984). On the power of alternation in finite automata. *Lecture Notes in Computer Science*, **176**, 322–9

IEEE (1988). *Proceedings 1987 Symposium on Logic Programming*. New York: IEEE

Kahn G. (1974). The semantics of a simple language for parallel programming. In *Inf. Processing '74, Proc. IFIP Cong.*, Vol. 77 (Rosenfeld J.L., ed.), pp. 471–5. New York: North-Holland

Karp R.M. and Miller R.E. (1966). Properties of a model for parallel computation: determinacy, termination and queuing. *SIAM J. of Applied Mathematics*, **14**, 1390–411

Krishnamurthy E.V. (1983). *Introductory Theory of Computer Science*. London: Macmillan

Lassez J.L., Nguyen V.L. and Sonenberg E.A. (1982). Fixed point theorems and semantics – a folktale, *Information Processing Lett.*, **14**, 112–16

Legendi T., Parkinson D., Vollmar R. and Wolf G. (1986). *Parallel Processing by Cellular Automata and Arrays*. Amsterdam: North-Holland

Manna Z. (1974). *Mathematical Theory of Computation*. New York: McGraw-Hill

Manna Z. and Waldinger R. (1985). *The Logical Basis for Computer Programming*. Reading MA: Addison-Wesley

McGettrick A.D. (1980). *The Definition of Programming Languages*. London: Cambridge University Press

Mendelsohn E. (1979). *Introduction to Mathematical Logic*. New York: van Nostrand

Milner R. (1980). A calculus of communicating systems. *Lecture Notes in Computer Science*, **92**

Olderog E.R. (1986). TCSP – theory of communicating sequential processes. *Lecture Notes in Computer Science*, **255**, 441–66

Pagnoni A. and Rozenberg G. (1983). Application and theory of Petri nets. *Informatik-Fachberichte*. New York: Springer

Peterson J.L. (1981). *Petri Net Theory and the Modelling of Systems*. Englewood Cliffs NJ: Prentice-Hall

Pratt V. (1985). Pomset model of parallel processing. *Lecture Notes in Computer Science*, **197**, 180–96

Pratt V. (1986). Modelling concurrency with partial orders. *International J. Parallel Programming*, **15**, 33–73

Pratt V.R. and Stockmeyer L.J. (1976). A characterization of the power of vector machines. *J. Computer System Science*, **12**, 198–221

Reisig W. (1985). *Petri Nets*. New York: Springer

Revesz G. (1988). *Lambda Calculus, Combinators and Functional Programming*. Cambridge: Cambridge University Press

Robinson A. (1963). *Introduction to Model Theory and the Metamathematics of Algebra*. Amsterdam: North-Holland

Rozenberg G. (1986). Advances in Petri nets. *Lecture Notes in Computer Science*, **222**

Rozenberg G. (1987). Advances in Petri nets. *Lecture Notes in Computer Science*, **266**

Salomaa A. (1985). *Computation and Automata*. London: Cambridge University Press

Schmidt D.A. (1988). *Denotational Semantics*. Newton MA: Allyn and Bacon
Shapiro E.Y. (1984). *Alternation and the Computational Complexity of Logic Programs*. CS84–06, Weizmann Institute of Science, Rehovot, Israel
Sharp J.A. (1985). *Dataflow Computing*. Chichester: Ellis Horwood
Staples J. and Nguyen V.L. (1985). A fixedpoint semantics or nondeterministic dataflow. *J. ACM*, **32**, 411–44
Stoy J.E. (1977). *Denotational Semantics*. Cambridge MA: MIT Press
Tick E. (1988). *Memory Performance of Prolog Architectures*. Boston MA: Kluwer
Tourlakis G. (1983). *Computability*. Reston VA: Reston Publishing Co.
Woods J.V. (1985). *Fifth Generation Computer Architectures*. Amsterdam: North-Holland
Yasuhara A. (1971). *Recursive Function Theory and Logic*. London: Academic Press

Chapter 4
Parallel Processes – Analysis and Semantics

4.1	Introduction	4.4	Tree semantics
4.2	Basics of semantics of concurrency	4.5	Temporal semantics
		4.6	Power domain semantics
4.3	Semantics of Petri net models	4.7	Actor semantics
			Summary

4.1 Introduction

In the previous chapter, we described several models for parallel–concurrent processes. Essentially we can classify these models into two kinds:

(1) operational or concrete models, for example Petri nets, state transition systems;

(2) algebraic (partial ordering) or abstract models (for example CCS, pomsets).

In order to use these models effectively, one needs to develop analytical or symbolic logic methods that will reveal the many different behavioural properties grouped under the following three categories (Section 1.8.2):

(1) **Invariance or safeness properties**
Partial correctness, mutual exclusion and absence of deadlock.

(2) **Eventuality or liveness properties**
Total correctness and termination, accessibility, absence of live-lock and starvation, and responsiveness.

(3) **Fairness properties**
Providing equitable or impartial treatment of all processes so that

no process is neglected; that is, 'any process which may be scheduled infinitely often will be executed infinitely often'.

The question of fairness typically arises in several contexts. Examples of the following kinds occur often:

(1)   the choice of an alternative in a non-deterministic algorithm;

(2)   the choice as to which process should get the next allocated slice of processor time in a multiprogrammed system;

(3)   in a resource allocation system, the choice as to which user should be granted a resource next so that no user is neglected (or starved);

(4)   in a mutual exclusion system, the choice of which process should be given next access.

In the case of a concurrent program written in specific programming or other descriptive languages, the above properties can be deduced only by understanding the meaning of the program. Typically, a program can be quite large and complicated. Therefore, it is desirable to decompose a program into modules; this will enable us to understand the meaning of the total program from the meaning of the smaller-size modules. This requires that a proper formal basis is to be chosen for the modules.

4.1.1   Formal basis – syntax, semantics and pragmatics

To provide such a formal basis, a language is usually partitioned into three aspects: syntax, semantics and pragmatics:

- **Syntax** defines the legal sentences that are admissible in the language; here the meaning of a sentence is not considered.

- **Semantics** defines the meaning or interpretation of each legal sentence.

- **Pragmatics** attempts to indicate how these sentences should be constructed and combined to achieve certain desired goals. In other words, pragmatics is the style or mode of usage of the language.

4.1.2   Purpose of formal semantics

A formal semantics provides a means for:

(1)   deducing safeness, liveness and fairness properties of a program, namely providing a proof system;

(2)   differentiating deadlock from successful termination;

(3)   distinguishing livelock from continuous behaviour;

(4)   distinguishing between non-terminating computations and partially defined computation;

(5)   deciding whether the compilation is correct, given a formal semantics of the target language into which a program is compiled.

4.1.3 Categories of formal semantics in sequential programming

In the case of sequential programming, the formal semantics is roughly classified into three categories:

4.1.3.1 Operational semantics

Here it is assumed that programs are generators of execution sequences on a well-defined hypothetical machine. Each execution sequence is a sequence of machine states. The set of execution sequences associated with each statement is described unambiguously by specifying the successor relationship that holds between consecutive states in any execution sequence. In other words, the meaning of each statement is defined by its effects on the hypothetical machine. The structure of the machine is kept so simple that there can be no misunderstanding on the way in which it works.

In summary, operational semantics defines the input–output relation computed by a program in terms of the individual operations evoked by the program inside a machine. The meaning of a program is the input–output relation obtained by executing the program on the machine.

4.1.3.2 Denotational semantics

This semantics is machine independent. Here a program is regarded as a function from an initial to a final state or as a relation between the initial state and the final state. The semantics is specified as a mapping from the program to the function or relation it computes. In other words, denotational semantics defines each language construct in terms of certain mathematical entities (numbers, truth values, functions) that model their meaning. The total meaning of a program is then reconstructed as a composition of the meanings of the basic constructs. If the program is recursively defined, then its meaning is the input–output function corresponding to the least or minimal fixed point of a transformation associated with the program.

4.1.3.3 Axiomatic or deductive semantics

This semantics does not bother about what a program is or what it does but concerns itself about what can be deduced about its behaviour or the function or relation it computes. Here the meaning is specified entirely in terms of the logical statements that can be made about the effect of executing a language construct.

4.1.4 Extending formal semantics to parallel programs

For sequential deterministic programs all the above approaches have proved useful. However, while extending these approaches to parallel non-deterministic programs, the following aspects are also to be considered.

4.1.4.1 Termination aspects

In a deterministic program there is only one possible execution sequence – it can terminate, abort or loop. In a parallel non-deterministic program there are many execution paths and the meaning of termination is not clear. Should one require that at least one path terminates and not care about the others or require that all the paths give correct answers? Also, the phenomenon of deadlock is to be distinguished from termination and we must have a method to do this.

4.1.4.2 Functionality

A parallel program, in general, cannot be considered as a function from an initial to a final state; this means that it is difficult to derive the meaning of a compound parallel program in terms of component properties. Hence the denotational approach to semantics is not directly applicable.

4.1.4.3 Nature of non-determinism

The description of a non-deterministic parallel process as an interleaving of execution sequences leads to a mathematically discontinuous function. In particular, when one considers a fair merge of two sequences S_1 and S_2, we have the following difficulty: we need to include a set of sequences which have increasingly long prefixes taken from S_1 before any element in S_2 is taken, and at the same time we need to have in the limit both sequences S_1 and S_2. This leads to a discontinuity.

The nature of non-determinism, namely the manner in which different choices can be made, affects the meaning of a program.

4.1.4.4   Nature of interprocess communication

Yet another aspect to be considered is the nature of interprocess communication. The three accepted methods are:

(1)   shared-variable concurrency;
(2)   message-passing concurrency;
(3)   dataflow concurrency.

With respect to each of these methods a suitable semantics has to be provided.

4.1.5   Difficulties and attempts

In view of the complexity involved in the study of different aspects, no widely accepted method exists for semantic modelling of concurrent processes. Each one of the different models earlier described attempts to capture precisely a particular type of behavioural property. Typically, in one model it is easy to treat one type of semantic property but difficult to reason about the others. This is because there is still no agreement at the basic level about what kind of mathematical object a process is. Therefore it is difficult to justify a preference for one semantics or proof system over another.

At present an enormous amount of work (represented by hundreds of published papers) is being carried out in this area. It is difficult for us to deal with this topic in great detail for two reasons:

(1)   it is a vast research area;
(2)   the mathematical preparation needed to understand these research papers is quite advanced.

Therefore in the following sections we shall simplify and qualitatively describe the basic principles used in some of the important approaches; a more enthusiastic reader can go into the details contained in the specialized papers and books on this topic (Apt, 1984; Melton, 1986; Brookes *et al.*, 1984; Brauer *et al.*, 1986a, 1986b; Rozenberg, 1984; Broy 1983, 1986; Kröger, 1987; Manes and Arbib, 1986; Venturini Zilli, 1987; Hennessy, 1986, 1988; Schmidt, 1988; Astesiano and Reggio, 1986).

4.2   Basics of semantics of concurrency

4.2.1   Exogeneous–endogeneous approaches

The behavioural semantics of concurrent processes is based on two different approaches:

(1)   definition of behaviour in terms of effects produced by actions and visible outside (called the **exogeneous** approach);

(2)   definition of behaviour that considers the effect of all actions, whether externally visible or not (called the **endogeneous** approach).

4.2.2   Different types of non-determinism

In addition, these approaches can be made for different types of non-determinism (Main (1986); see remarks in Section 3.5.6.1):

(1)   Ephemeral non-determinism: this arises from the transients in a distributed network but settles down after a while. In other words, ephemeral non-determinism arises from transient instabilities.

(2)   Discrete probabilistic non-determinism: here probabilistic choices are made in conditional and iterative statements of 'while' programs.

(3)   Oracle non-determinism: here the choices are beyond our control.

(4)   Demonic non-determinism: here the choices are made in such a way that every program that might possibly fail to terminate does in fact fail to terminate; this kind of non-determinism is also called Smyth's non-determinism.

(5)   Angelic non-determinism: here the choices are made in such a way that every program that might possibly terminate does in fact terminate; this kind of non-determinism is called Hoare's non-determinism. It is a dual to Smyth's non-determinism.

(6)   Erratic non-determinism: here the choices are made in such a way that a program that might or might not terminate does in fact terminate; this kind of non-determinism is called Plotkin's non-determinism.

4.2.3   Formal semantics of concurrency – categories

The formal semantics of concurrency is roughly classified under three categories, each category having an operational component.

4.2.3.1   Behavioural semantics

Here the meaning of a statement in a program is the set of possible behaviours and the total behaviour is explicitly constructed from the behaviour of the features of its components. This notion combines denotational semantics and operational semantics.

This type of semantics, although well suited for sequential programming, is not satisfactory for concurrent programming.

For instance, the behaviour of the compound process

cobegin P$_1$ || P$_2$ coend

is obtained by forming the interleaving of processes P$_1$ and P$_2$. As already mentioned, the interleaving process is not mathematically understood.

4.2.3.2   Action semantics

Here a behaviour is defined in terms of a sequence of actions starting from some state. Hence a statement can be defined as the set of all possible behaviours that can be obtained from these actions starting from the specified starting states. This semantics is similar to the operational semantics in sequential programming and can express parallelism more effectively.

For instance, the behaviour of

cobegin P$_1$ || P$_2$ coend

is the union of sets of possible actions of P$_1$ and P$_2$. However, this semantics too can be unsatisfactory, since it cannot express fairness.

4.2.3.3   Action–axiom semantics

Here the meaning of a statement consists of a set of actions together with a set of time-dependent (or temporal) logic axioms. The temporal logic is effective in axiomatically stating the conditions under which an action must eventually occur.

For example, a fair coin flipper requires two axioms:

(1)   at any time, a head must eventually occur;
(2)   at any time, a tail must eventually occur.

This semantics combines features of axiomatic and operational semantics used in sequential programming.

Temporal logic semantics together with a well-founded ordering method seem to be well suited for analysing fairness (Kröger, 1987) (see Section 4.5).

4.2.4   Semantics of different models

The two different categories of models, that is (i) concrete models (Petri nets, state transition systems) and (ii) abstract models (algebraic structures, partial ordering), can both be described under the different semantic schemes.

For example, the firing sequences in a Petri net correspond to interleaved behaviour, while the notion of a process in a Petri net captures the partial ordering semantics.

The algebraic models use the concept of power domains to establish operational equivalence and to prove specific properties.

The temporal logic approach can be used to describe action–axiom semantics.

Also, category theory and topology have played a significant role in the semantics of concurrent processes (Melton, 1986; Apt, 1984; Brookes *et al.*, 1984).

In this chapter we shall briefly introduce:

(1)   the semantics of Petri nets,

(2)   tree semantics,

(3)   temporal semantics,

(4)   power domain semantics, and

(5)   actor semantics.

Since the whole subject of the semantics of concurrency is still under development, we confine ourselves to only basic principles of these different semantics. This will help the reader to appreciate the different lines of thinking that are currently being pursued to understand the very complex and controversial problem of the semantics of concurrency.

4.3   Semantics of Petri net models

We first define some of the most commonly analysed properties of Petri nets.

4.3.1   Properties of Petri nets

In all future discussion, we assume that the Petri nets have a finite number of places and transitions.

4.3.1.1   Reachability

When a transition in a Petri net is fired, the token distribution changes according to the transition rules mentioned in Section 3.5. A sequence of transition firings results in one marking after another. We say that a marking m_1 is reachable from an initial marking m_0 if there exists a sequence of firings that can transform m_0 to m_1. The set of all possible markings reachable from m_0 by any possible transition is denoted by $R(m_0)$, the reachability set.

The determination of the reachability set is an exponential-space hard problem (see Chapter 6).

4.3.1.2 Controllability

A Petri net is said to be completely controllable if any marking is reachable from any initial marking. Some necessary conditions are available for the controllability of general Petri nets. A marked graph is completely controllable iff the underlying graph is a tree or a forest (Murata, 1984).

4.3.1.3 Boundedness

A Petri net is said to be k-bounded for the initial marking m_0 if each place of the Petri net gets at most (a finite number) k tokens for every marking reachable from m_0.

4.3.1.4 Safeness

A Petri net which is 1-bounded is called safe. That is, under any marking configuration a place has no more than one token. This property ensures that no overflows occur in buffers under any firing sequence.

4.3.1.5 Liveness

As mentioned earlier, the concept of liveness is related to the absence of deadlock. A Petri net is live if, starting from m_0, it is always possible to fire any transition by progressing through some firing sequences. Various classifications of liveness are possible (Peterson, 1981; Murata, 1984; Reisig, 1985).

4.3.1.6 Persistence

A Petri net is persistent if at any marking in $R(m_0)$ an enabled transition can be disabled only from its own firing.

4.3.1.7 Coverability

A marking m is said to be coverable if there exists a marking m_1 reachable from the initial marking m_0 such that $m_1(p) \geqslant m_0(p)$ for each place p (here $\geqslant$ means the partial ordering relation 'greater than or equal to' is with respect to each component of the vector).

The coverability is related to potential fireability. Let m be a marking that enables a transition t with the minimum number of tokens; then t is potentially fireable iff m is coverable. In other words, t is dead iff m is not coverable.

This property determines whether violations of mutual exclusion occur in each system and tests for deadlock.

4.3.1.8 Synchronic distance

This provides a measure for the mutual dependences between two transitions t_1 and t_2 and is useful for studying fairness when resources are shared.

The synchronic distance $d(t_1, t_2)$ between two transitions t_1 and t_2 is defined by

$$d(t_1, t_2) = \text{maximum} \, |N(\sigma, t_1) - N(\sigma, t_2)|$$

where $N(\sigma, t_i)$ denotes the number of appearances of transition t_i ($i = 1, 2, \ldots, n$) in a firing sequence σ; it measures the maximum difference that can arise in the appearance of t_1 and t_2 over all possible firing sequences and subsequences. Hence it serves as a measure for assessing the fairness.

4.3.1.9 Conservativeness

A Petri net that conserves a total number of tokens in all its places for all possible reachable markings is called conservative. This means that no tokens are gained or lost and the sum of components in a marking (vector) remains a constant. This concept is useful when the number of tokens denotes the number of resources and the resources are to be conserved.

4.3.2 Analysis methods

Two major methods are available for analysing and understanding the properties of Petri nets. These are

(1)   the reachability tree method, and
(2)   the linear algebraic method.

The reachability tree method inspects whether a sequence of firings can take a specified initial vector to a new specified vector by explicit tree search on the reachability set.

The linear algebraic method reformulates the problem to solving a homogeneous equation $\mathbf{A}^T\mathbf{x} = \mathbf{0}$, where $\mathbf{A}$ is the incidence matrix (Section 3.5.3) of size $n \times m$ (m, number of places; n, number of transitions), T denotes the transpose and x is the unknown vector. This method is complicated by the fact that the homogeneous equation $Ax = 0$ possesses a non-trivial solution only when A^T is singular. In addition, what we require is a minimal integral x out of the possible infinitely many solutions.

The reachability tree method can be used to solve the safeness, boundedness, conservation and coverability problems. However, it cannot in general be used to solve the reachability or liveness problem of unbounded nets or to determine which of the firing sequences are possible.

The linear algebraic method has also several drawbacks. It is applicable to only non 'self-loop' Petri nets (since the incidence matrix will not be able to represent the self-loop). Secondly, this method does not contain the sequencing information of the firing vector. Also, many spurious solutions arise which are difficult to eliminate.

The linear algebraic method can be used for checking boundedness, controllability and conservativeness. Also, it is very well suited for the simpler case of Petri nets, namely the marked graphs.

4.3.3   Reachability tree method

The reachability tree offers a pictorial representation of the reachability set of a Petri net. It essentially describes a Petri net in terms of states and state changes.

The reachability tree is a tree in which the node labels are the different markings of a Petri net and each directed arc label represents a transition that results in a new marking from a given marking.

To construct the reachability tree we choose a root node whose label is the initial marking of the Petri net. From this marking we draw a set of directed arcs denoting the various transitions that result in new markings.

The procedure is repeated until every reachable marking is produced. However, two problems can arise:

(1)   the resulting tree can become infinite owing to possible loops (repeated markings);

(2)   the number of tokens in a given place may grow arbitrarily large.

To accommodate these two possibilities we use the following rules; these rules enable us to have a shorthand notation to represent the infinite tree and an infinite number of tokens.

Rule 1: representing arbitrarily large tokens

Some transitions may result in the build-up of an arbitrarily large number of tokens in a place. This is indicated by a special symbol

w (a kind of infinity). The removal or addition of a finite number of tokens from w will not then alter the value w. In other words, $w \pm a = w$, $a \ll w$.

Rule 2: truncating the tree at terminal nodes

The terminal nodes are those nodes which correspond to markings that can no longer enable transitions. We then stop growing the tree at this node.

Rule 3: truncating the tree at duplicated nodes

If the new marking created is the same as one of the earlier markings and the new node is on a path from the root which contains the node with the same marking then the new node is a duplicate. Also, since this marking is the same as the previous marking, all markings reachable from it have already been enumerated; hence we terminate the generation of the tree at this node. This rule truncates the tree at a finite depth (for a detailed proof of the method, see Peterson (1981)).

Remark

This method gives what is known as 'trace semantics' or 'tree semantics' since it generates all possible traces of events and their results.

We illustrate the above method by an example (Peterson, 1981).

4.3.3.1   Example

Consider the Petri net shown in Figure 4.1(a). The initial marking is $(1, 0, 1, 0)$. Using this we construct the reachability tree of Figure 4.1(a) in Figure 4.1(b). Note that the node $(1, w, 0, 0)$ is dead whereas $(1, w, 1, 0)$ is identical to the previous node $(1, w, 1, 0)$, the grandfather node. Hence we call $(1, w, 0, 0)$ the terminal node and $(1, w, 1, 0)$ the duplicate node and then halt.

4.3.3.2   Inferring Petri net properties from the reachability tree

(1)   Safeness–boundedness: the labels of the nodes of the reachability tree can be inspected to find whether the token counts are k-bounded or 1-bounded (safe).

(2)   Conservativeness: we can check whether a net is conservative by inspecting the node labels and determining whether the sum of the components is invariant.

(3)   Unboundedness: if any node label contains w then the net is unbounded and non-conservative.

(4)   Coverability: the markings can also be inspected for coverability with respect to each place.

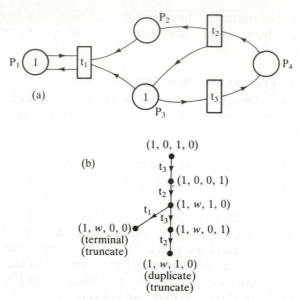

Figure 4.1 (a) A Petri net; (b) the reachability tree.

4.3.3.3 Limitations

The reachability tree cannot, in general, be used to solve the liveness problem or reachability problem or to determine which of the firing sequences are possible.

Further, it is possible that two different Petri nets have the same reachability trees; this is due to the use of the w symbol. Hence the reachability tree cannot be readily used to detect deadlock.

However, certain definite conclusions can be drawn in some cases. For instance, if a reachability tree has only terminal nodes, it is not live; if a marking **m** appears in a reachability tree it is reachable. If a marking is not covered by some node of the reachability tree then it is not reachable.

4.3.4 Linear algebraic method

Another approach to the analysis and understanding of Petri nets is based on the incidence matrix representation and the use of linear algebra. This approach consists in solving a system of linear homogeneous equations for positive integral solutions in a way very similar to balancing chemical equations or solving a dimensional analysis problem in physics. In this book, we shall only briefly introduce this method; for fuller details reference is made to Reisig (1985), Murata (1984), Lautenbach (1986), Krückeberg and Jaxy (1987) and Murthy and Schroder (1989).

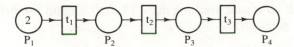

Figure 4.2   Reachability problem.

As mentioned earlier in this chapter, the linear algebraic method is subject to several limitations:

(1)   The solution to a homogeneous system of the form $\mathbf{Ax} = \mathbf{0}$ exists only when $\mathbf{A}$ is singular. Hence the solution is not unique and most numerical methods cannot be used directly without any modification.

(2)   We require only the positive integral solutions which are linear combinations of the solution vectors obtained. Therefore special methods that produce exact results are to be used.

(3)   The linear algebraic method does not contain the sequencing information of firing vectors.

(4)   Also, the linear algebraic method is applicable to only special classes of nets such as self-loop-free nets and marked graphs. General Petri nets are not easily amenable to matrix analysis.

(5)   The matrix approach provides only the necessary condition for reachability, not a sufficient condition.

4.3.4.1   Reachability

Let $\mathbf{A}$ be an $n \times m$ incidence matrix of a self-loop-free Petri net. Let $\mathbf{m}_0$ be the initial marking vector at the m places. Then the new marking $\mathbf{m}_1$ when a transition t_i is fired is given by

$$\mathbf{m}_1 = \mathbf{m}_0 + \mathbf{A}^\mathrm{T}\mathbf{f}_i$$

Here $\mathbf{A}^\mathrm{T}$ is the transpose of $\mathbf{A}$ and $\mathbf{f}_i$ is an $n \times 1$ unit firing vector $(t_1, t_2, \ldots, t_i, \ldots, t_n)$ and $t_i = 1$ if t_i is fired and $t_i = 0$ if t_i is not fired; also $t_j = 0$ $(i \neq j)$.

For example, for the Petri net shown in Figure 4.2, the incidence matrix $\mathbf{A}$ is given by (see Section 3.5.3)

$$
\mathbf{A} = \begin{array}{c} \\ t_1 \\ t_2 \\ t_3 \end{array}
\begin{array}{cccc} p_1 & p_2 & p_3 & p_4 \\ \left[\begin{array}{cccc} -1 & 1 & 0 & 0 \\ 0 & -1 & 1 & 0 \\ 0 & 0 & -1 & 1 \end{array}\right] \end{array}
$$

Starting with an initial marking $\mathbf{m}_0 = (2, 0, 0, 0)$ and the firing of t_1 will result in $\mathbf{m}_1$ given by

$$\mathbf{m}_1 = \begin{bmatrix} -1 & 0 & 0 \\ 1 & -1 & 0 \\ 0 & 1 & -1 \\ 0 & 0 & 1 \end{bmatrix} \begin{bmatrix} 1 \\ 0 \\ 0 \end{bmatrix} + \begin{bmatrix} 2 \\ 0 \\ 0 \\ 0 \end{bmatrix} = \begin{bmatrix} 1 \\ 1 \\ 0 \\ 0 \end{bmatrix}$$

Thus, to prove reachability using the matrix method we must show that for any arbitrary marking $\mathbf{m}_k$, after k transitions with firing vectors $\mathbf{f}_1, \mathbf{f}_2, \ldots, \mathbf{f}_k$, we should have:

$$\mathbf{m}_1 = \mathbf{m}_0 + \mathbf{A}^T\mathbf{f}_1 \geqslant 0$$
$$\mathbf{m}_2 = \mathbf{m}_1 + \mathbf{A}^T\mathbf{f}_2 \geqslant 0$$
$$\ldots$$
$$\mathbf{m}_k = \mathbf{m}_{k-1} + \mathbf{A}^T\mathbf{f}_k \geqslant 0$$

or

$$\mathbf{m}_k = \mathbf{m}_0 + \mathbf{A}^T(\mathbf{f}_1 + \mathbf{f}_2 + \ldots + \mathbf{f}_k)$$
$$= \mathbf{m}_0 + \mathbf{A}^T\mathbf{f} \geqslant 0$$

where

$$\mathbf{f} = \sum_{i=1}^{k} \mathbf{f}_i$$

is the firing count vector; the ith entry of $\mathbf{f}$ denotes how many times the transition t_i has fired to reach $\mathbf{m}_k$ from $\mathbf{m}_0$. Thus

$$\mathbf{A}^T\mathbf{f} = \mathbf{m}_k - \mathbf{m}_0 = \mathbf{d} \qquad (4.1)$$

is the difference vector.

It is well known from linear algebra (see Rao and Mitra (1971)) that an inhomogeneous equation such as Equation 4.1 is consistent if and only if every solution $\mathbf{x}$ of the homogeneous system

$$\mathbf{A}\mathbf{x} = 0 \qquad (4.2)$$

is orthogonal to $\mathbf{d}$; in other words for consistency

$$\mathbf{A}^T \mathbf{A}^{T-} \mathbf{d} = \mathbf{d} \qquad (4.3)$$

where $\mathbf{A}^{T-}$ is called the generalized inverse (g-inverse) of $\mathbf{A}^T$ and satisfies

$$\mathbf{A}^T \mathbf{A}^{T-} \mathbf{A}^T = \mathbf{A}^T$$

(see Rao and Mitra (1971) and Gregory and Krishnamurthy (1984)). We use the generalized inverse approach here as it simplifies the treatment and provides a simpler computational algorithm.

Thus from Equation 4.3 we obtain

$$\mathbf{d}^T(\mathbf{I} - \mathbf{A}^-\mathbf{A}) = \mathbf{0} \qquad (4.4)$$

as the consistency condition. Hence if $\mathbf{m}_k$ is reachable from $\mathbf{m}_0$ in a Petri net then

$$\mathbf{d}^T(\mathbf{I} - \mathbf{A}^-\mathbf{A}) = \mathbf{0} \text{ where } \mathbf{d} = \mathbf{m}_k - \mathbf{m}_0$$

In other words, Equation 4.4 is a necessary condition for reachability of $\mathbf{m}_k$ from $\mathbf{m}_0$.

Using this we can write the converse, that is a sufficient condition for non-reachability; a marking $\mathbf{m}_k$ is not reachable from $\mathbf{m}_0$ ($\neq \mathbf{m}_k$) if $\mathbf{d}$ is a linear combination of the columns of $\mathbf{I} - \mathbf{A}^-\mathbf{A}$.

The usual method to solve Equation 4.2 is by the use of the Smith canonical form. This method is quite involved because of an intermediate expression swell arising from the use of integer arithmetic and gaussian elimination without division (see Krückeberg and Jaxy (1987)).

The algorithm described here, however, is suitable for rational or exact arithmetic to evaluate a weak generalized inverse and uses a divide-and-conquer strategy of finding the g-inverse of $\mathbf{A}$ column by column. This controls the growth of the numbers. Also, since $\mathbf{I} - \mathbf{A}^-\mathbf{A}$ needs to be integral, this matrix is suitably scaled up in the final stage to obtain the integer entries. This is quite easy since $\mathbf{I} - \mathbf{A}^-\mathbf{A}$ usually contains very few non-zero entries.

Then, for an arbitrary choice of $\mathbf{x}$ the solution of Equation 4.2 is easily obtained.

4.3.4.2 Algorithm

This algorithm is based on the following definition and theorem (Murthy and Schroder, 1989).

Definition

Let $\mathbf{A}$ be an $m \times n$ matrix with integer elements denoted by

$$\mathbf{A} = [\mathbf{a}_1, \mathbf{a}_2, \ldots, \mathbf{a}_n]$$

where $\mathbf{a}_i$ $(i = 1, 2, \ldots, n)$ denotes the ith column of size $m \times 1$. Also, let

$$\mathbf{A}_i = [\mathbf{a}_1, \mathbf{a}_2, \ldots, \mathbf{a}_i]$$

denote the matrix which contains the first i columns of $\mathbf{A}$ starting with $\mathbf{A}_1 = \mathbf{a}_1$. Then

$$\mathbf{A}_{i-1} = [\mathbf{A}_{i-2} : \mathbf{a}_{i-1}], i = 3, 4, \ldots, n$$

where $\mathbf{A}_{i-1}$ is an $m \times (i-1)$ matrix and $\mathbf{a}_{i-1}$ is an $m \times 1$ vector.

Theorem (Rao and Mitra, 1971)

Let $\mathbf{A}_i$ be an $m \times i$ matrix and $\mathbf{a}_i$ be an $m \times 1$ vector. $\mathbf{A}^-$ is generated using the following recursive equations (for $i \geq 1$):

$$\mathbf{e}_{i+1} = (\mathbf{I} - \mathbf{A}_i \mathbf{A}_i^-)^{\mathrm{T}} (\mathbf{I} - \mathbf{A}_i \mathbf{A}_i^-) \, \mathbf{a}_{i+1} \tag{4.5}$$

$$\mathbf{d}_{i+1} = \mathbf{A}_i^- \, \mathbf{a}_{i+1} \tag{4.6}$$

$$\mathbf{b}_{i+1} = \begin{cases} \mathbf{e}_{i+1}^{\mathrm{T}} / \mathbf{e}_{i+1}^{\mathrm{T}} \mathbf{a}_{i+1} & \text{if } \mathbf{e}_{i+1}^{\mathrm{T}} \mathbf{a}_{i+1} \neq 0 \\ \mathbf{0} & \text{otherwise} \end{cases} \tag{4.7}$$

$$\mathbf{A}_{i+1}^- = \begin{bmatrix} \mathbf{A}_i^- - \mathbf{d}_{i+1} \mathbf{b}_{i+1} \\ \mathbf{b}_{i+1} \end{bmatrix} \tag{4.8}$$

To begin the recursion, we set

$$\mathbf{A}_1^- = \mathbf{0}, \text{ if } \mathbf{a}_1 = \mathbf{0}; \text{ else, } \mathbf{A}_1^- = \mathbf{a}_1^{\mathrm{T}} / \mathbf{a}_1^{\mathrm{T}} \mathbf{a}_1$$

Note that the value of $\mathbf{e}_{i+1}$ is critical to the computation of $\mathbf{A}_{i+1}^-$. If ordinary floating point arithmetic is used, the round-off errors interfere with the computation; accordingly, it is advisable to use either rational or exact arithmetic (Gregory and Krishnamurthy, 1984).

Also, it can be proved that the rank of $\mathbf{I} - \mathbf{A}^- \mathbf{A}$ is $k = n - r$ where r is the rank of $\mathbf{A}$ and $\mathbf{I} - \mathbf{A}^- \mathbf{A}$ will be an $n \times n$ matrix with $n - r$ linearly independent columns.

4.3.4.3 Example

Consider the following 3×4 incidence matrix of a Petri net with three transitions and four places:

$$
A = \begin{array}{c} \\ t_1 \\ t_2 \\ t_3 \end{array} \begin{array}{cccc} p_1 & p_2 & p_3 & p_4 \\ \left[\begin{array}{cccc} -1 & 0 & 1 & -1 \\ 1 & -1 & 0 & 1 \\ 1 & 0 & -1 & 1 \end{array} \right] \end{array}
$$

Using the above algorithm we obtain

$$
I - A^-A = \begin{bmatrix} 0 & 0 & 1 & -1 \\ 0 & 0 & 1 & 0 \\ 0 & 0 & 1 & 0 \\ 0 & 0 & 0 & 1 \end{bmatrix}
$$

of rank 2. It is easily verified that if

$$
m_0 = \begin{bmatrix} 1 \\ 1 \\ 0 \\ 0 \end{bmatrix}
$$

$$
m_1 = \begin{bmatrix} 2 \\ 0 \\ 0 \\ 1 \end{bmatrix}
$$

then

$$
d = \begin{bmatrix} 1 \\ -1 \\ 0 \\ 1 \end{bmatrix}
$$

Hence $d^T (I - A^-A) = (0, 0, 0, 0)$. This shows that m_1 is reachable from m_0.

4.3.4.4 S-invariants and T-invariants

A vector x $(m \times 1)$ of integers is called an S-invariant of the Petri net if

$$\mathbf{A}\mathbf{x} = \mathbf{0} \qquad \text{(note that } \mathbf{A} \text{ is of size } n \times m)$$

A vector $\mathbf{y}$ ($n \times 1$) of integers is called a T-invariant of the Petri net if

$$\mathbf{A}^T\mathbf{y} = \mathbf{0} \qquad \text{(note that } \mathbf{A}^T \text{ is of size } m \times n)$$

4.3.4.5   Inferring Petri net properties

Using the linear algebraic technique the following properties can be inferred.

(1)   **Controllability**

A Petri net is completely controllable if rank $\mathbf{A} = m$. Hence this property can be easily inferred. This property ensures that any marking is reachable from any initial marking.

It can be proved that a marked graph (Section 3.5.8.1) where each place has exactly one incoming and one outgoing arc of unit weight and the cyclic conservation property is satisfied is completely controllable.

(2)   **Conservative or S-invariant net**

A Petri net is an S-invariant net or conservative iff there exists an m-vector of positive integers $\mathbf{x}$ such that

$$\mathbf{A}\mathbf{x} = \mathbf{0}$$

(3)   **Consistency**

A Petri net is said to be consistent or a T-invariant net if there exists a marking $\mathbf{m}_0$ and a firing sequence s from $\mathbf{m}_0$ back to $\mathbf{m}_0$ such that every transition occurs at least once in s.

This property is true iff there exists an n-vector $\mathbf{y}$ of positive integers such that

$$\mathbf{A}^T\mathbf{y} = \mathbf{0}$$

(4)   **Structural boundedness**

A Petri net is structurally bounded if it is bounded for any initial marking $\mathbf{m}_0$.

It can be proved (see Murata (1984) and Reisig (1985)) that a Petri net is structurally bounded iff there exists an m-vector $\mathbf{x}$ of positive integers such that

$$\mathbf{A}\mathbf{x} \leqslant \mathbf{0}$$

(5)   **Repetitive**

A Petri net is said to be repetitive if there exists a marking $\mathbf{m}_0$ and a firing sequence s from $\mathbf{m}_0$ such that every transition occurs infinitely often in s; this is useful for the study of fairness.

It can be shown that a Petri net (Murata, 1984) is repetitive iff there exists an n-vector $\mathbf{y}$ of positive integers such that

$$\mathbf{A}^T \mathbf{y} \geq \mathbf{0}.$$

Remark

In summary:

- $\mathbf{Ax} = \mathbf{0}, \mathbf{x} > 0$ is a conservative net;
- $\mathbf{Ax} \leq \mathbf{0}, \mathbf{x} > 0$ is a structurally bounded net;
- $\mathbf{A}^T \mathbf{y} = \mathbf{0}, \mathbf{y} > 0$ is a consistent net;
- $\mathbf{A}^T \mathbf{y} \geq \mathbf{0}, \mathbf{y} > 0$ is a repetitive net.

Thus conservativeness is a special case of structural boundedness and consistency is a special case of repetitiveness.

4.3.4.6   Inadequacy of linear algebraic methods

In the beginning of Section 4.3.4 we indicated some of the limitations arising in the use of linear algebraic techniques. Lautenbach (1986) has shown that the linear algebraic techniques are inadequate to solve more general problems such as liveness. This result is not surprising since the modelling and decision power of the linear algebraic techniques that use linear substitution and simplification are no more than the modelling and decision power of a context-free production system.

4.4   Tree semantics

In the last section we studied in detail the semantics of Petri net models based on the reachability tree and the linear algebraic approaches.

In this section we introduce the concept of tree semantics that bears a similarity to the reachability tree approach. We then illustrate its use for the semantics of DILAG (Section 3.5.5.2) programs. The tree semantics is direct and is based on a transition tree representation which explicitly represents the non-deterministic choices. It can be used to study fairness and probabilistic programs.

4.4.1   Application to DILAG

A typical repetition statement such as:

$$P :: *[\quad []\, i : A_i \rightarrow B_i] \qquad i \in I$$

can be mapped into a tree whose root s_0 is an initial state. The various non-deterministic choices are then represented along the different branches s_{0i}. Similarly, for every other succeeding state s_{0i} we repeat the above operation. For example,

$$P :: *[\ 1 : a \to x := x + 1$$
$$[\ ]\ 2 : a \to a := False$$
$$]$$

with $(a, x) := (true, 0) = s_0$ will have a tree T given in Figure 4.3. This tree has an initial state $x = 0$ and $a = true$; then the computation proceeds by choosing the direction 1 or 2 as required. Note that the tree can represent an infinite computation path such as 111 . . . .

The semantic tree is a useful aid for studying fairness.

4.4.2 Fairness

We can define three kinds of fairness (Francez, 1986) for a repetition statement that starts from an initial state and takes an infinite path.

(1)   **Impartial** (unconditionally fair)
      We define that the choices are impartial iff every direction is chosen along an infinite path in the tree infinitely often.

(2)   **Just** (weakly fair)
      We define that the choices are just iff every direction continuously enabled along an infinite path is chosen infinitely often along an infinite path.

(3)   **Fair** (strongly fair)
      We define that the choices are fair iff every direction infinitely often enabled along an infinite path is chosen infinitely often along that infinite path.

For a detailed study of the subject of fairness see Francez (1986).

4.4.3 Application to probabilistic programs

Probabilistic non-determinism can be introduced in DILAG and its semantics studied using a semantic tree.

A typical repetition statement could be represented by

$$P :: *[\ \ [\ ]\ p_i : A_i \to B_i]\ \ \ \ i \in I$$

where $0 \leqslant p_i \leqslant 1$ and $\Sigma_i\, p_i = 1$. Here the choices are made probabilistically and p_i is the probability of selecting the ith statement.

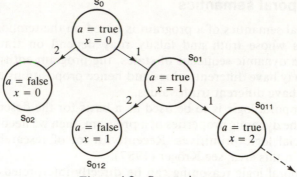

Figure 4.3   Semantic tree.

4.4.3.1   Example

We now illustrate a probabilistic program with an example (Francez, 1986):

$$P :: b := 0$$
$$*[\tfrac{1}{2} : b \leq 1 \rightarrow b := 0$$
$$[\,]$$
$$\tfrac{1}{2} : b \leq 1 \rightarrow b := b + 1$$
$$]$$

Its tree is given in Figure 4.4. From this tree we see that, from state b = 0 the probability is $\tfrac{1}{4}$ to reach the state b = 2 which is halt.

Hence the probability for non-termination of the program P is

$$\underset{k \to \infty}{\text{Lim}}\, (1 - \tfrac{1}{4})^k = (\tfrac{3}{4})^k = 0$$

for infinite repetition or the program terminates with probability 1.

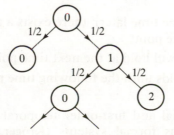

Figure 4.4   Probabilistic program.

4.5 Temporal semantics

The temporal semantics of a program is based on the temporal logic of propositions whose truth and falsity may depend on time. Since a program is a dynamic sequence of states, the program entities, such as variables, may have different values and hence propositions about these values may have different truth values.

If temporal logic is to be used as a basis for the description and analysis of the dynamic properties of a program, then we need to develop certain special logic primitives. Recently, a lot of research has been carried out in this area; see Kröger (1987).

Temporal logic reasoning can be directly interpreted on infinite trees and so can be used to represent the evolution in time of the program states.

This approach is endogeneous, that is it considers the set of complete computation sequences (for trees) as given and reasons directly about the behaviour of the whole program. Thus given a program the reasoning is done in two steps:

(1)   define the set of all its computations;

(2)   prove any required property in terms of these histories, independently of the programs.

Therefore this approach is most suitable for dealing with programs presented as transition systems in contrast with the exogeneous systems that are better suited for well-structured programs.

Recently some attempts have been made to use temporal semantics in a more structured–compositional way. Temporal logic is best suited for studying liveness properties of which termination is a special case. Temporal logic has been axiomatized using operators such as:

(1)   next time: A holds at time point immediately after a reference point;

(2)   henceforth (always): A holds at all time points after the reference point;

(3)   eventually (some time later): there exists a time at which A holds after a reference point;

(4) A at next B: A will hold at the next time point that B holds;

(5) A until B: A holds until the following time point when B holds.

Both the propositional and first-order temporal languages have been recently developed as formal systems (Kröger, 1987) and used in programming (Moszkowski, 1986)

4.6   Power domain semantics

The use of semantic domains for programming languages was introduced by Scott and Strachey in the late 1960s. The purpose of the theory of domains is to give models for spaces on which we can define computable functions. In the case of deterministic sequential programming the kinds of spaces needed for denotational semantics involve higher-order function (function of a function) spaces and also spaces which are defined by recursive equations (Section 3.3.6.9). Domains which contain such equations and their solutions are known as reflexive domains. Reflexive domains play a vital role in the denotational semantics of deterministic programs, since the meaning of such programs can then be considered as the valuation of a function from a domain D to itself. The use of domain theory has several advantages:

(1)   The definitions are precise and simple.

(2)   Properties of programs can be proved as theorems.

(3)   It is a constructive approach in which we build a total program from a set of component programs whose meaning is understood.

When extending the domain theory to non-deterministic programs the function space needs to be enlarged for possible interpretations. This enlargement is similar to what we do in ordinary mathematics, where the equation $x^2 + 1 = 0$ has no interpretation over the integers or reals but has an interpretation over the complex numbers. For this purpose, we embed the set of reals in the set of complex numbers. Analogously, to handle non-determinism an extra algebraic structure is added to the complete partially ordered sets (cpo). This is called a power domain.

The power domain concept is analogous to the power set describing all the possible interleavings with corresponding evaluations. However, here partial orderings are introduced to describe the progress of a non-deterministic computation.

There are various ways in which one can add an extra algebraic structure for including non-determinism. These have been studied by Hoare (1985), Plotkin (1976) and Smyth (1978); as a result, a set of suitable conditions for adding such an algebraic structure has been arrived at. These are as follows.

(1)   The domain contains all the desired primitive data types.

(2)   The domains chosen are closed under the desired operators (analogous to the complex field from the point of view of solution of equations and convergence), such as cartesian products, disjoint union, function mapping and separated sum, for each data type.

(3)   There is a solution for recursive equations. Such a solution is canonical or can be expressed in a standardized form.

(4)   There is a flexible and intuitive theory of computability through finitary approximation.

(5)   The domain is natural to motivate and simple to describe.

(6)   The embedding function from the domain to the power domain is universal; that is, the algebraic structure is preserved and there exists a unique morphism between the two structures.

Plotkin (1976) was the earliest to suggest a characterization of the power domain. Several other alternative power domains due to Hoare (1985) and Smyth (1978) have also been proposed and these have been formalized using category theory techniques (Gunter, 1986). All these approaches essentially seek to guarantee the existence of least solutions to continuous equations for the denotation of while constructs.

For a detailed study of power domains the above-cited references may be consulted.

4.7   Actor semantics

The actor paradigm consists of a set of computational agents called **actors**. Each actor usually consists of an operation and a firing rule. The actors communicate among themselves through message passing. The order of arrival of messages (operands) is indeterminate, leading to an inherent non-determinism in the evolution of the system. This non-determinism is due to different possible arrival orderings for the messages (or operands). The message-passing discipline is constrained so that the eventual delivery of all communications sent is guaranteed. This paradigm also provides for dynamic creation and reconfiguration of actors in the system.

The actor paradigm exploits the object-oriented methodology of programming which has shown increasing promise in programming language design (Agha, 1984, 1986).

Actor theory differentiates between objects whose behaviour changes over their lifetime and those that are behaviourally constant. Thus on the one hand it shares with Milner's calculus of communicating systems (CCS) the use of recursively defined behaviour and on the other it extracts maximum possible concurrency from the concept of immutable and permanent objects which are the backbone of functional programming. Also, actor theory allows explicit consideration of causality and causal reasoning in contradistinction to models such as Petri nets and dataflow where the relationship between the elements is static.

Complexity of computations in actor systems stems from the pattern of communication between individual actors and not from the behaviour of the individual actor alone. It has been conjectured that the actor model is the most general model of concurrent computation and all other models can be derived as special cases.

A series of languages have been developed to exploit the actor paradigm and to provide higher level language constructs to support concurrent programming. These languages may find applications in artificial intelligence (Agha, 1986)

SUMMARY

In this chapter we introduced the different categories of formal semantics used in sequential programming. We then explained how these concepts can be extended for parallel programming under different types of non-determinism and communication modes.

The study of different styles of semantics was then taken up. The two different methods of analysis of Petri nets, namely the reachability tree method and the linear algebraic method, were explained in detail. Then the method of tree semantics was introduced together with its applications to fairness in non-deterministic and probabilistic programs. Also, the temporal semantics based on temporal logic was briefly introduced. Following this, brief descriptions of power domain semantics and actor semantics were given.

EXERCISES

4.1   Find the reachability tree of the following Petri net:

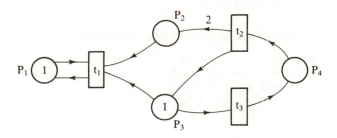

4.2   Show that the following Petri net has the same reachability tree as in Exercise 4.1. What do you infer from this?

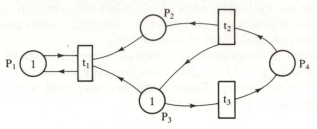

4.3   Can the following Petri net deadlock?

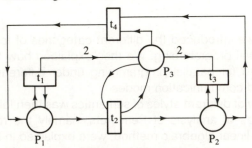

4.4   Write down the incidence matrices of the Petri nets given in Exercises 4.1–4.3.

4.5   Write a program to compute the generalized inverse A^- of an incidence matrix A, based on the algorithm in Section 4.3.4.2.

4.6   Use the program in Exercise 4.5 to find the S and T invariants in Exercises 4.1–4.3.

4.7   Using the *g*-inverse concept can we determine which of the Petri nets in Exercises 4.1–4.3 are controllable, conservative and repetitive? If not, describe why.

4.8   Describe the various types of fairness and explain them from a sociological point of view.

4.9   Consider the following probabilistic program:

```
P :: b := 1
   *[1/3  : b ≤ 1 → b := 0
    [] 1/3 : b ≤ 1 → b := b + 1
    [] 1/3 : b = 2 → b := b - 1
    ]
```

Draw its semantic tree and analyse it.

4.10 Analyse the fairness of a simple uniform random number generator that is used for tossing a six-faced die, by constructing a semantic tree.

4.11 What kind of primitive operators are needed to devise a temporal logic program?

4.12 Give a practical example of a simple problem that needs a temporal logic solution.

4.13 Explain with an example the concept of domains and recursive equations in domains.

4.14 The well-known Newton's iterative method is applied to a polynomial equation $x^2 + 4 = 0$ (which has a complex pair of roots $\pm 2i$) using real arithmetic. What kind of interpretation can you offer for the computed results in the domain of real numbers?

4.15 There are two different valuation systems, known as archimedean (absolute-value metric) and non-archimedean (p-adic metric), under which we can find the completion (that is, every Cauchy sequence converges) of the rational numbers. Study these systems in order to understand the concept of power domains (Schikhof, 1984).

4.16 An important method to factorize a polynomial with integer coefficients and integer or rational roots is Hensel's lifting technique. How is it related to the concept of power domains (Krishnamurthy, 1985)?

4.17 A deterministic program can be considered as a function from a domain D to D. For non-deterministic programs show that this is not true. Also, convince yourself why this function is either $D \rightarrow 2^D$ or $2^D \rightarrow 2^D$ (where 2^D is the power set of D, that is the set of all subsets of D) to take care of the different possibilities.

4.18 Study the principles of an object-oriented programming such as Smalltalk.

4.19 Study how communication takes place between objects in Smalltalk.

4.20 Study any actor language and compare it with an object-oriented language.

References

Agha G. (1984). Semantic considerations in the actor paradigm of concurrent computation. *Lecture Notes in Computer Science*, **197**, 151–79

Agha G. (1986). *Actors: a Model of Concurrent Computation in Distributed Systems*. Cambridge MA: MIT Press

Apt K.R. (1984). *Logics and Models of Concurrent Systems*, NATO ASI Series. New York NY: Springer

Astesiano E. and Reggio G. (1986). A syntax directed approach to the semantics of concurrent programming languages. In *Proceedings Information Processing 1986* (Kugler H.J., ed.), pp. 571–6. New York: Elsevier

Brauer W., Reisig W. and Rozenberg G. (1986a). Petri nets: central models and their properties. *Lecture Notes in Computer Science*, **254**

Brauer W., Reisig W. and Rozenberg G. (1986b). Petri nets – applications and relationship to other models of concurrency. *Lecture Notes in Computer Science*, **255**

Brookes S.D., Roscoe A.W. and Winskel G. (1984). Seminar on concurrency. *Lecture Notes in Computer Science*, **197**

Broy M. (1983). *Control Flow and Dataflow – Concepts of Distributed Programming*, NATO ASI Series. New York NY: Springer

Broy M. (1986). A theory for nondeterminism, parallelism, communication and concurrency. *Theoretical Computer Science*, **45**, 1–61

Francez N. (1986). *Fairness*. New York NY: Springer

Gregory R.T. and Krishnamurthy E.V. (1984). *Methods and Applications of Error-free Computation*. New York NY: Springer

Gunter C.A. (1986). Comparing categories of domain. *Lecture Notes in Computer Science*, **239**, 101–21

Hennessy M. (1986). Proving systolic systems correct. *ACM Trans. Programming Languages Systems*, **8**, 344–87

Hennessy M. (1988). *Algebraic Theory of Processes*. Cambridge MA: MIT Press

Hoare C.A.R. (1985). *Communicating Sequential Processes*. Englewood Cliffs NJ: Prentice-Hall

Krishnamurthy E.V. (1985). *Error-free Polynomial Matrix Computations*. New York NY: Springer

Kröger F. (1987). *Temporal Logic of Programs*. New York NY: Springer

Krückeberg F. and Jaxy M. (1987). Mathematical models for calculating invariants in Petri nets. *Lecture Notes in Computer Science*, **266**, 104–31

Lautenbach K. (1986). Linear algebraic techniques for place/transition nets. *Lecture Notes in Computer Science*, **254**, 142–67

Main M.G. (1986). Free constructions of power domains. *Lecture Notes in Computer Science*, **239**, 162–83

Manes E.G. and Arbib M.A. (1986). *Algebraic Approaches to Program Semantics*. New York NY: Springer

Melton A. (1986). Mathematical foundations of programming semantics. *Lecture Notes in Computer Science*, **239**

Moszkowski B. (1986). *Executing Temporal Logic Programs*. London: Cambridge University Press

Murata T. (1984). Modelling and analysis of concurrent systems. In *Handbook of Software Engineering* (Ramamoorthy C.V. and Vick C.R., eds.). New York NY: van Nostrand

Murthy V.K. and Schroder H. (1989). Systolic arrays for parallel matrix g-inversion and finding Petri net invariants. *Parallel Computing*, to be published

Peterson J.L. (1981). *Petri Net Theory and the Modelling of Systems*. Englewood Cliffs NJ: Prentice-Hall

Plotkin G.D. (1976). A power domain construction. *SIAM J. Computing*, **5**, 452–87

Rao C.R. and Mitra S.K. (1971). *Generalized Inverse of Matrices and its Applications*. New York NY: Wiley

Reisig W. (1985). *Petri Nets*. New York NY: Springer

Rozenberg G. (1984). Advances in Petri nets. *Lecture Notes in Computer Science*, **222**

Schikhof W.H. (1984). *Ultrametric Calculus – an Introduction to p-adic Analysis*. London: Cambridge University Press

Schmidt D.A. (1988). *Denotational Semantics*. Newton MA: Allyn and Bacon

Smyth M.B. (1978). Power domains. *J. Computer System Sciences*, **16**, 23–6

Venturini Zilli M. (1987). Mathematical models for semantics of parallelism. *Lecture Notes in Computer Science*, **280**

Chapter 5
Parallel Processors – Structure and Organization

5.1   Introduction

In Section 1.6 we outlined some of the key issues that need consideration in parallel architectural organization and design. To summarize, these key issues are as follows:

(1)   whether the architecture is meant for general-purpose or special-purpose computers;

(2)   grain size (granularity) – the capability of the basic modules and their density;

(3)   topology – interconnection or communication geometry;

(4)   nature of coupling – light, moderate or tight;

(5)   control–data mechanisms;

(6)   task allocation and routing methodology;

(7)   reconfigurable structure;

(8)   language issues;

(9)   nature of technology – VLSI or optical;

(10)   performance measures and evaluation.

A detailed consideration of these key issues obviously results in an enormous variety of possible structures and organization for parallel processors (see Uhr (1984)). In order to provide a suitable description for the structure and organization of these processors, it is desirable to devise a nomenclature or a taxonomical system similar to that used in zoology, botany or chemistry. Such a taxonomical system is a useful guide for the designers and users; this will be introduced in the next section.

In the later sections we shall describe some important processor organizations.

5.2   Taxonomy of parallel processors

A number of different taxonomical systems have evolved over the last 25 years based on the different attributes.

5.2.1   Flynn's taxonomy

One of the earliest approaches to naming and classification is due to Flynn. In Flynn's taxonomy, parallel computers are grouped under four major categories (Flynn, 1966, 1972):

(1)   single-instruction stream single-datastream (SISD) machines;

(2)   single-instruction stream multiple-datastream (SIMD) machines;

(3)   multiple-instruction stream single-datastream (MISD) machines;

(4)   multiple-instruction stream multiple-datastream (MIMD) machines.

The features of these four categories were described in Section 1.2.3. Flynn's taxonomy has several drawbacks, since it cannot precisely discriminate different categories. Therefore several other efforts have been made, notably by Kuck (1978); Basu (1987); Johnson (1988) and Skillcorn (1988); Kung (1982) suggests that the manner in which an algorithm is realized should be an attribute in the taxonomy of architecture.

Based on the above studies we construct a taxonomical tree for parallel machines. It is to be noted that a precise classification scheme is difficult to achieve because of the complexity of parallelism. However, our aim here is to provide a taxonomical tree that contains the required attributes, but each such attribute is not necessarily disjoint and the classification may not be very precise.

5.2.2 Taxonomy tree

The four major attributes used in constructing the taxonomical tree are:

(1)   granularity (grain size);
(2)   nature of the algorithm-realization module (hardware or mixed hardware–software);
(3)   topology and nature of coupling;
(4)   control.

The granularity determines the number as well as the size and capability of the basic processors used. It can vary from simple microprocessor-like components to full-fledged central processing units (CPUs).

The realization of an algorithm can be either entirely by hardware modules or by mixed hardware–software modules.

The topology determines the interprocessor communication network. It can be very simple (for example ring, bus) or extremely complex with a high degree of interconnection among a very large number of processors.

The coupling is tight if memory is shared and there is a clock control; otherwise, it is light.

The control can be synchronous (centralized with a clock control) or asynchronous (decentralized). Most hardware-based processors that have a complex interconnection geometry use synchronous control. The asynchronous control is usually used in software-based modules, dataflow machines or other lightly connected machines.

Based on these four major attributes we can construct a taxonomical tree (Figure 5.1). In this tree the first level choice is granularity. The granularity can be considered

(1)   at data level (also called 'fine'),
(2)   at operation level (also called 'medium'), or
(3)   at task level (also called 'coarse').

When specifying hardware modules, the granularity denotes the processor capability and density. Large granularity systems have less than 500 processors with high-precision floating-point operations. Medium granularity systems have between 500 and 5000 processors with high-precision floating-point operations. Fine granularity systems have more than 5000 processors with smaller precision floating-point operations. When specifying a program module it refers to the amount of computation executed by a module, before the next module takes over.

The three options for granularity can be elaborated thus:

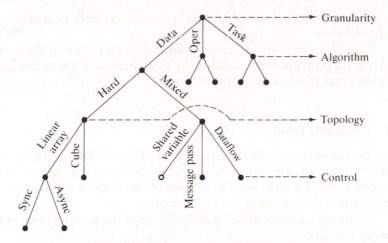

Figure 5.1   Taxonomy tree.

(1)   data level: here the module effects the same operation on multiple data items simultaneously as in a vector addition;

(2)   operational level: here the module executes independent instructions simultaneously;

(3)   task level: here the module can execute some tasks concurrently and asynchronously with other tasks.

The second level of the taxonomical tree determines the nature of algorithm realization, namely, whether

(1)   an algorithm is realized entirely using hardware modules, or

(2)   an algorithm is realized using mixed software–hardware modules.

In the first case we need to consider the coupling among the processors, while in the second case we need to consider both the coupling as well as the manner in which instructions are software realized; these decisions are to be made at the next level.

At the third level we make a choice of a suitable topology and the nature of coupling. For fully hardware modules, a simple or complex communication geometry (or coupling) is chosen, for example pipelines, linear arrays, arrays or trees.

For the mixed software–hardware module system, firstly a choice is to be made on the nature of the interconnection–coupling (with a range of variation) between different hardware modules, secondly a choice is made on how the instructions are executed within each software or hardware module (sequential, pipeline or parallel), and thirdly a choice is needed on the specific mode of communication between the different software modules (as to whether it is a shared-variable or a message-passing or a dataflow mode).

Finally, at the fourth level we need to make a choice of the nature of the control (synchronous, dataflow or asynchronous); there can again be a wide range of variations in this choice.

5.2.3   Taxonomy table

We use the taxonomy tree to classify some well known architectures. This is given in Table 5.1. This table indicates the choices at the various levels. No precise naming is attempted by the use of this table; it only serves as a guide for the classification of the architectures.

We provide a more detailed description of the architectures in the following sections.

5.2.4   Limitations

The taxonomy table (Table 5.1) shown opposite uses only four major attributes. These are inadequate to classify several other interesting architectures. For example, the connection machine (Section 1.6), hypercube architectures and associative processors are not easily classified. If one wants to bring in a precise classification of these complex architectures, additional attributes such as task allocation, routing, reconfigurability, language issues, nature of technology and performance measures are to be considered. However, since such factors themselves are not precisely definable, their introduction may add only further complexity rather than clarity in description.

5.3   Basic parallel architectures

In this section we describe some basic parallel architectures that are widely used at present (Hwang and Briggs, 1984):

(1)   multiprocessors;
(2)   vector processors;
(3)   pipeline processors;
(4)   array processors;
(5)   systolic processors;
(6)   wavefront array processors;
(7)   cube architectures;
(8)   pyramid architectures;
(9)   prism architectures.

Table 5.1 Taxonomy table.

Number	Conventional name	First level	Second level	Third level	Fourth level
1	Multiprocessor	Task	Mixed	Simple geometry, shared variable, lightly coupled	Asynchronous
2	Vector processor	Operational	Hardware	Linear array, tight coupled	Synchronous
3	Pipeline processor	Data	Hardware	Simple geometry, moderately coupled	Synchronous
4	Array processor	Data	Hardware	Two-dimensional geometry, tight coupled	Synchronous
5	Systolic processor	Data	Hardware	Complex geometry, tight coupled	Synchronous
6	Wavefront processor	Data	Hardware	Two-dimensional geometry, tight coupled	Dataflow
7	Cube	Task	Hardware	Simple geometry, moderately coupled	Synchronous–asynchronous
8	Dataflow	Operational	Mixed	Simple geometry, dataflow, light to moderate coupling	Asynchronous–dataflow

5.3.1 Multiprocessors

This is a general term for a computer with more than one processor. Usually the processors are connected through a kind of communication system to a common shared memory, and a shared input–output system. A common global operating system controls the tasks performed on each processor.

The operating system also provides synchronization between the different processors and each processor is autonomous. The synchronization operation is usually done using the test set, semaphores or other shared-variable method (Section 2.6).

In Flynn's taxonomy, the multiprocessor is an MIMD machine. According to the taxonomy tree it is a machine having a task level granularity, mixed hardware–software with simple light interconnection and shared variable communication, and asynchronous control.

For a detailed study of multiprocessors, see Desrochers (1987), Ernston (1977) and Satyanarayanan (1980).

5.3.2 Vector processors

The vector processors usually deal with vector operations; that is, all the elements of a vector are subject to a particular operation simultaneously. A vector processor is usually an attachment to a mainframe machine.

The vector processor architecture contains several processors each capable of dealing with a certain number of elements n each of size m bits and outputting the result. Occasionally pipelining is used when larger vectors are encountered.

There is a simple control unit that controls communication to the mainframe machine and the execution of local programs. Most of the other resources are provided by the mainframe machine (also known as the front end).

The vector processor is an SIMD machine. According to the taxonomy tree it is a machine with an operational level granularity and tightly coupled hardware and it is synchronous within its processing elements. It is to be noted that the mainframe controls the job stream and operation of the vector processor.

For a detailed study of vector processors see Hwang and Briggs (1984) and te Riele et al. (1987).

5.3.3 Pipeline processors

The pipeline processor consists of a number of different processors connected at different stages, somewhat like a pipeline or an assembly line. Each processor performs a specific function during a specified period of time.

Pipeline processors can be classified as either

(1)   a single-function pipeline, or
(2)   a multifunction pipeline.

The single-function pipeline processor performs one kind of operation on the stream of data at each stage of the pipeline. In a multifunction pipeline different operations can be performed at different stages like the assembly line of an automobile factory. The granularity of a pipeline processor is therefore at the operational level or at the data level (medium to fine). The algorithm realization is by hardware modules and the topology is a moderately interconnected linear network. The control is necessarily synchronous, since different stages have to be perfectly synchronized.

Pipelining is one of the most successfully applied techniques in vector machines; see Kogge (1981).

5.3.4   Array Processors

This name is given to a set of processors that are interconnected to form a rectangular mesh or a grid. The intersection points in the grid are called **nodes**.

Obviously, each node has four directly connected neighbours, except those nodes along the boundaries. This kind of structure is useful for applications in matrix processing and picture processing where each node can be identified with the matrix element or a picture element (pixel).

The array processor has a control unit that controls the instructions within its processing elements in the array. The access to the array processor is through a host computer interface. The control unit synchronizes the operations of different processing elements.

In some cases it is desirable to have the nodes along the boundaries communicate more effectively by connecting the processor elements across the different boundaries. If the top row and bottom row processors are connected directly, then the array becomes a horizontal cylindrical net. Similary, if the left column and right column processors are connected directly, then the resulting structure is a vertical cylindrical net.

By using both the above connections, namely the top row and the bottom row as well as the left and right columns, a torus-shaped net called a **hypertorus** is obtained.

Figure 5.2   Spiral structured arrays.

Also, the patterns of connections can be made to resemble spirals of various kinds (Figure 5.2) by suitably skewing the connections.

The various configurations such as cylinder, torus and spiral are useful for many different algorithms that require special kinds of inter-processor communication; see Kung (1988).

The array processor is a machine with a data level concurrent hardware module, two-dimensional array geometry and a synchronized control.

5.3.5   Systolic processors

In Section 3.10 we introduced a basic model known as the systolic automaton for synchronous, deterministic parallel computing. Two categories of this model, namely the systolic tree and systolic mesh automata, and their modelling and decision power were described. In this section, we describe their practical realization and organization.

The term systolic computation was introduced by H. T. Kung and C. E. Leiserson in 1978 (Mead and Conway, 1980; Kung, 1982; IEEE, 1987). This term is used because of its analogy with a blood circulatory system in which the heart sends and receives a large amount of blood as a result of the frequent and rhythmic pumping of small amounts of blood through the arteries and veins. In this analogy, the heart is the source and destination of data (global memory) and the arterial–venous network corresponds to the processors and communication links.

Systolic architectures are extensions of the pipelining concept. While a pipeline is a one-dimensional, unidirectional flow, the systolic system permits multidimensional, multidirectional flow including feedback. In other words, data can be used and re-used and both partial results and new data may move within the system.

The major attributes of the systolic system are:

(1)   Each data item can be used and re-used before the final result reaches the memory.

(2)   Several data items can be processed concurrently.

(3)   The operations performed by the processors at each step are simple.

(4)   The architecture has a regular geometry, and the flow of control and data is regular and consistent across the processors.

(5)   The regular and localized communication geometry reduces routing costs, power, time and chip area required to implement a computation.

(6)   A systolic array is usually an attachment to a host computer. Therefore, I/O time, costs and access are to be taken into account and to be balanced with the computation. This balancing can be done very well with a systolic array designed for special-purpose algorithms.

5.3.5.1   VLSI realization and cost effectiveness

The systolic processors are well suited for VLSI implementation. In this sense they are 'algorithms cast in silicon'. This makes them very highly suitable for applications in signal–image processing, pattern recognition, matrix arithmetic, graph and sorting problems.

The casting of special-purpose algorithms in silicon turns out to be very cost effective. In fact a systolic array with thousands of processors can be built at a total price of US$10–100 thousand (IEEE, 1987; Moore *et al.*, 1987).

Recently, Carnegie–Mellon University and General Electric have designed and produced a programmable, systolic array computer known as Warp that can carry out 100 MFLOPS (million floating point operations per second).

Also, Carnegie–Mellon University and Intel are jointly developing a 600K transistor VLSI chip called Warp chip that can be used as a building block for a variety of processor arrays.

5.3.5.2   Designing systolic processors

A systolic array is usually built as a special-purpose algorithmic device although some generalization is possible. To synthesize a systolic array from the algorithm description (called the **mapping** strategy for design) the designer should be familiar with systolic computing, algorithms, technology and applications. Although recently systematic design techniques have become available for automation (Fortes, 1985; Quinton, 1987), these techniques are not completely satisfactory. Hence the designer has to consider several aspects.

(1)   **Homogeneous–heterogeneous**
       The choice of basic modules (called nodes) for realizing the algorithm – whether these modules are functionally identical (homogeneous) or different (heterogeneous). The homogeneous

systems are easy to build, test and maintain; also, for programmable machines homogeneity simplifies the software.

Heterogeneous systems allow the processors to carry out
different functions, but they are not very well suited for VLSI
implementation.

(2)   **Module or node complexity**
The module complexity is also referred to as the grain size – it
determines the basic function of each node and the number of
nodes packed in a system.

For example, each node may perform only multiplication
and addition of eight-bit numbers and there may be 4000 of them.

(3)   **Communication**
The choice of connection network or geometry.

(4)   **Order and timing of data**
The sequencing operations that must be built in and the control
signals and timing. Usually the control is like that in an SIMD
machine.

(5)   **Input/output**
The I/O and memory access complexities are to be considered to
get the best performance.

In addition to the above factors, one has to take into account
factors such as reliability and fault tolerance. Also, methods for solving a
larger problem size without building a larger sized systolic array have to
be found; otherwise, the practical application of systolic arrays may be
extremely limited.

Recently there have been attempts to develop universal building
blocks for the design of different systolic arrays (Kung, 1988; Fortes,
1985). Such a universal building block together with programming tools
and flexibility in communication would provide a great impetus in
systolic computing. Also, methods have been developed to prove systolic
systems correct (Hennessy, 1986).

5.3.5.3   A systolic matrix multiplier

We now consider an example of the systolic multiplication of two
matrices **A** $(k \times m)$ and **B** $(m \times n)$. The algorithm for matrix multiplication that is most suited is based on outer products (rather than the
conventional inner product method) (Krishnamurthy and Klette, 1981).

Here we evaluate

$$\mathbf{AB} = \sum_{p=1}^{m} \mathbf{C}(p)\mathbf{R}(p)$$

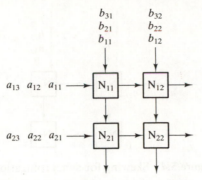

Figure 5.3   Systolic matrix multiplier.

where $\mathbf{C}(p)\mathbf{R}(p) = c_{pj}r_{pj}$, $p = 1, 2, \ldots, k$, and $j = 1, 2, \ldots, n$. Here $\mathbf{C}(p)$ is a $k \frown n$ matrix with all the columns identical with the pth column of $\mathbf{A}$ and $\mathbf{R}(p)$ is a $k \frown n$ matrix with all the rows identical with the pth row of $\mathbf{B}$.

For example, if

$$\mathbf{A} = \begin{bmatrix} a_{11} & a_{12} & a_{13} \\ a_{21} & a_{22} & a_{23} \end{bmatrix} \qquad \mathbf{B} = \begin{bmatrix} b_{11} & b_{12} \\ b_{21} & b_{22} \\ b_{31} & b_{32} \end{bmatrix}$$

$$\mathbf{AB} = \mathbf{C}(1)\mathbf{R}(1) - \mathbf{C}(2)\mathbf{R}(2) - \mathbf{C}(3)\mathbf{R}(3) = \mathbf{N}$$

$$= \begin{bmatrix} a_{11}b_{11} & a_{11}b_{12} \\ a_{21}b_{11} & a_{21}b_{12} \end{bmatrix} + \begin{bmatrix} a_{12}b_{21} & a_{12}b_{22} \\ a_{22}b_{21} & a_{22}b_{22} \end{bmatrix} + \begin{bmatrix} a_{13}b_{31} & a_{13}b_{32} \\ a_{23}b_{31} & a_{23}b_{32} \end{bmatrix}$$

A systolic matrix multiplier is shown in Figure 5.3. The input streams of the rows of $\mathbf{A}$ arrive from the left, and the input streams of the columns of $\mathbf{B}$ arrive from the top of the nodes N_{11}, N_{12}, N_{21} and N_{22}. Each of these nodes has the capability for multiplying two input numbers and holding the result until the next set of inputs arrives for multiplication; then the sum is accumulated and the process is repeated.

The most important task, however, is to synchronize the timings for each multiplication, communication of the values, and accumulation of the sum. To synchronize these timings, we use a technique called **skewing** of the matrices $\mathbf{A}$ and $\mathbf{B}$ as shown in Figure 5.4. This technique pads the sequences with zeros and ensures that the right pairs interact at the right time step to produce the right result.

Note that the product matrix $\mathbf{N}$ is finally available at the nodes N_{11}, N_{12}, N_{21} and N_{22}. Thus in this case the matrix is entirely mapped in one-to-one correspondence to the processor array.

The time taken to multiply two matrices of size $k \times m$ and $m \times n$ using kn processors is $m + (k - 1) + (n - 1)$ time units. This result is

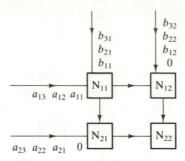

Figure 5.4   Skewing for synchronization.

easily proved using the fact that the last computations are carried out after a lapse of $(k - 1) + (n - 1)$ units, because of the skewing of the matrices, and it takes m units of time to multiply two vectors of size m.

Note that a conventional single-processor matrix multiplication requires kmn operational time units; in the case of the systolic multiplier we use kn processors (or more space) to reduce the time to $m + n + k - 2$.

5.3.5.4   Instruction systolic arrays

The systolic arrays have their limitations. Their special-purpose nature makes them less flexible; that is, an array designed for a specific purpose cannot be used for another purpose; for instance a sorting systolic array cannot multiply a matrix. In other words, systolic arrays can execute only one algorithm for a fixed set of parameters and a fixed problem size.

In order to introduce flexibility, the concept of instruction systolic arrays (ISAs) has been proposed by Lang (1986, 1987).

Principles of ISA   The ISA as its name indicates is also a systolic array. However, instead of data, here the instructions are pumped through the processor array. This is done by using a separate arrangement to pump an instruction stream from the top, called the top program (TP) and an orthogonal stream of boolean selectors from the left called the left program (LP). An instruction is executed in a processor only if an instruction in the TP meets a selector bit in the LP with a value 1; if the selector bit is 0 it inhibits the instruction. Such an arrangement requires that the processors have the capability to execute different instructions; however, the separation of the program stream and a selector stream enables the execution of different programs on the same processor array (Figure 5.5).

ISA architecture   The basic architecture of the ISA is an $n \times m$ mesh-connected array of identical (homogeneous) processors (Figure 5.6). The

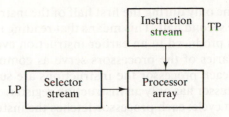

Figure 5.5 Instruction systolic array.

processors have simple control units and can execute instructions from a fixed simple instruction set. The processor array is synchronized by a global clock and the execution of each instruction is assumed to take the same time duration.

Each processor has some data registers D, including a designated communication register R. Two processors P and Q communicate by sharing R: first P writes the required data in its register R_p in one instruction cycle and its neighbour Q reads the contents of R_p in the following instruction cycle. Thus each processor P can only write in its own register R_p, while other neighbours can read the register R_p. All neighbouring processors are permitted to read the same register simultaneously. The read–write conflicts are eliminated by dictating that

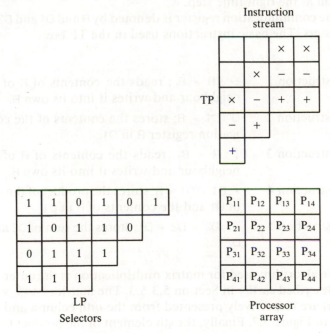

Figure 5.6 ISA architecture.

reading can be done only during the first half of the instruction cycle and writing only in the second half. This means that reading results in the 'old contents' that was produced in an earlier instruction cycle.

The boundaries of the processors serve as communication links for I/O data. For each processor the instructions are supplied from the outside. Each processor has only an instruction register. At the beginning of each instruction cycle, each processor fetches the instruction from the instruction register of its top neighbour. This is done synchronously, so that rows of instructions are shifted through the processor array from the top to the bottom. The processors in the top row of the array are supplied with instructions from a memory outside.

In a similar manner, the column of selector bits is shifted through the array from left to right.

A processor executes its instruction if its selector bit is 1; otherwise it is idle, leaving the contents of the registers unchanged.

We now illustrate the ISA principle using the familar example of matrix multiplication.

Matrix multiplier   An ISA matrix multiplier is shown in Figure 5.7. It is assumed that the two matrices **A** and **B** of size $k \times m$ and $m \times n$ respectively are available as input queues on the left and top.

The processor array is of size $k \times n$ and the selector bits and instruction set interact at the processor array performing the required instruction at the right time step.

The communication register is denoted by R and D1 and D2 are two data registers. The basic instructions used in the TP are:

- Instruction 1 $\rightarrow$: R = R_L; reads the contents of R of the left neighbour and writes it into its own R.

- Instruction 2   D : D1 = R; stores the contents of the communication register R in D1.

- Instruction 3 $\downarrow$: R = R_T; reads the contents of R of the top neighbour and writes it into its own R.

- Instruction 4 $*$: D1 = D1 $\times$ R; stores the product of the contents of D1 and the contents of R in D1.

- Instruction 5   + : D2 = D2 + D1; stores the sum of D2 and D1 in D2.

The algorithm used for matrix multiplication is the outer product method described earlier in Section 5.3.5.3. The matrices **A** ($k \times m$) and **B** ($m \times n$) are respectively presented from the mth column and nth row as shown in Figure 5.7. Finally, the ijth element of the product **C** appears

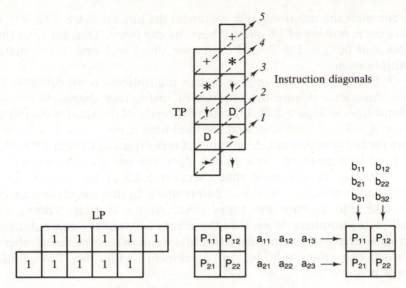

Figure 5.7   ISA matrix multiplier.

in processor P_{ij}. In Figure 5.7, we have chosen $k = 2$, $m = 3$ and $n = 3$ for the sake of simplicity in explanation.

The configuration of the instruction sequence (TP) and the selector stream (LP) is as shown at time step 0. At each time step 1, 2, . . . the TP moves down by one cell while the LP moves right by one cell. Their interaction at the processors results in appropriate computations at the appropriate time step, as below:

- At time step 1, the first instruction puts a_{13} in R of P_{11}.

- At time step 2, a_{13} is stored in D1 of P_{11}, and a_{23} is stored in R of P_{21}; also, a_{13} is read in R of P_{12}.

- At time step 3, b_{31} is read in R of P_{11}; a_{13} is stored in D1 of P_{12}; a_{23} is stored in D1 of P_{21}.

- At time step 4, $a_{13} \times b_{31}$ is computed and placed in D1 of P_{11}.

- At time step 5, the register D2 in P_{11} accumulates the product $a_{13} \times b_{31}$. Also, $a_{23} \times b_{31}$ is computed in P_{21} and $a_{13} \times b_{32}$ in P_{12}.

- At time step 6, the products are accumulated in P_{21} and P_{12}. The operation $a_{23} \times b_{32}$ is completed in P_{22}.

- At time step 7, the accumulation of product is done in P_{22}; also, both TP and LP leave the processor array now, completing the first cycle of iteration, namely multiplying one column of A by a row of B.

To complete the remaining task we repeat the process twice. This will require the repetition of TP and LP basic blocks twice. Thus the total time taken will be $2 \times 5 + 7 = 17$ units for the 2×3 and 3×2 matrix multiplication.

For a $k \times m$ and $m \times n$ matrix multiplication we compute the time thus: let r denote the number of instruction diagonals (broken oblique lines in Figure 5.7). Then the first cycle of iteration is completed in $r + n + k - 2$ time units and the total time is $mr + n + k - 2$ units. Here the factor m denotes the number of repetitions of LP and TP blocks. Thus we have an $O(m + n + k)$ ISA algorithm using kn processors.

It may be observed that (Section 5.3.5.3) the systolic array computation took $m + n + k - 2$ time units. In that calculation we did not take into account the times involved for shifting, adding and multiplying numbers. If we take these into account the computational timing will have to be modified to rm instead of m (r being the number of instructions); this will be in agreement with the ISA timing ($mr + n + k - 2$).

Remarks

The ISA design is analogous to the ballet planning which consists in fitting a story to a given music and a scenario. In the ISA, the problem corresponds to the story, the algorithm to the ballet, the timing steps to the dance movements and the VLSI layout to the scenario. Thus the TP and LP are analogous to the choreography which allows the story to flow with a perfect blend of dance and music in a given scenario. Based on this analogy, the TP and LP pair may be called 'choreograms'.

5.3.6   Wavefront array processors

The systolic array is entirely controlled by a global clock. Therefore, the synchronization of different computations requires careful planning to ensure correct timing. When the systolic arrays become very large, such planning may be extremely difficult. To obviate this difficulty wavefront array processors have been suggested by Kung (1988).

A wavefront array (WFA) can be described as a systolic array in which the dataflow computation is embedded. Thus the computation is essentially data driven and not control driven. This means the successive instructions are not triggered by an external clock but by the availability of the required operands and resources.

A wavefront array has the following features:

(1)   There is no global clock and the computations are self-timed and data driven; hence it is globally asynchronous, that is synchronization is distributed.

(2)   The computing network has a modular, regular structure with local interconnections.

(3)   It is programmable using the handshaking or message-passing languages such as occam.

(4)   The computational activity starts at one corner of the processor array and propagates downward, travelling like a wavefront; this diagonal motion of the wave across the array is called a **sweep**. Each processing element waits for the arrival of the primary wavefront, executes the required computation and then generates the result as a secondary wavefront. This is equivalent to the dataflow principle.

(5)   Since each sweep carries out certain partial computations, the total computation may be realized as a sequence of sweeps. Hence the wavefront processing is pipelineable.

We now illustrate WFA processing using the example on matrix multiplication (Section 5.3.5.3).

5.3.6.1   Wavefront matrix multiplier

The wavefront matrix multiplier is shown in Figure 5.8. Here we multiply a $k \times m$ matrix A and an $m \times n$ matrix B. A is stored at the left memory module and B is stored at the top memory module. We assume that the processor array size is $k \times n$ to compute the product P. In Figure 5.8 we choose $k = 3$, $m = 3$ and $n = 4$ for simplicity.

The columns of A and the rows of B are taken one by one to generate the product $C(i)R(i)$ at each sweep of the wavefront for $i = 1, 2, \ldots, m$.

At the first sweep the product $C(1)R(1)$ is formed. To do this initially all the processors $P_{ij}^{(0)} = 0$ for all (i, j). Processor P_{11} starts computing $P_{11}^{(1)} = P_{11}^{(0)} + a_{11}b_{11}$. Then the computational activity propagates for P_{12} and P_{21} to compute:

$$P_{12}^{(1)} = P_{12}^{(0)} + a_{11}b_{12}$$
$$P_{21}^{(1)} = P_{21}^{(0)} + a_{21}b_{11}$$

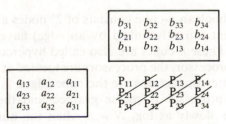

Figure 5.8 Wavefront matrix multiplier.

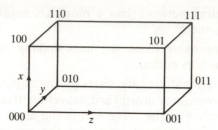

Figure 5.9   Boolean 3-cube.

The next secondary wavefront activates P_{31}, P_{22}, P_{13} to compute the other elements; then similarly the remaining elements of $C(1)R(1)$ are computed by P_{32}, P_{23}, P_{14} and P_{33}, P_{24} and P_{34}.

After the processor P_{11} completes its task for the first wavefront, the second sweep can begin to compute $C(2)R(2)$. Similarly, the m sweeps are carried out. After the m sweeps the product matrix is obtained.

5.3.6.2   ISA and WFA

The ISA and WFA are quite closely related. The ISA can simulate a WFA very easily by choosing a proper LP and TP. In fact, ISA is more flexible than WFA since it can permit irregular movements of data and computation and also inhibit certain computations. It is possible to incorporate the dataflow principle in ISA. However, this is currently a research topic (Megson and Evans, 1987).

5.3.7   Cube architectures

The cube architectures come in several different forms. They are all variations of the basic architecture called a boolean n-cube or binary cube (Welty and Patton, 1985; Seitz, 1985).

A three-dimensional unit cube is shown in Figure 5.9; the eight vertices are labelled using 3-bit binary numbers, in a coordinate system with x, y, z directions as shown. Such a cube is also called a boolean 3-cube.

A general boolean n-cube consists of 2^n nodes and any two nodes which are adjacent (directly linked by an edge) have node labels that differ in one bit. These n-cubes are also called hypercubes.

In a cube processor, the processors are located at the vertices of the n-cube and the interconnections are the cube edges.

The cube processor is coarse grained and the interconnection complexity grows slowly as $\log_2 N = n$ when the number of nodes N increases exponentially ($N = 2^n$).

The control in a cube architecture can be synchronous or asynchronous as required in any application. Thus it can function as an SIMD or an MIMD machine.

5.3.7.1 Cosmic cubes

The cosmic cube developed by Seitz and Fox at the California Institute of Technology is a concurrent VLSI processor with $2^6 = 64$ nodes arranged in a binary hypercube architecture (Seitz, 1984).

Each node is a single computer based on Intel 8086–8087 microprocessor chips containing 128 kB of RAM memory on the processor board. The machine has an MIMD architecture. Each node runs asynchronously with no shared memory and is connected to its six neighbours in the hypercube topology.

An important difference between the cosmic cube and other MIMD processors is that the cosmic cube uses the message-passing rather than the shared variable method for communication. The message passing is handled by explicit communication and synchronization primitives invoked by the programmer (see Welty and Patton (1985) and Seitz *et al.* (1988)).

5.3.7.2 Variants of cube architecture – CCC

An important variant of the cube architecture is called the cube-connected cycles (CCC) architecture. Here each corner of the 2^p-cube contains a cycle of 2^q processors, making the total number of processors 2^{p+q}.

For example, if $p = 2$ and $q = 2$ we have the cube-connected cycle shown in Figure 5.10.

The CCC architecture retains a constant connectivity value at each vertex and is highly suited for area-efficient VLSI implementation. Also, it offers a very versatile interconnection pattern to implement graph and other related algorithms (Uhr, 1984; Preparata and Vuillemin, 1981; Seitz, 1984).

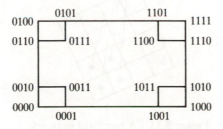

Figure 5.10 2^{2+2} CCC processor.

5.3.8 Pyramid architecture

A pyramid belongs to the class of cellular computers and is well suited to image processing work (Burt, 1984).

Basically, a pyramid is a stack of cellular arrays that tapers exponentially in size. For example, the base of the pyramid is a $2^n \times 2^n$ array; then the successively higher levels contain $2^{n-1} \times 2^{n-1}$, $2^{n-2} \times 2^{n-2}, \ldots, 2 \times 2$ and 1 processors. The total number of cells in a pyramid is $4^n(1 + \frac{1}{4} + \frac{1}{16} + \ldots) < \frac{1}{3} \times 4^{n+1}$.

For example, if $n = 4$, the pyramid has a total of 341 cells with 256 cells in its base.

In Figure 5.11 a pyramid network of base size $2^2 \times 2^2$ is shown. The upper level processors are connected to the lower level using $2^n \times 2^n$ connections with each vertex in the upper level connected to each of the 2×2 meshes in the lower level.

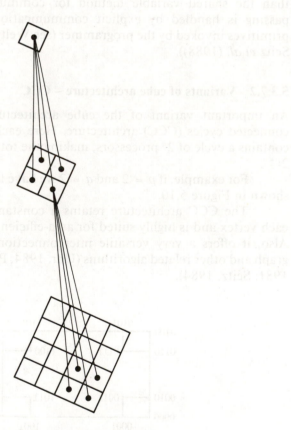

Figure 5.11 A pyramid network.

5.3.9 Prism architecture

A prism is a stack of cellular arrays, all of the same size. The height of the stack is the same as in the case of a pyramid; for example, if the base size is $2^n \times 2^n$, the number of levels is n, so that there are $n \times 4^n$ cells in the prism.

Here each cell is connected to its neighbours on its own level and also to the three cells on the level above; specifically, cell (i, j) on level k is connected to cells (i, j), $(i + 2^k, j)$ and $(i, j + 2^k)$ on level $k + 1$ (which implies that it is also connected to cells (i, j), $(i - 2^{k-1}, j)$ and $(i, j - 2^{k-1})$ on level $(k - 1)$. In these connections it is understood that addition is modulo 2^n. For example, if $k = 4$, $i = 24$ and $n = 5$ then $24 + 16 > 32$; the result is taken modulo 32 and equals 8. The levels of the prism are numbered bottom up from 1 to n.

Rosenfeld (1985) has shown that a prism machine can be very useful for image processing. Also, Rosenfeld (1985) has shown that a prism can simulate a pyramid in a linear time. This is useful in several applications.

The prism machine can compute the discrete Fourier transform of a $2^n \times 2^n$ input image in $O(n)$ time.

The prism requires more cells than a hypercube or a pyramid; however, it has a simpler interconnection structure in which each cell has only a small number of neighbours, and in particular there are only three connections (per cell) between levels. Therefore, it turns out to be a useful architecture.

5.4 Algorithm-structured networks

In the previous section we described several basic parallel architectures which are of a rather general nature. These general architectures usually do not mirror the structure of the algorithms they execute. Therefore, a certain special class of networks known as 'algorithm-structured networks' have been designed. These networks mirror the structure of the algorithms they execute (see Section 5.5 for examples). Although this is a definite advantage, some of these networks require many more interconnections than regular mesh-connected arrays in order to move data rapidly from any one processor to another. This means that, in some of these algorithm-structured networks, connecting wires may occupy more area in a VLSI chip than the processor area. Accordingly one has to balance these two factors, namely the processor area and the wire area.

The most important among the class of algorithm-structured networks are

(1)   H-tree structures,

(2)   shuffle exchange structures,

(3)   butterfly structures.

5.4.1   H-trees

Trees permit a variety of tasks where information is sorted, compared or reorganized. Hence there has been major effort in designing planar VLSI layouts for trees.

Usually a complete binary tree on a grid is organized as a recursive pattern with a primitive that looks like the letter 'H' (Figure 5.12). Hence such trees are called H-trees.

In Figure 5.12, the H-trees of order 1 and 2 are shown. From these H-trees it is easy to visualize how to increase the order of the H-trees recursively.

The H-tree layout is very well suited for several applications. An H-tree layout for a complete binary tree of n leaves has an area of order n and provides the most efficient (with more processor area than wire area) layout for VLSI chip design (Ullman, 1984).

5.4.2   Shuffle exchange and butterfly architectures

The mesh and the tree processors are planar layouts occupying more processor area than wire area. We now describe some organizations that take $O(n^2)$ area where n is the number of nodes laid out in the plane and $O(n^{3/2})$ volume in three-space. The two most important processor organizations belonging to this category are:

(1)   the shuffle exchange architecture (SEA), and

(2)   the butterfly architecture (BA).

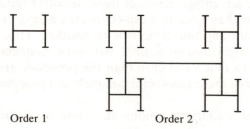

Order 1   Order 2

Figure 5.12   H-trees.

The SEA contains 2^k nodes and among them two kinds of interconnections called shuffle and exchange are used. We shall describe this in Section 5.4.2.1.

The BA contains $2^k(k + 1)$ nodes; these are organized into 2^k columns and $k + 1$ rows. For $k = 1$, the BA and SEA are identical. We shall describe the BA in Section 5.4.2.2.

5.4.2.1   Shuffle exchange architecture

Here we have 2^k processors labelled $0, 1, \ldots, 2^k - 1$. The connections between these processors are of two kinds as defined below:

- **Exchange**
  Every even-numbered processor i is connected to the odd-numbered processor $i + 1$ and every odd-numbered processor j is connected to the even-numbered processor $j - 1$.

- **Shuffle**
  Every processor i is connected to $2i$ (modulo $2^k - 1$); also, for $i = 2^k - 1$, processor $2^k - 1$ is connected to itself; note that processor 0 is connected to itself.

An SEA for $k = 3$ is shown in Figure 5.13. The exchange connections are 0–1, 2–3, 4–5 and 6–7, while the shuffle connections are 0–0, 1–2, 2–4, 3–6, 4–1, 5–3, 6–5 and 7–7.

In other words, if x is the binary representation of a node label and is given by

$$x = a_m \times 2^m + a_{m-1} \times 2^{m-1} + \ldots + a_0$$

then a shuffle connection is made to x^1 which has a left-ring-shifted binary representation of x; or,

$$x^1 = a_{m-1} \times 2^m + a_{m-2} \times 2^{m-1} + \ldots + a_0 \times 2 + a_m$$

The SEA is useful for sorting (see Section 5.5.2).

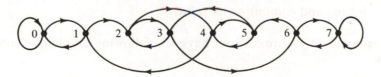

Figure 5.13   Shuffle exchange network.

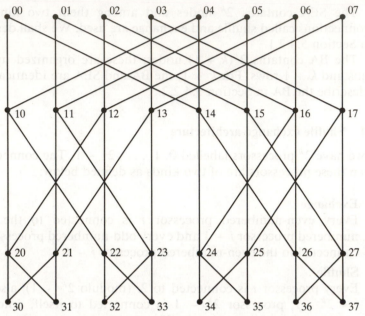

Figure 5.14   8-column × 4-row BA.

5.4.2.2 Butterfly architecture

The butterfly network contains $2^k(k + 1)$ processors arranged in 2^k columns and $k + 1$ rows. For $k = 3$, this architecture will have $2^3 \times 4 = 32$ processors; this arrangement with eight columns and four rows is shown in Figure 5.14. This network resembles a butterfly pattern, hence the name.

Let (i, j) denote the processor number where $0 \leq i \leq k$ is the row index and $0 \leq j \leq 2^k - 1$ is the column index. The interconnections among the nodes satisfy the following rule. Each node (i, j) on row $i > 0$ is connected to a pair of nodes on the upper row $i - 1$ thus:

(1) a direct column connection to $(i - 1, j)$, and

(2) an oblique connection to $(i - 1, r)$ with $r - j = \pm 2^{k-i}$, where k is the maximum row index; the determination of r for a given j is made unique by complementing the $(k - i)$th binary positional bit in j and computing its value.

For example, in Figure 5.14 we have the following 24 oblique connections:

$(0, 0) \rightarrow (1, 4); (0, 1) \rightarrow (1, 5); (0, 2) \rightarrow (1, 6); (0, 3) \rightarrow (1, 7)$
$(1, 0) \rightarrow (0, 4); (1, 1) \rightarrow (0, 5); (1, 2) \rightarrow (0, 6); (1, 3) \rightarrow (0, 7)$

$(2, 0) \rightarrow (1, 2); (2, 1) \rightarrow (1, 3); (2, 2) \rightarrow (1, 0); (2, 3) \rightarrow (1, 1)$
$(2, 4) \rightarrow (1, 6); (2, 5) \rightarrow (1, 7); (2, 6) \rightarrow (1, 4); (2, 7) \rightarrow (1, 5)$
$(3, 0) \rightarrow (2, 1); (3, 1) \rightarrow (2, 0); (3, 2) \rightarrow (2, 3); (3, 3) \rightarrow (2, 2)$
$(3, 4) \rightarrow (2, 5); (3, 5) \rightarrow (2, 4); (3, 6) \rightarrow (2, 7); (3, 7) \rightarrow (2, 6)$

Notice that in each case the oblique connection is made to a node whose right (column) index r differs by $\pm 2^{3-i}$ where i is the row index; the r value is easily obtained by inverting the 2^{3-i}th positional bit in j.

5.4.2.3 BA–CCC–SEA – their interrelationship

There is a close relationship between the CCC architecture (Section 5.3.7.1) and the BA.

The CCC is a k-dimensional hypercube whose 2^k nodes are actually cycles of k nodes formed by a column of a butterfly network in which the rows 0 and k coincide, forming a ring. However, in the CCC, a node (i, j) has an oblique connection to a node (i, r) where r is the binary representation of j with the 2^{k-i}th bit inverted, as described earlier. Thus the CCC is a modified form of the BA (Figure 5.15).

Like the SEA, the CCC is useful for sorting; since BA and CCC are interconvertible, they are both very useful for several applications. The SEA is identical to the BA for $k = 1$, that is there are four nodes and they are connected as shown in Figure 5.16. This simple network (Figure 5.16) is also known as a butterfly switch or an exchange switch.

Remark

There are several other interconnection schemes such as banyan, omega and baseline which are closely related to butterfly; Wu and Feng (1980) have demonstrated that all these networks are topographically related.

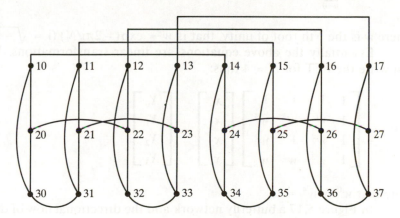

Figure 5.15 Cube-connected cycles.

Figure 5.16   Butterfly and shuffle exchange network for $k = 1$.

5.5   Applications for algorithm-structured networks

In the previous section we described some important networks such as butterfly and shuffle exchange networks. It was mentioned that these architectures can mirror the structure of the algorithms they execute. In this section we shall illustrate this aspect with some examples. For recent research papers, see Albrecht and Melhorn (1987).

5.5.1   Fast Fourier transform

The most important application of the butterfly architecture is for computing the Cooley–Tukey fast Fourier transform (FFT) which plays a significant role in signal processing (Ullman, 1984).

The discrete FFT pair is written as

$$X_n = \frac{1}{N} \sum_{m=0}^{N-1} x_m w^{mn}, \quad n = 0, 1, \ldots, N-1$$

$$x_m = \sum_{n=0}^{N-1} X_n w^{-mn}, \quad m = 0, 1, \ldots, N-1$$

where w is the Nth root of unity, that is $w = \exp(-2\pi i/N)$ $(i = \sqrt{-1})$.

Essentially the above equations are linear transformations. We can write the FFT for $N = 4$ thus:

$$\frac{1}{4} \begin{bmatrix} 1 & 1 & 1 & 1 \\ 1 & w & w^2 & w^3 \\ 1 & w^2 & 1 & w^2 \\ 1 & w^3 & w^2 & w \end{bmatrix} \begin{bmatrix} x_0 \\ x_1 \\ x_2 \\ x_3 \end{bmatrix} = \begin{bmatrix} X_0 \\ X_1 \\ X_2 \\ X_3 \end{bmatrix}$$

Note that $w^0 = w^4 = 1$.

In Figure 5.17 a butterfly network and the directional flow of data

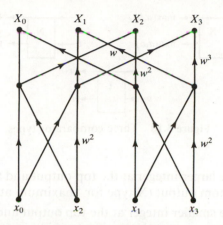

Figure 5.17 FFT for N = 4 in a butterfly processor.

are shown. The weights marked along the edges are the multiplication factors; if the weight is unity, it is not marked. The BA shown in Figure 5.17 uses a 4-column × 3-row network; that is, it is a BA with k = 2.

Comparison of Figures 5.14 and 5.17 reveals that the butterfly elements can be used as a basic structure and computations can be carried out by pipelining them. The complexity of a BA for an n-processor system increases at the rate $n \log_4 n$. Currently the BA is available as custom VLSI chips.

Recently Bolt Beranek and Newman Inc. have developed a butterfly parallel processor for the US Defense Agency (Babb, 1988). Programmable versions of these machines are available.

5.5.2 Sorting

One of the most widely used computing activities is sorting. An enormous amount of work has been carried out on devising parallel sorting algorithms (Akl, 1985; Bitton *et al.*, 1984; Richards, 1986). Unfortunately, our scope in this book is restricted and we shall not be able to deal with this topic at any great length. Our aim here is to illustrate the use of the SEA in sorting.

The basic algorithm used for parallel sorting is due to Batcher (1968) and is called the bitonic merge (Nassimi and Sahni, 1979). This algorithm can take multiple inputs and produce multiple outputs. Stone (1971) implemented this algorithm using the perfect shuffle interconnection among a number of decision elements called 'comparators'. The comparators are one of the following three types, where each can take an input of two positive integers and can

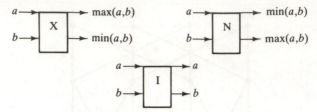

Figure 5.18   Three comparator types.

(1)   output the larger integer at the top output and the smaller integer at the bottom output (X type for 'maximum at top'), or

(2)   output the smaller integer at the top output and the larger integer at the bottom output (N type for 'minimum at top'), or

(3)   output the integers in the same order as the inputs (I type for 'identity').

The three types of comparators are shown in Figure 5.18.

The X-, N- and I-type comparators are then interconnected using the shuffle interconnections as shown in Figure 5.19.

The sorter shown in Figure 5.19 sorts $2^k = n$ elements (where $n = 8$, $k = 3$). In general, the sorting network requires a total of $(n/2)k^2$ comparators arranged in $n/2$ rows and k^2 columns. The network has an

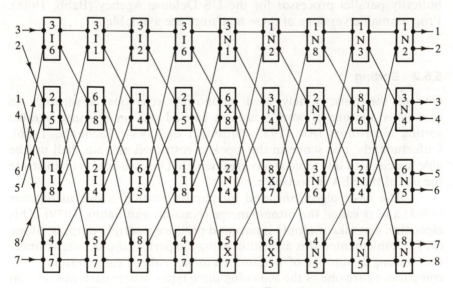

Figure 5.19   Stone–Batcher shuffle exchange sorter.

asymptotic complexity of $O((\log n)^2)$ comparison exchanges. Thus it provides a speed-up factor of $n/\log n$ over the sequential algorithm of $O(n \log n)$ time.

The shuffle connection between the different comparators in Figure 5.19 follows the rule described earlier in Section 5.4.2.1, namely

$$0-0, \ 1-2, \ 2-4, \ 3-6, \ 4-1, \ 5-3, \ 6-5, \ 7-7$$

Figure 5.19 illustrates the sorting of the eight-element input

$$(3, 2, 1, 4, 6, 5, 8, 7) \text{ to } (1, 2, 3, 4, 5, 6, 7, 8)$$

The shuffle exchange network has serious drawbacks; it has a low degree of regularity and modularity and requires long wires. As a result one needs an $O[n^2/(\log n)^2]$ chip area for VLSI design (Ullman (1984); see also Leighton (1983)).

For a detailed study of the complexity of sorting networks, see Akl (1985) and Parberry (1987).

5.5.3 CCC and its applications

The CCC architecture turns out to be a very versatile network for solving a large class of problems that include FFTs, sorting and other related algorithms. By combining the principles of pipelining, CCC can emulate the SEA (Preparata and Vuillemin, 1981).

The CCC is well suited for VLSI design since it has a regular structure and the layout area turns out to be $(\log n)^{1/2}$ superior to the shuffle exchange network.

5.6 Supercomputer architectures

For the sake of completeness, we now briefly introduce a higher level architecture popularly known as 'supercomputers'. The supercomputer architecture has been largely motivated by the increasing computational demands of the scientific and engineering communities (Hwang, 1987; Lubeck et al., 1985).

The two basic architectures that are used to build supercomputers are the vector processor and the array processor. These supercomputers can be thought of as parallel 'mainframe' computers built from identical powerful processors whose instruction execution is based on a concurrent alternative to the traditional sequential control flow architecture.

Vector-processor-based systems are produced by several companies – Cray 1, CDC Cyber 200, Fujitsu VP-100/VP-200, Hitachi S-810 and NEC SX-1/SX-2. These systems have the ability to vectorize the FORTRAN code.

The array processor architecture is not yet fully commercial: the Illiac IV, ICL DAP and Goodyear Staran belong to this category.

The supercomputers are usually programmed using three different approaches (Perrott and Aliabadi, 1986) (see also Chapter 7):

(1)   Those based on detecting parallelism: here the user writes a program in a parallel extension of FORTRAN, such as Cyber FORTRAN, CFT or IVTRAN, and the compiler determines which parts of the program can be executed in parallel (or vectorized).

(2)   Those which specify parallelism directly: this involves the use of machine parallelism languages such as CFD and DAP FORTRAN, where the syntax reflects the underlying machine architecture (Perrott, 1987).

(3)   Those which exploit problem parallelism: the language Actus, which expresses the problem parallelism directly in its syntax and is machine independent, is used.

For a detailed study on supercomputing, see Riganati and Schnek (1984), Dongarra (1987) and te Riele *et al.* (1987).

5.7 Dataflow architecture

In Section 3.9.2 we described the dataflow computing model. Since 1970, MIT and University of California in USA, CERT-ONERA in France, NTT and ETL in Japan and the University of Manchester, UK, have been very seriously pursuing this line of thought and have developed dataflow machines.

It is claimed that the dataflow architecture is highly suited for supercomputing as well as for natural programming in higher level languages called the 'single-assignment rule' languages. In such languages a variable is assigned a value by one statement only in a program fragment. This allows the data dependences in a program to be easily detectable and so the statements may be specified in any order.

The dataflow architectures have yet to gain commercial interest and exploitation. The following references may be consulted for full details: Gajski *et al.* (1982), Sharp (1985, 1988), Gurd *et al.* (1985, 1987) and Veen (1986).

5.8 Connection machine, logical and functional architectures

5.8.1 Connection machine

The connection machine designed by Hillis (1985) and currently marketed by Thinking Machines Corporation, Cambridge, MA, is a data level parallel computing system (Section 1.6). Data parallel computing associates one processor with each data element. This style of computing is useful for data-intensive problems since it reduces the computing time in proportion to the number of data elements in the computation; also, it reduces the programming effort in proportion to the complexity of expressing a naturally parallel problem statement in a serial manner.

The connection machine (model CM2) hardware consists of 64 000 processors each with 8 kilobytes of memory and an arithmetic–logic unit that can operate on variable length operands. There are two forms of communication within these processors:

(1)   **Router**
This allows any processor to communicate with any other processor. Every processor can therefore access any memory location of any other processor. This permits all the local memories to be treated as a single large memory.

(2)   **NEWS (north–east–west–south) grid**
This is a structured communication system with a rectangular fixed two-dimensional mesh-connected network where each processor has four neighbours (Section 5.3.4) to facilitate local four-neighbour communication.

The assembly language used in the connection machine is Paris (parallel instruction set); this is the target language of higher level language compilers. The parallel languages available now are *LISP, C* and FORTRAN 8X which are respectively the parallel dialects of Common LISP, C and FORTRAN 77 (see Section 7.3.6).

The system software is based on the operating system or environment of the front end computer such as the Digital Equipment Corporation VAX 8000 or Symbolics 3600 LISP Machine.

5.8.2 Logic and functional architectures

A number of architectures have been proposed for the execution of functional, logic and object-oriented languages. For a detailed review see Vegdahl (1984), Treleaven *et al.* (1982), Treleaven and Vanneschi (1987) and Karia (1987).

Also, attempts are underway to design concurrent logic programming machines. The concurrent PROLOG machine Bagel suggested by Shapiro (1983, 1987) at the Weizmann Institute of Science, Israel, combines the concepts of systolic programming, dataflow-like synchronization, guarded command indeterminacy and graph reduction (see also Woods (1985), Wise (1986), Tick (1988) and IEEE (1988)).

5.9   Comparative analysis of architectures

We described several different parallel computer architectures. In order to compare their performance, several metrics have been proposed in recent years (Levitan, 1985). However, as yet no suitable metric is available to determine the performance of an algorithm in any one type of parallel architecture.

Some of the important metrics suggested by Levitan are as follows:

(1)   **Diameter**
This is the worst-case time to get a message from one processor to another in a network.

(2)   **Bandwidth**
This is the total number of messages that can be sent or received by processors in the system in one instruction execution unit of time. In other words it is the maximum number of unique messages that can be generated or consumed in unit time in a network.

(3)   **Narrowness**
This is a measure for congestion in a network. It is calculated as follows: the network is partitioned into two sets of processors X and Y where $N(X)$ and $N(Y)$ are the numbers of processors in set X and set Y respectively. Let us assume that $N(Y) \leqslant N(X)$. Then count the number of interconnections between X and Y; call this $N(XY)$; then find the maximum value of $N(Y)/N(XY)$ for all possible partitionings of the processors.

(4)   **Gannon's bisection bandwidth**
To obtain this measure, the set of processors is partitioned into two halves. We also assume that the underlying task is for each processor in one partition to send a message to another processor in the other partition. The time taken for this task is called a bisection bandwidth.

Table 5.2 gives the metrics described above for different architectures (Levitan, 1985) (see also Cosnard *et al.* (1986)). The use of these

Table 5.2 Metrics for architectures.

Architecture	Diameter	Bandwidth	Narrowness	Gannon bandwidth
Serial	1	1	1	1
Linear array	N	N	N	1
Tree	$\log N$	N	N	1
Shuffle	$\log N$	N	1	N
Full interconnection	1	N	$1/N$	N^2

measures for practical problems is discussed in Levitan (1985). For other performance measures, see Stone (1988).

SUMMARY

In this chapter we studied the structure and organization of parallel processors. After a preliminary introduction to a taxonomical tree for the classification of different parallel architectures, we described several basic parallel architectures such as multiprocessors, vector processors, pipeline processors, array processors, systolic processors, wavefront array processors, cube architectures, and pyramid and prism architectures.

The special class of networks known as algorithm-structured networks was then introduced. The most important among these are the H-trees and the butterfly and shuffle exchange networks. The practical applications of these networks were then considered.

We then mentioned briefly the different higher level architectures – such as supercomputers, dataflow architectures, and functional, connection and logic architectures.

Finally, we introduced basic measures that determine the performance of an algorithm in any one of the parallel architectures.

EXERCISES

5.1 Design a systolic array machine to find the successive powers of a boolean matrix and to accumulate them to find the transitive closure.

5.2 Design a systolic matrix transposer.

5.3 Design an instruction systolic array for matrix transposition.

5.4   Design a wavefront array for finding the transitive closure, as in Exercise 5.1.

5.5   Draw a cube-connected cycle configuration for 2^{p+q}. $p = 3, q = 2$.

5.6   Draw a butterfly network for performing the fast Fourier transform with $N = 8$.

5.7   Describe the use of multiprocessors for sieving out the prime numbers (Bokhari (1987); see Exercise 1.11).

5.8   Design a systolic array to compute the different convergents of the finite continued fraction specified by

$$a_0 + \cfrac{1}{a_1 + \cfrac{1}{a_2 + \cfrac{1}{a_3 + \dots}}} = [a_0, a_1, \dots, a_n]$$

(see Exercises 1.18 and 2.7).

5.9   Design a systolic array to generate the Fibonacci sequence specified by

$$f_n = f_{n-1} + g_n$$
$$g_n = f_{n-1} + g_{n-1}$$

with

$$f_0 = 1, g_0 = 0$$

5.10 Generate the Farey sequence of order N, using the mutual recursion given in Section 1.9.4.4, with systolic arrays.

5.11 Design a systolic array for evaluating a polynomial of degree n.

5.12 Construct a pipeline array to compute the Moore–Penrose inverse A^+ using the algorithm described in Exercise 2.8 (De Vel and Krishnamurthy, 1987).

5.13 Write a program to simulate the shuffle exchange network method of sorting. Examine its performance for various sizes of the inputs.

5.14 Write a program to simulate the butterfly network for $N = 16$ and to perform Fourier transformations.

5.15   Compare the different vector processor systems such as the Cray 1, CDC Cyber 200 and Fujitsu VP-100.

5.16   Study how a sequential program written in FORTRAN is executed in parallel in a vector machine.

5.17   Study the language Actus and examine how it introduces parallelism in Pascal.

5.18   What is a single-assignment rule? What are its advantages?

5.19   Study Hillis' work on connection machines. Where do these machines find applications?

5.20   Study the suggestions of Shapiro (1983) on concurrent PROLOG machine.

References

Akl S.G. (1985). *Parallel Sorting Algorithms*. New York NY: Academic Press

Albrecht A. and Melhorn K. (1987). Parallel algorithms and architectures. *Lecture Notes in Computer Science*, **269**

Babb II R.G. (1988). *Programming Parallel Processors*. Reading MA: Addison-Wesley

Basu A. (1987). Parallel processing systems: a nomenclature based on their characteristics. *Proc. IEE (UK)*, **134**, 143–7

Batcher K. (1968). Sorting networks and their applications. *Proc. AFIPS SJCC*, **32**, 307–14

Bitton D., de Witt D.J., Hsiao D.K. and Menon J. (1984). A taxonomy of parallel sorting. *ACM Computing Surveys*, **16**, 287–318

Bokhari S.H. (1987). Multiprocessing the sieve of Eratosthenes. *IEEE Computer*, **20**, 50–8

Burt P. (1984). The pyramid as a structure for efficient computation. In *Multiresolution Image Processing and Analysis* (Rosenfeld A., ed.). New York NY: Springer

Cosnard M., Quinton P., Robert Y. and Tchuente M. (1986). *Parallel Algorithms and Architectures*. Amsterdam: North-Holland

Desrochers G.R. (1987). *Principles of Parallel and Multiprocessing*. New York NY: McGraw-Hill

De Vel O.Y. and Krishnamurthy E.V. (1987). An iterative pipelined array architecture for generalized matrix inversion. *Information Processing Lett.*, **26**, 263–7

Dongarra J.J. (1987). *Experimental Parallel Computing Architectures*. Amsterdam: North-Holland

Ernston P.H. (1977). Multiprocessor organization. *Computing Surveys*, **9**, 103–29

Flynn M.J. (1966). Very high speed computing systems. *Proc. IEEE*, **54**, 1901–9

Flynn M.J. (1972). Some computer organizations and their effectiveness. *IEEE Trans. Computers*, **21**, 948–60

Fortes J.A. (1985). Systematic approaches to the design of algorithmically specified systolic arrays. In *Proc. 1985 Int. Conf.*, ASASP. New York NY: IEEE

Gajski D.D., Padua D.A., Kuck D.J. and Kuhn R.H. (1982). A second opinion on dataflow machines and languages. *IEEE Computer*, **15**, 58–68

Gurd J.R., Kirkham C.C. and Watson I. (1985). The Manchester prototype dataflow computer. *Comm. ACM*, **28**, 34–52

Gurd J.R., Barahona P.M.C.C., Bohm A.P.W. *et al.* (1987). Fine grain parallel computing: the dataflow approach. *Lecture Notes in Computer Science*, **272**, 82–152

Hennessy M. (1986). Proving systolic systems correct. *ACM Trans. Programming Languages Systems*, **8**, 344–87

Hillis W.D. (1985). *The Connection Machine*. Cambridge MA: MIT Press

Hwang K. (1987). Advanced parallel processing with supercomputer architectures. *Proc. IEEE*, **75**, 1348–79

Hwang K. and Briggs F.A. (1984). *Computer Architecture and Parallel Processing*. New York NY: McGraw-Hill

IEEE (1987). Systolic arrays. *IEEE Computer*, **20**

IEEE (1988). *Proc. 1987 Symp. on Logic Programming*. New York NY: IEEE

Johnson E.E. (1988). Completing an MIMD multiprocessor taxonomy. *Computer Architecture News*, **16**, 44–8

Karia R.J. (1987). Towards a parallel architecture for functional languages. *Lecture Notes in Computer Science*, **272**, 270–86

Kogge P.M. (1981). *The Architecture of Pipelined Computers*. New York NY: McGraw-Hill

Krishnamurthy E.V. and Klette R. (1981). Fast parallel realization of matrix multiplication. *EIK*, **17**, 279–92

Kuck D. J. (1978). *The Structure of Computers and Computations*, Vol. 1. New York NY: Wiley

Kung H.T. (1982). Why systolic architectures? *IEEE Computer*, **15**, 37–46

Kung S.Y. (1988). *Array Processors*. Englewood Cliffs NJ: Prentice-Hall

Lang H.W. (1986). The instruction systolic array. *Integration – the VLSI J.*, **4**, 65–74

Lang H.W. (1987). ISA and SISA: two variants of general purpose systolic array architectures. In *Proc. 2nd Int. Conf. on Supercomputing*, Vol. 1, pp. 460–5

Leighton F.T. (1983). *Complexity Issues in VLSI*. Cambridge MA: MIT Press

Levitan S.P. (1985). Evaluation criteria for communication structures in parallel architectures. In *Proc. 1985 Int. Conf. on Parallel Processing*. New York NY: IEEE

Lubeck O., Moore J. and Mendez R. (1985). A benchmark comparison of three supercomputers: Fujitsu VP-200, Hitachi S810/20, and Cray X-MP/2. *IEEE Computer*, **18**, 10–23

Mead C.E. and Conway L. (1980). *Introduction to VLSI Systems*. Reading MA: Addison-Wesley

Megson G.M. and Evans D.J. (1987) LISA: a parallel processing architecture. *Lecture Notes in Computer Science*, **237**, 361–75

Moore W., McCabe A. and Urquhart R. (1987). *Systolic Arrays*. Bristol: Adam Hilger

Nassimi D. and Sahni S. (1979). Bitonic sort on a mesh connected parallel computer. *IEEE Trans. Computers*, **27**, 1–7

Parberry I. (1987). *Parallel Complexity Theory*. London: Pitman

Perrott R.H. (1987). *Parallel Programming*. Wokingham: Addison-Wesley

Perrott R.H. and Aliabadi A.Z. (1986). Supercomputer languages. *Computing Surveys*, **18**, 5–22

Preparata F.P. and Vuillemin J. (1981). The cube connected cycles: a versatile network for parallel computation. *Comm. ACM*, **24**, 300–9

Quinton P. (1987). An introduction to systolic architectures. *Lecture Notes in Computer Science*, **272**, 387–401

Richards D. (1986). Parallel sorting. *SIGACT News* (Summer 1986)

Riganati J.P. and Schnek B.P. (1984). Supercomputing. *IEEE Computer*, **17**, 97–114

Rosenfeld A. (1985). The prism machine: an alternative to the pyramid. *J. Parallel and Distributed Computing*, **2**, 404–11

Satyanarayanan M. (1980). *Multiprocessors – a Comparative Study*. Englewood Cliffs NJ: Prentice-Hall

Seitz C.L. (1984). Concurrent VLSI architectures. *IEEE Trans. Computers*, **33**, 1247–65

Seitz C.L. (1985). The Cosmic cube. *Comm. ACM*, **28**, 22–33

Seitz C.L., Athas W.C., Dally W.J. *et al.* (1988). *Message Passing Concurrent Computers: their Architecture and Programming*. Reading MA: Addison-Wesley

Shapiro E.Y. (1983). *Lecture Notes on the Bagel, a Systolic Concurrent Prolog Machine*. Technical Report TR-035, ICOT, Tokyo

Shapiro E.Y. (1987). *Concurrent Prolog – Collected Papers*, 2 vols. Cambridge MA: MIT Press

Sharp J.A. (1985). *Dataflow Computing*. Chichester: Ellis Horwood

Sharp J.A. (1988). *Introduction to Distributed and Parallel Processing*. London: Blackwell Scientific

Skillcorn D.B. (1988). A taxonomy for computer architectures. *IEEE Computer*, **21**, 46–57

Stone H.S. (1971). Parallel processing with the perfect shuffle. *IEEE Trans. Computers*, **20**, 153–61

Stone H.S. (1988). *High Performance Computer Architecture*. Reading MA: Addison-Wesley

te Riele H.J.J., Dekker Th.J. and van der Vorst H.A. (1987). *Algorithms and Applications on Vector and Parallel Computers*. Amsterdam: North-Holland

Tick E. (1988). *Memory Performance of Prolog Architectures*. Boston MA: Kluwer

Treleaven P.C. and Vanneschi M. (1987). Future parallel computers. *Lecture Notes in Computer Science*, **272**

Treleaven P.C., Brownbridge D.R. and Hopkins R.P. (1982). Data driven and demand driven computer architecture. *ACM Computing Surveys*, **14**, 93–143

Uhr L. (1984). *Algorithm Structured Computer Arrays and Networks*. New York NY: Academic Press

Ullman J.D. (1984). *Computational Aspects of VLSI*. Rockville MD: Computer Science Press

Veen A.H. (1986). Dataflow machine architecture. *ACM Computing Serveys*, **18**, 365–98

Vegdahl S.R. (1984). A survey of proposed architectures for the execution of functional languages. *IEEE Trans. Computers*, **33**, 1050–71

Welty L. and Patton P.C. (1985). Hypercube architectures. In *AFIPS, Proc. National Conf.*, Vol. 54, pp. 495–501

Wise M.J. (1986). *Prolog Multiprocessors*. Englewood Cliffs NJ: Prentice-Hall

Woods J.V. (1985). *Fifth Generation Computer Architectures*. Amsterdam: North-Holland

Wu C. and Feng T. (1980). The reverse exchange interconnection network. *IEEE Trans. Computers*, **29**, 801–11

Chapter 6
Parallel Computation – Complexity Aspects

6.1 Introduction

One of the most important practical considerations in computing is the amount of computational resources needed to solve a problem. Two common measures for the computational resources used by an algorithm are time, that is the number of steps executed by the algorithm, and space, that is the amount of memory used by the algorithm. Given a specific decidable problem, one therefore obtains an upper bound on the required time and space by exhibiting a particular algorithm which solves the problem and then bounding its resources. However, in judging the optimality of algorithms, it is also necessary to have the corresponding lower bounds on the computational complexity of the problem.

Sequential complexity theory in both its 'abstract' and 'concrete' forms deals with both the time and the space requirements to solve classes of problems in sequentially programmed machines. Abstract complexity theory has an axiomatic framework suggested by Rabin (1960) and developed further by Blum (1967). Concrete complexity theory deals with practical aspects of running time and space required by an algorithm.

247

A class of problems is considered tractable if the running time is a polynomial function of the input size of the given instance of a problem. This takes us to the question 'what is input size?'. Clearly, for every problem we can take the length of the input data in some alphabet as the size of the input. For example, if the inputs are numbers, the length of the binary notation can be used as the input size; for graphs, the adjacency matrix size can be treated as the input size. Using some such convention, if n is the input size, the number of operations for polynomial time algorithms is of the form $P(n)$ (P is a low degree polynomial of the form $a_0 + a_1 n + \ldots + a_k n^k$). We designate this class of problems having deterministic polynomial time algorithms by P.

A class of problems is said to be intractable if the running times of the known algorithms are no less than exponential where the number of operations is of the order k^n (k = a constant).

The distinction between the tractable and the intractable problems can now be made more explicit. When a deterministic sequential computer is used, the tractable problems can be solved significantly more rapidly by increasing the speed of the computer; however, for intractable problems, increasing the speed of the deterministic sequential machine has practically negligible effects. In fact the intractability turns out to be essentially independent of the encoding scheme used for inputting the problem and the deterministic sequential machine model used. Similarly, all the tractable problems can be solved in polynomial time in all deterministic sequential machine models. This belief that all the deterministic sequential machine models have polynomial-related execution times is called the 'sequential computation thesis'.

The intractability leads to the definition of a class of problems other than the class P, known as the **NP** class. The NP class (for non-deterministic polynomial class) of problems can be solved in polynomial-bounded time by using a non-deterministic algorithm. Within this NP class, there is a subclass called the **NP-complete** problems. The NP-complete problems are mutually reducible. That is, if a fast deterministic algorithm for solving any one problem is available, then such an algorithm can be used to devise algorithms to solve other NP-complete problems.

The theory of NP-completeness was developed in two fundamental papers by Cook (1971) and Karp (1972). Since then an enormous number of problems have been shown to be NP-complete and those come from a wide variety of areas. Typical examples are the travelling salesman problem, the boolean satisfiability problem, reachability for 1-conservative Petri nets and fault detection in logic circuits (for a detailed exposition see Garey and Johnson (1979), Cook (1983), Stockmeyer (1987) and Machtey and Young (1978)).

Proving that an NP problem is NP-complete ensures that the problem is not in P (does not have a deterministic polynomial time algorithm) unless every NP problem is in P. Thus NP-completeness provides a lower bound for complexity. An important open question, however, is whether P = NP. This appears to be a difficult question to answer.

A complexity class that is broader than NP is the class PSPACE of problems solvable using a polynomial amount of space on a deterministic TM. In other words, $P \subset NP \subset PSPACE$; it is believed that these inclusions are strict.

In analogy with NP-completeness, we call a problem PSPACE-complete (PSC) if it is in PSPACE and all problems in PSPACE can be reduced to it.

A practical problem in PSC is the problem of quantified satisfiability. Here a boolean expression of the form (with alternating universal and existential quantifiers) $\forall x_1 \exists x_2 \forall x_3 \ldots \exists x_{2n} B(x_1, x_2, \ldots, x_{2n})$ where B is in conjunctive normal form ('and' of a set of clauses made up of 'or' of literals) is given. We are required to find whether the expression is satisfiable; that is, whether for all choices of truth values for x_1 there is a choice of truth value for x_2, such that for all choices for x_3 etc., and finally there is a choice for x_{2n} which leaves all the clauses true at least for one literal.

The above problem is nothing but a two-person game played between an existential (E) player and a universal (U) player, who take turns setting the values of even- and odd-suffixed variables respectively. The E player tries to make the formula true, while the U player tries to make it false. The question is whether the E player has a winning strategy. This problem is PSC.

6.2 Parallel speed-up

The NP class, as already mentioned, stands for the non-deterministic polynomial class of problems. That is those problems that can be solved either by non-deterministic Turing machines or by non-deterministic algorithms in polynomial time. Such algorithms are endowed with the power of choosing the correct alternatives among N different alternatives, so that the correct solution can be reached.

For example, suppose that the problem is to determine whether an undirected graph is k-colourable (an undirected graph is said to be k-colourable if all its vertices can be coloured using k different colours, so that no two adjacent vertices receive the same colour). A non-deterministic algorithm may start by colouring the first vertex with an arbitrary colour; then at each step, it colours one or more vertices and checks that up to that point no two adjacent vertices have been assigned the same colour. Each time the algorithm colours a new vertex, it has k choices. The non-deterministic algorithm in such a case carries out the computation in 'parallel': this is done by using independent copies of the algorithm simultaneously all along the paths from the root to the leaves of the tree of possibilities (where each path from the root to a leaf represents the computation) to check out one possible solution.

This ability of the non-deterministic algorithm to choose a path that leads to a correct solution may be thought of as a guess made by the algorithm. Accordingly, we can say that a non-deterministic algorithm solves a problem if there are some sequences of guesses or a path in the tree of possibilities to reach the solution. In practice, however, a non-deterministic machine that solves a problem in polynomial time is not constructively feasible. In order to simulate such a machine in reality, we need to use k^N deterministic processors, where k is the number of branches at each level and N is the depth of the tree of possibilities. In such a case each possible outcome can be computed by the tree of concurrent deterministic machines. Such an approach in fact converts a non-deterministic polynomial time algorithm to a deterministic systematic search of a solution space of exponential size.

The above argument shows that, to solve an NP-complete problem, the number of processors required grows exponentially with the input size of the problem. This means we reduce the time complexity at the expense of using more space for processors whose number grows exponentially. At this point we may recall the prophetic remark of the philosopher Charles Babbage (Babbage, 1864):

> It is impossible to construct machinery occupying unlimited space; but it is possible to construct finite machinery, and to use it through unlimited time. It is this substitution of the infinity of time for the infinity of space which I have made use of to limit the size of the engine and yet to retain its unlimited power.

We may call this Babbage's thesis. This thesis states that the time and the space complexity are related and can be traded for one another. The miniature size of VLSI permits this space–time trade-off since we can pack a very large number of processors into a given area. So the central issue in parallel and concurrent processing using a large number of processors is the design of algorithms whose performance can be somehow related to the time complexity of the single-processor sequential algorithm, T_1. Ideally, we require that a parallel algorithm which takes a problem and uses N processors in time T_N is related to T_1 by the relation $T_N = T_1/N$. In other words, based on common sense, one expects that a multiple processor with N independent processors should be able to compute the solution of a problem N times faster than a single processor. This is called 'ideal speed-up'. However, in practice this speed-up ratio T_1/T_N turns out to be far less than N for the following reasons:

(1)   Processors competing for the same communication paths with other processors or to a shared memory can slow down because of the non-availability of paths.

(2)   Since simultaneous reading and writing from a file can cause conflicts the processors are forced to wait for mutual exclusion.

(3)   Processors need to be conditionally synchronized when different tasks are to be coordinated.

(4)   The sequential component in an algorithm limits the speed of the total process; in other words, if T_s and T_p are respectively the time spent on serial and parallel components of an algorithm in a single processor, then the maximum speed-up S_N that can be achieved using N processors in parallel for the parallel component is given by:

$$S_N \leqslant \frac{T_s + T_p}{T_s + T_p/N} = \frac{1}{x + (1 - x)/N}$$

where $x = T_s/(T_s + T_p)$ and $0 \leqslant x \leqslant 1$.

Note that x is a fraction of the computations performed sequentially. For example, if $x = 1/k$, where $k > 1$, then $S_N \leqslant k$, even if N is very large; obviously, for $x = 0, S_N = N$. This is called 'Amdahl's law' (see Gustafson (1988)).

We now introduce some measures for efficiency of speed-up and also consider some simple problems that can be speeded up.

6.3   Efficiency of speed-up and communication complexity

In the previous section we said that there is always a trade-off between the number of processors utilized and the computation time. In order to determine the efficiency of processor utilization, the following measure may be chosen:

$$E = \frac{T_1}{NT_N}$$

where T_1 is the time complexity of the fastest sequential algorithm, N is the number of processors used and T_N is the parallel time complexity. Note that $0 < E \leqslant 1$; also, $E = 1$ corresponds to the best speed-up, namely $T_N = T_1/N$.

However, the above measure turns out to be too crude to be useful, since every parallel algorithm has a strong dependence on the underlying architecture that determines the communication as well as computational complexity. This means that, in order to analyse and measure the efficiency of parallel algorithms, the architectural model of computation also has to be specified.

One can, for instance, introduce the following simple-minded architectural specifications:

(1)   The parallel processor system consists of N individual processors (N can be bounded or unbounded).

(2)   The computational problem to be solved by the parallel processor system can be represented as sequences of binary arithmetic and logical operations.

(3)   Each of the N processors can execute any one of the operations at any time.

(4)   Every operation takes the same unit of time.

(5)   Other processes such as data transfers, control and communication delays are not taken into account.

(6)   There are no data access conflicts.

Based on the above specifications Munro and Paterson (1973) proved the following theorem.

6.3.1 Theorem (Munro–Paterson)

If the sequential computation of a single result consists of x arithmetic operations, $T_1 = x \geqslant 1$, the parallel computation using N processors requires

$$T_N \geqslant \begin{cases} [\log x + 1] & \text{if } x < 2^{[\log N]} \\ \dfrac{x + 1 - 2^{[\log N]}}{N} + \log N & \text{if } x \geqslant 2^{[\log N]} \end{cases}$$

where the logarithm is to base 2 and [ ] denotes the higher integral part of the value inside.

6.3.2 Example

Consider the addition of eight numbers. The sequential addition takes 7 units of time while the parallel scheme (Figure 6.1) takes 3 units of time using four processors. Here $x = 7$ and $N = 4$, and hence $x \geqslant 2^2$; thus $T_4 = 3$.

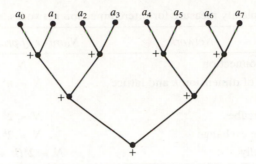

Figure 6.1   Parallel addition.

The above example essentially manipulates the evaluation tree in order to construct an equivalent arithmetic expression that can be evaluated in parallel.

Also, one may wonder whether it is still possible to achieve speed-up when a sufficient number of processors are unavailable. This is given by the following theorem due to Brent (1974).

6.3.3   Theorem (Brent)

If a computation can be performed in time T with x operations and sufficiently many processors, then the same computation can be performed in time T^1 with N processors, where $T^1 = [T + (x - T)/N]$; here, $[\ ]$ denotes the higher integral part of the value inside.

For example, in the addition of eight numbers, if we use only three processors, we shall require

$$T^1 = [3 + (7 - 3)/3] = 5$$

In the architectural specifications of the simplified model described above, we have ignored the data communication aspects. This is really a crucial issue to be taken into account when finding the complexity of a parallel computation. We shall discuss this aspect briefly in the following subsection.

6.3.4   Communication complexity

The complexity of communication is difficult to evaluate in a shared-memory asynchronous computational model. However, when synchronous interconnection networks are used to realize the algorithms, the complexities are more easily evaluated. When implementing a synchronous parallel algorithm in a standard interconnection network, it is useful

Table 6.1   Complexity measure for interconnection networks.

Number	Network	Number of processors	C
1	Full connection	N	$N - 1$
2	Mesh of dimension k and lattice size n	$N = n^k$	$2k$
3	Hypercube	$N = 2^k$	k
4	Shuffle exchange	$N = 2^k$	3
5	Butterfly	$N = 2^k(k + 1)$	4

to include the communication complexity costs with the time and space complexities.

The number of interconnections per processor (C) serves as a useful measure for the complexity of an interconnection network. We give this measure in Table 6.1 for some of the standard interconnection networks earlier studied in Chapter 5.

In the following section, we describe some basic parallel computational models to study the complexity aspects in greater detail.

6.4   Parallel complexity models

In the previous section, we gave a very simple example of a problem involving the addition of eight numbers; for this problem, the sequential algorithm took 7 time steps, while the parallel algorithm took $\log_2 7 = 3$ steps using four processors. In other words, a sequential problem with time complexity of order n (denoted by $O(n)$) was solved using $n/2$ processors in parallel in $O(\log n)$ time. Naturally, the question arises as to whether every problem in class P (that is, having a sequential polynomial time algorithm) can be solved using $O(\text{poly}(n))$ processors in a parallel time $O(\text{poly}(\log n))$ where $\text{poly}(\log n)$ is a polynomial in $\log n$.

The answer to the above question requires a suitable definition of the concept of 'parallel time' and a precise specification of the computational model used. Several parallel computational models have been proposed for this purpose. Among these the most popular model is the parallel version of the sequential random access machine (RAM) to be described below.

6.4.1   RAM model

An RAM model is a one-accumulator computer in which the instructions are not permitted to modify themselves.

An RAM consists of a read-only input tape, a single processor, a write-only output tape, a program and a memory unit. The memory unit consists of an infinite number of registers R_0, R_1, . . . , each of which can hold an integer of an arbitrary size. The program is a finite sequence of labelled instructions, not stored in the memory but read from the input tape. The basic instruction set has the following form, where $*$ denotes the standard binary operations on integers.

- $R_i \leftarrow$ constant (load register with constant)
- $R_i \leftarrow R_j * R_k$ (binary operation)
- $R_i \leftarrow R_{R_j}$ (indirect load)
- $R_{R_i} \leftarrow R_j$ (indirect store)
- $R_i \leftarrow$ PID (store process identity register)
- Halt (end)
- Go to label m if $R_i \geqslant 0$ (conditional jump)

Note that the RAM machine is as powerful as Church's universal machine (Section 3.3.6.10), since the processor has all the necessary instructions.

The input is read from the input tape that is marked as a sequence of squares and the output is written in the output tape again marked as a sequence of squares.

The advantage of the RAM model is that it is as powerful yet more realistic than a Turing machine, since the RAM resembles modern computers more closely.

The RAM programs can simulate both deterministic and non-deterministic Turing machines with time bounds preserved within a polynomial and space bounds preserved to within a constant factor. We now describe the parallel version of the RAM model (PRAM).

6.4.2 PRAM model and its variants

The PRAM model consists of N deterministic RAM processors P(i), i = 1, 2, . . . , N, all operating in parallel and communicating via a shared memory. The number of processors N is a function of the input size n. Each processor i has an infinite number of general-purpose registers as in the RAM and a unique read-only memory (ROM) X(i). The shared memory cells C(i) are infinite. A PRAM program consists of a finite list of instructions, where each instruction is of the form:

(1)   perform an internal computation;
(2)   transfer of control;

(3)   read a value from the shared memory;

(4)   write a value in the shared memory.

Categories (1) and (2) are local instructions to each P(i) (earlier described in Section 6.4.1), whereas categories (3) and (4) are communication instructions between different processors.

At each step, each processor is in some state. The actions and the next state of each processor at each step depend on its current state and the values it reads from ROM X(i) and the shared memory. The various variants of the PRAM model differ in the way they handle the write conflicts:

- Variant 1: CREW (concurrent read exclusive write) – here, the write conflicts are avoided by mutual exclusion.

- Variant 2: COMMON – here all the processors simultaneously write the same value in the same cell.

- Variant 3: ARBITRARY – an arbitrary processor succeeds in writing.

- Variant 4: PRIORITY – the processor with the minimum index succeeds in writing.

In using the PRAM model, the following terminology is used:

(1)   Processor bound $P(n)$: the number of processors used as a function of the input size n.

(2)   Word size $W(n)$: the machine is said to have a word size $W(n)$ if the size of any number during the computation is less than $2^{W(n)}$. It is assumed that $W(n)$ is at least $\log(P(n))$.

(3)   Time bound $T(n)$: this is the number of instructions executed before all processors have halted.

The study of parallel models leads to the following three new concepts: the parallel computation thesis, P-completeness and Nick's class of problems. We shall now explain these concepts. For a detailed study of parallel complexity, see Parberry (1987).

6.5   Parallel computation thesis, P-completeness and Nick's class

6.5.1   Parallel computation thesis

Investigations of a variety of parallel models have shown that, if no explicit upper bound is placed on the number of processors, then the class of problems accepted by the PRAM in time poly$[T(n)]$ is precisely the class of problems accepted by deterministic Turing machines (DTM) in space poly$[T(n)]$ (Fortune and Wyllie, 1978). A similar result is true for the alternating Turing machines (ATM) (Section 3.11), namely

$$\text{ATM}\{\text{poly}[T(n)]\} = \text{DTM}\{\text{space poly}[T(n)]\}$$

These investigations led to the formulation of the parallel computation thesis (Goldschlager, 1982) analogous to the sequential computation thesis. The parallel computation thesis states that a problem can be solved in time polynomial $T(n)$ by a parallel machine (with unlimited number of processors) if and only if it can be solved in space polynomial in $T(n)$ by a sequential machine (with unlimited time). This thesis has not been proved. If one adopts this thesis the question we asked earlier in the beginning of Section 6.4, namely whether every problem in P can be solved in a parallel time O[poly$(\log n)$], is equivalent to the question:

is P $\subseteq$ DSPACE[poly$(\log n)$]?

(Here DSPACE denotes the space requirement for a deterministic Turing machine or RAM model.)

6.5.2   P-completeness

The relationship between the time and space complexities gives rise to the class of problems called P-complete. If a problem A is P-complete then

$$A \in \text{DSPACE}[\text{poly}(\log n)] \text{ iff } P \subseteq \text{DSPACE}[\text{poly}(\log n)]$$

As a result, proving a problem to be P-complete is viewed as evidence that the problem cannot be solved in poly$(\log n)$ parallel time. Thus P-complete problems probably do not have an exponential speed-up in parallel.

6.5.3   Validity of the parallel computation thesis

It is necessary to point out that the parallel computation thesis has been verified only for those parallel models with the following property; if a parallel computation has t parallel steps then at most $2^{O(t)}$ processors can participate in the computation. Thus, for the parallel computation thesis to hold, $P(n) = 2^{O[T(n)]}$.

In fact Blum (1983) points out that the parallel computation thesis can fail if many more than $2^{O[T(n)]}$ processors are employed. Therefore, at present it is a convention to call those models which employ no more than $2^{O[T(n)]}$ processors 'reasonable' models.

6.5.4   Some P-complete problems

The P-complete problems are in a sense the most difficult ones in P. If any one of these problems can be computed in poly(log n) space then so can every member of P. (Hence P-complete problems are also known as 'log space complete for P'.)

One of the well-known problems that is P-complete and hence not solvable in poly(log n) space is the circuit value problem (CVP). This problem determines the value of an output from a given combinational circuit with certain specified inputs. Formally, such a problem can be defined as a sequence of equations among m boolean variables X_1, X_2, ..., X_m. Each equation is of the form $X_i = 1$, $X_i = 0$ or $X_i = X_j * X_k$, for some j, $k < i$, where * is any one of the sixteen 2-ary boolean connectives (such as **and**, **or**, **nor**, **exclusive or**) and each variable appears exactly once on the left-hand side of each equation. Variables can occur any number of times in the right-hand sides of the equations.

Given such a sequence of equations, we may assign truth values to all the variables in order X_1, X_2, ..., X_m. The condition j, $k < i$ ensures that there are no cyclic dependences among the variables. The CVP is the set of such sequences of equations such that $X_m = 1$. Ladner (1975) proved that the CVP is P-complete.

Goldschlager (1977) proved that the monotone CVP defined like the CVP but confining * to **and** and **or** is also P-complete.

6.5.5   Nick's class (N-class)

A basic question (we asked several times) in parallel computation is: which problems can be solved substantially faster using many processors rather than a single processor? Nicholas Pippenger (Pippenger, 1979) formalized this question by defining a class known as NC (Nick's class) which can be solved ultrafast in parallel machines in poly(log n) time using poly(n) processors.

Pippenger showed that NC is the class of problems solvable by deterministic Turing machines in polynomial time whose tape head makes at most poly(log n) reversals.

Another characterization is that NC is the class of problems accepted by alternating Turing machines which accept simultaneously within space O(log n) and time poly(log n).

6.5.6 Some NC problems

The following problems are in NC:

(1)   matrix inversion;

(2)   determinant evaluation;

(3)   arithmetic operations (+ , – , × , ÷) on binary numbers;

(4)   sorting;

(5)   graph connectivity;

(6)   finding greatest common divisors of polynomials (gcd).

Placing problems in NC is a very active research area, since it tells us whether ultrafast algorithms can be designed (see Cook (1985)). Many useful problems are yet to be classified including the very well known problem of finding the gcd of two integers; it is not yet known whether finding the gcd is in NC. For recent surveys, see Vishkin (1983) and Karp and Ramachandran (1988).

Remark
One may observe that only the NC problems are ideally suited for solution by synchronous and systolic machines.

6.6 Realizability of parallel machines

In Section 6.5.4 we mentioned that the CVP and monotone CVP are P-complete. These results have the following consequences in designing parallel machines using bases of boolean functions.

Goldschlager and Parberry (1986) have shown that a 2-ary boolean function basis is P-complete if it contains

(1)   at least one of the following functions (called 'hard'): nand, nor, implies, not implies, implied by, not implied by; or

(2)   the following two functions (called 'moderate'): and, or; or

(3)   a moderate function and one of the easy functions of the form: not x, not y, exclusive or, equivalence.

The remaining bases of two-input boolean functions are not believed to be P-complete (unless P = SPACE[poly(log n)]).

If a basis is P-complete then the CVP over that basis is probably inherently sequential. Only the P-complete basis functions can be used to build general-purpose parallel machines. The remaining bases are not suitable for building general-purpose parallel machines. (For further studies, see Schoning (1986) and Wegener (1987).)

6.7   Universal interconnection patterns

In Section 6.3.4 we mentioned that the interconnection pattern among the different processors is of great importance in determining the communication complexity of a given algorithm. It is natural therefore to examine whether we can design a universal interconnection structure that can simulate any one of the desired interconnections, for example a butterfly or a shuffle or a hypercube.

Goldschlager (1982) describes a class of parallel machines called 'conglomerates' that include all parallel machines which could feasibly be built with fixed interconnections. Then he shows that there is a universal conglomerate structure which can simulate any other basic conglomerate in linear time.

Such an approach will be useful in developing a programmable interconnection pattern (see Parberry (1987)).

6.8   VLSI computational complexity

Another important topic for study is the derivation of complexity bounds for VLSI implementation. The practical use of many new algorithms and computer science theory depends heavily on the design of VLSI chips that can perform computation with maximal efficiency. This means the information transfer as well as the signal propagation times are both minimized in the realization of VLSI chip algorithms (see Bertolazzi and Luccio (1984) and Leighton (1983)).

In order to study the efficiency of a VLSI chip, different models are used. The main difference among these models is the manner in which the signal propagation time is modelled. Most authors evaluate a VLSI algorithm under the constant or logarithmic model, that is the signal propagation time is assumed to be at most proportional to the logarithm of the wire length. Some authors prefer the use of a linear model in which the signal propagation time is assumed to be proportional to the wire length.

Two fundamental parameters decide the efficiency of a VLSI chip: the area of the circuit and the time taken to produce the output for a given input. The area gives the space complexity, while the time taken gives the time complexity. Intuitively, since the time and space complexities can be traded for one another we can write $f_1(T)f_2(S) = $ a constant of suitable dimension, where $f_1(T)$ and $f_2(S)$ are time and space complexities.

The practical complexity measures used for a VLSI chip are the area (A) or the time (T) or the products AT or AT^2. Most of the designs evaluate these complexity measures based on one of the signal propagation models.

6.8.1 Notation for complexity bounds

In evaluating the measures, the following notations are used to specify the asymptotic order – whether upper, lower or exact estimates.

Let f, g be functions defined on the set of natural numbers (N).

(1) $f(n) = O[g(n)]$: means $f(n)$ is order at most $g(n)$ if and only if there are constants $c > 0$ and $N > 0$ such that, for all $n \geqslant N$, $f(n) \leqslant cg(n)$. That is, O gives the upper bound.

(2) $f(n) = \Omega[g(n)]$: means $f(n)$ is order at least $g(n)$ if and only if there are constants $C > 0$ and $N > 0$ such that, for $n \geqslant N$, $f(n) \geqslant Cg(n)$. That is, Ω gives the lower bound.

(3) $f(n) = \Theta[g(n)]$: means $f(n)$ is order exactly $g(n)$ if and only if $f(n) = O[g(n)]$ and $f(n) = \Omega[g(n)]$. That is, Θ gives the exact bound.

The above mappings O, Ω, Θ introduce classes of functions of similar complexity ignoring constant factors. These are therefore useful for the asymptotic evaluation of the complexities.

6.8.2 VLSI hardware model

There are several ways in which a VLSI chip can be abstracted to construct a model.

On the higher level of abstraction, the VLSI chip can be viewed as a computation graph whose vertices are information processing devices (gates) and whose arcs are wires, that are electrical connections used for information transfer, power supply and distribution of clock pulses. Usually there is a global clock synchronizing the actions of these information-processing devices.

On the lower level of abstraction, the computational graph is a geometric object embedded in the euclidean plane. Here the information-processing devices (called gates or nodes) and the wires are represented as areas in the plane. The wires are represented by connected sets of rectangular arcs (called 'a wire segment'). The computation graph is thus a geometric object embedded in the plane dictated by the design rules of technology used (see Mead and Conway (1980)).

Then suitable assumptions are made on the measurements of area and time, nature of node functions, the communication protocol and the nature of the input–output for each algorithm realized.

Based on these assumptions the lower bounds for area–time trade-off have been obtained for several problems such as fast Fourier transform (FFT), matrix multiplication, sorting and binary arithmetic.

Another important aspect of VLSI computation is the layout

Table 6.2 Area complexity measures.

Network	Area
Complete binary tree	$\Omega(n \log n)$
H-tree	$O(n), \Omega(n)$
Mesh of trees	$O(n \log^2 n), \Omega(n \log n)$
Planar graph	$\Omega(n \log n)$
Shuffle exchange	$O(n^2/\log^2 n)$
Butterfly	$O(n^2), \Omega(n^2)$

complexity. Given a computational graph, here we want to know what is the minimum area required to embed it in the euclidean plane. Such a study has given rise to good upper bounds for the minimal area for graphs such as trees and planar graphs.

In Table 6.2, we give some bounds on the areas of some of the important VLSI layouts for some standard n-input node networks (see Ullman (1984)), using the notation of Section 6.8.1. Also, in Table 6.3 we give the time bounds for processing some standard problems in VLSI (Ullman, 1984).

6.9 Physical complexity and neural networks

The complexity aspects earlier described are all concerned with the number of time steps and the space required to perform a given computation. Hence these are essentially the logical and computational related complexities. However, associated with each computation is the expenditure of energy. This energy – called the computation energy – can also provide us with a measure for the efficiency of an algorithm, as well as the computational architecture and the mapping of the algorithm onto the architecture. Any approach that results in lowering the energy cost of computation for a specified technology will then imply an improvement in one of the above-mentioned factors (such as the efficiency of the

Table 6.3 Some typical time complexities.

Algorithm	Time complexity
Sorting on butterfly	$O[t(n) \log^2 n]$, $t(n)$ = comparison time
FFT on butterfly or shuffle exchange	$O[t(n) \log n]$, $t(n)$ = arithmetic operation time
Mesh-connected array $\sqrt{n} \times \sqrt{n}$ merge sort	$O(\sqrt{n})$

algorithm or the computational architecture or the mapping strategy used).

There is a close relationship between energy dissipation and the thermodynamic entropy. When very large networks of processors are synthesized, not only the mathematical principles but also the physical laws play an important role. The recognition of the close relationship of computing and information processing to statistical thermodynamics has led to the development of a new computational model known as the Boltzmann machine; this physical machine performs an action based on threshold potentials, probabilistic decision and global energy minimization.

The Boltzmann machine consists of a large number of processors among which their mutual strength of communication can be increased or decreased to perform computations. Such a machine is modelled as a graph in which the vertices are the processors and the edges are the links. Each vertex is labelled with a threshold value and each edge has a weight, both of which are integers. Each processor can be in either the off or the on state.

The computation is synchronous and proceeds thus: at time t, a processor computes the sum of the weights of the edges that link it to its neighbours; then, at time $t + 1$, this processor fires or assumes the on state with the following probabilities P:

$P \to 0$, if (sum of weights – threshold) < threshold
$P = \frac{1}{2}$, if (sum of weights – threshold) = threshold
$P \to 1$, if (sum of weights – threshold) > threshold

At the initial step, some specific processors are held in on or off states to represent the input binary string. The output is similarly encoded in the states of a distinguished set of output vertices on completion of the computation. The computation terminates when the global energy of the system is a minimum.

Thus the three key features of this model are:

(1)   probabilistic decisions;
(2)   threshold potential computation;
(3)   termination at minimal global energy.

The Boltzmann model is actively studied for understanding the function of the human brain (Ackley *et al.*, 1985) and also for the design of massively parallel processors that can be used in artificial intelligence. Such a model is also known by the name 'connectionist model' or 'neural network model'.

Remark

At this point we may highlight some of the important differences between massively parallel machines and the brain. In the brain, the number of processors is close to ten billion which is far more than that in any proposed machine. The clock rate in the brain is in the range of 5–50 milliseconds, while in the machine it is less than a microsecond. Yet, complex pattern recognition problems are solved by the brain much faster than by a machine. This may be attributed to the richness and randomness of the interconnections in the brain.

The striking dissimilarities between the brain and machines have attracted the attention of scientists for a very long time. But only very recently have these studies become feasible due to the availability of massively parallel hardware for simulating and understanding the neural networks and their behaviour. For further reading on this subject, see Rumelhart *et al.* (1986).

SUMMARY

This chapter dealt with the complexity aspects of parallel computation. After a short introduction to the polynomial class (P) and the non-deterministic polynomial class (NP) in sequential algorithms, we described the time–space complexity of parallel algorithms and parallel speed-up. Then we explained how the efficiency of parallel algorithms can be measured and speed-up can be achieved for some specific problems. A brief description of the communication complexity of a special class of networks was then included.

The parallel computational models PRAM and its variants were then described. With these as the basis concepts such as the parallel computation thesis, P-completeness and the NC of problems were then introduced.

Also, some basic concepts concerning the realizability of parallel machines using boolean basis functions were then explained.

We then outlined the current attempts to design a universal interconnection machine that can simulate any specific interconnection such as a butterfly or shuffle exchange network.

Another important area of study is VLSI computational complexity. The measures used for determining the complexity of VLSI chips in realizing specific algorithms were introduced.

Finally, we briefly explained the concept of physical complexity and its role in the design of very large machines. In this context, we mentioned the connectionist or neural network model, Boltzmann machine, that is used for studies in artificial intelligence.

EXERCISES

6.1   Convince yourself that if an algorithm has a sequential fraction of computations of 10% then the parallel speed-up that can be achieved is at most 10.

6.2   Verify the Munro–Paterson theorem (Munro and Paterson, 1973) for parallel computation using N processors.

6.3   Verify Brent's theorem (Brent, 1974) for parallel computation using fewer than the required number of processors.

6.4   Compute the communication complexity in pyramid and prism networks.

6.5   Represent the following arithmetic expression as a directed acyclic graph and find out the best possible parallel computation time with a required number of processors and fewer than the required number of processors:

$$((a + b) \times c + ((a + b) + e) \times (e + f)) \times ((a + b) \times c)$$

6.6   A boolean 2-ary function $f(x, y)$ is monotonic if, for all $x_1 \leqslant x_2$ and $y_1 \leqslant y_2$, $f(x_1, y_1) \leqslant f(x_2, y_2)$. Which of these 16 functions are monotonic?

6.7   A boolean 2-ary function $f(x, y)$ is linear if it can be expressed as $f(x, y) = a_0 \oplus a_1 \wedge x \oplus a_2 \wedge y$ where $\oplus$ denotes exclusive or, $\wedge$ denotes 'and', and $a_0, a_1, a_2 \in \{0, 1\}$. Which of the sixteen 2-variable boolean functions are linear?

6.8   A set of boolean functions is called functionally complete if every other boolean function not in the set can be realized using only those functions in the set. Find the functionally complete sets.

6.9   Study Goldschlager's work (1982) on the universal interconnection pattern. Write a simulation program to generate either the shuffle exchange network or the butterfly network. (See also Parberry (1987).)

6.10   Study from Ullman's book (Ullman, 1984) why the butterfly and shuffle exchange architectures are more expensive to realize in VLSI.

6.11   Demonstrate that the matrix inversion can be carried out in poly$(\log n)$ time using poly(n) processors.

6.12   Demonstrate that the greatest common divisor of two polynomials is in the NC.

6.13   Study the algorithms for finding the greatest common divisor of integers (Knuth, 1981). What is the best available algorithm? Is parallel speeding feasible?

6.14   The well-known Ackermann function is given by the conditional expression

$$A(m, n) = \{m = 0 \to n + 1, n = 0 \to A(m - 1, 1),$$
$$A[m - 1, A(m, n - 1)]\}$$

What is the inherent difficulty that arises in speeding up this computation with many processors?

6.15   Study the parallel spanning tree algorithms. What is the order of complexity?

6.16   Study the various parallel sorting algorithms and their complexities. (See Bitton *et al.* (1984).)

6.17   A magic square of order N is an arrangement of integers in an $N \times N$ matrix form such that the sums of elements in each row or column or the two principal diagonals are equal. Customarily the integers are taken to be distinct in each cell and drawn from $\{1, 2, \ldots, N^2\}$. What is the complexity of the sequential algorithm to construct the magic square? If we use N^2 processors can we speed it up? (See Goodman and Hedetniemi (1977).)

6.18   There are six computational rules for substituting and evaluating recursive expressions; these are

    (1)   leftmost innermost rule (call by value),
    (2)   parallel innermost rule,
    (3)   leftmost (call by name) rule,
    (4)   parallel outermost rule,
    (5)   free argument rule,
    (6)   full substitution rule.

Read about these rules from Manna (1974). When parallel

computation is carried out will there be a difference among the values obtained from different rules?

6.19 Draw the computation tree for $E := a/[b/(c \times d \times e \times f \times g) + h]$. What is the best possible modification of this tree for parallel processing?

6.20 Draw a computation graph for computing the value of:

$$a = p - q$$
$$b = a/p$$
$$c = q \times b$$
$$d = a + b$$
$$e = (a \times b) - c$$
$$f = d \times e$$

What is the best possible organization of the processors to evaluate the expression quickly?

6.21 Let $p(x) = a_0 + a_1 x + \ldots + a_n x^n$; given x_i, what is the best way to evaluate $p(x_i)$ using many processors in $O(\log n)$ time?

6.22 Let $\mathbf{A} = ((a_{ij}))$ be an $n \times n$ matrix. The determinant of $\mathbf{A}$ is the number

$$\text{Det}(\mathbf{A}) = \sum_{\sigma} \text{sign}(\sigma)\, a_{1,\sigma(1)}\, a_{2,\sigma(2)} \ldots a_{n,\sigma(n)}$$

where the sum is over all permutations σ of $\{1, 2, \ldots, n\}$. The permanent of $\mathbf{A}$ is defined by

$$\text{per}(\mathbf{A}) = \sum_{\sigma} a_{1,\sigma(1)}\, a_{2,\sigma(2)} \ldots a_{n,\sigma(n)}$$

omitting the $\pm$ signs of the permutation σ. The evaluation of the determinant is in the NC, whereas the evaluation of per$(\mathbf{A})$ is not. Why? (See Valiant (1979).)

6.23 A polynomial $P(x)$ of degree n is in Newton's form if $P(x) = a_0 + a_1(x - x_1) + \ldots + a_n(x - x_1) \ldots (x - x_n)$. Devise a parallel algorithm to evaluate this polynomial.

6.24 Find a fast algorithm for computing $x^m \bmod p$ where x, m, p are positive integers.

6.25 Find a fast parallel algorithm to compute the characteristic equation of a matrix. What is its order of complexity?

References

Ackley D.H., Hinton G.E. and Sejnowski T.J. (1985). A learning algorithm for Boltzmann machines. *Cognitive Science*, **9**, 147–69

Babbage C. (1864). *Passages from the Life of a Philosopher*, p. 124. London: Longman, Roberts and Green

Bertolazzi P. and Luccio F. (1984). *VLSI: Algorithms and Architectures.* Amsterdam: North-Holland

Bitton D., Dewitt D.J., Hsiao D.K. and Menon J. (1984). A taxonomy of parallel sorting. *Computing Surveys*, **16**, 287–318

Blum M. (1967). A machine independent theory of the complexity of recursive functions. *J. ACM*, **14**, 322–36

Blum N. (1983). A note on parallel computation thesis. *Information Processing Lett.*, **17**, 203–5

Brent R.P. (1974). The parallel evaluation of general arithmetic expressions. *J. ACM*, **21**, 201–6

Cook S.A. (1971). The complexity of theorem proving procedures. In *Proc. 3rd ACM Symp. on the Theory of Computing*, pp. 151–8

Cook S.A. (1983). An overview of computational complexity, *Comm. ACM*, **26**, 401–7

Cook S.A. (1985). A taxonomy of problems with fast parallel algorithms. *Information and Control*, **64**, 2–22

Fortune S. and Wyllie J. (1978). Parallelism in random access machines. In *Proc. 10th Ann. ACM Symp. on Theory of Computing*, pp. 114–18

Garey M.R. and Johnson D.S. (1979). *Computers and Intractability.* San Francisco CA: Freeman

Goldschlager L.M. (1977). The monotone and planar circuit value problems are log space complete for P. *SIGACT News*, **9**, 25–9

Goldschlager L.M. (1982). A universal interconnection pattern for parallel computers. *J. ACM*, **29**, 1073–86

Goldschlager L.M. and Parberry I. (1986). On the construction of parallel computers from various bases of boolean functions. *Theoretical Computer Science*, **43**, 43–58

Goodman S.E. and Hedetniemi S.T. (1977). *Introduction to the Design and Analysis of Algorithms.* New York NY: McGraw-Hill

Gustafson J.L. (1988). Re-evaluating Amdahl's law. *Comm. ACM*, **31**, 532–3

Karp R.M. (1972). Reducibility among combinatorial problems. In *Complexity of Computations* (Miller R.E. and Thatcher J.W., eds.), pp. 85–104. New York NY: Plenum

Karp R.M. and Ramachandran V. (1988). *A Survey of Complexity of Algorithms in Shared Memory Machines.* University of California, Berkeley

Knuth D.E. (1981). *The Art of Computer Programming*, Vol. 2. Reading MA: Addison-Wesley

Ladner R.E. (1975). The circuit value problem is log space complete for P. *SIGACT News*, **1**, 18–20

Leighton F.T. (1983). *Complexity Issues in VLSI.* Cambridge MA: MIT Press

Machtey M. and Young P. (1978). *An Introduction to the General Theory of Algorithms.* Amsterdam: North-Holland

Manna Z. (1974). *Mathematical Theory of Computation*, pp. 375–6. New York NY: McGraw-Hill

Mead C.E. and Conway L. (1980). *Introduction to VLSI Systems*. Reading MA: Addison-Wesley

Munro I. and Paterson M. (1973). Optimal algorithms for parallel polynomial evaluation. *J. Computer Systems Science*, **7**, 189–98

Parberry I. (1987). *Parallel Complexity Theory*. London: Pitman

Pippenger N. (1979). On simultaneous resource bounds. In *Proc. 20th IEEE Symp. on the Foundations of Computing Science*, pp. 307–11

Rabin M.O. (1960). *Degree of Difficulty of Computing a Function and a Partial Ordering of Recursive Sets*. Technical Report, Hebrew University, Jerusalem

Rumelhart D.E. and McClelland J.L. (1986). *Parallel Distributed Processing: Explorations in the Microstructure of Cognition*. Cambridge MA: Bradford Books

Schoning U. (1986). Complexity and structure. *Lecture Notes in Computer Science*, **211**

Stockmeyer L. (1987). Classifying computational complexity of problems. *J. Symbolic Logic*, **52**, 1–43

Ullman J.D. (1984). *Computational Aspects of VLSI*. Rockville MD: Computer Science Press

Valiant L.G. (1979). The complexity of computing the permanent. *Theoretical Computer Science*, **8**, 189–202

Vishkin V. (1983). *Synchronous Parallel Computation – a Survey*. Technical Report 71, Courant Institute of Mathematical Sciences, New York NY

Wegener I. (1987). *The Complexity of Boolean Functions*. New York NY: Wiley

Chapter 7
Parallel, Concurrent and Distributed Programming

7.1 Introduction

The purpose of this chapter is to introduce the reader to the topics of parallel, concurrent and distributed programming. Obviously this area is too vast to be covered in a short chapter. We shall therefore confine ourselves to the basic principles of these three different categories of programming. Within each category we provide a brief introduction to the representative languages that are currently used and the particular architectural configuration that is compatible with the language primitives.

7.2 Synchronous parallel programming

The first category of programming we shall study is the synchronous parallel programming. This kind of programming is essentially meant for matrix and vector processing in supercomputers. These supercomputers which are essentially array and vector processors perform lockstep or synchronous processing. The properties of the algorithms and the primitive nature of the data structure used, namely the array structure, result in a regular control flow. Accordingly there is no necessity to have the mutual exclusion or conditional synchronization operations that are needed in usual multiprocessor systems which carry out concurrent or distributed processing. Also, the communication problem is more concerned with the movement of data between different streams and hence turns out to be simpler.

The programming languages designed for array and vector processing can be classified into three groups:

(1)   those based on detecting parallelism;
(2)   those which specify parallelism directly;
(3)   those which exploit the problem parallelism.

7.2.1 Parallelism detection approach

Here the languages used are the parallel extensions of FORTRAN. Examples of this kind are: IVTRAN for the Illiac IV, CFT for the Cray 1 and CDC Cyber FORTRAN. These languages attempt to extract the parallelism within the sequential DO loop statements in FORTRAN. Such an approach has the advantage of using many readily available software packages, thereby reducing the developmental costs. However, this approach has the disadvantage that we need to restructure the codes to suit the compiler and for memory management.

7.2.2 Direct specification approach

In this approach, the languages have a syntactic ability that reflects the machine architecture. Examples of this kind are CFD and DAP FORTRAN.

CFD is an extension of FORTRAN and reflects the architecture of the Illiac IV; DAP FORTRAN reflects the architecture of the ICL distributed array processor DAP. The programmer has to know the architectures of these machines and the data structures in order to write efficient programs.

The disadvantage of this approach is that, if the parallelism of the problem does not match the machine parallelism, the user must reorganize the data structures; also, the programs are not portable, that is cannot be directly transferred from one machine to another and run.

7.2.3 Problem parallelism approach

This approach enables the expression of parallelism in a manner which is suitable for the problem and can be easily exploited by the parallel machines. The Actus language recently developed by Perrott (1987) is based on this approach. It provides a number of language features which facilitate the expression of the parallelism inherent in problems suited to the type of environment in array and vector processors.

Actus is a high level language based on Pascal. It provides parallel data structures to define the parallel nature of the data in a problem; also, it provides statements to manipulate this data parallelism. Further, the language is independent of the machine architecture. Also, the syntax developed can handle both array and vector processing and enables portability of the programs developed.

The advantage of using Actus is that the parallel nature of a problem is expressed directly in its syntax. This ensures that the computational resources are used efficiently. From the user point of view, removal of the machine and compiler dependences is a friendly feature. Further, the Actus language permits program and data structuring and can also provide compile time and run-time checking. Thus it is very useful for programming supercomputers.

For a detailed discussion of Actus, see Perrott (1987).

7.3 Synchronous parallel programming languages

In this section, we give a brief introduction to the features of some of the synchronous parallel programming languages in the different groups mentioned in the previous section.

7.3.1 Cyber FORTRAN

Cyber 200 FORTRAN is a higher level language based on an extension of FORTRAN for use in the Cyber 205. The compiler tries to detect which parts of a sequential FORTRAN program can be executed by the pipelined units.

The action of parallelizing a sequential computation is known as vectorization. In Cyber 200 FORTRAN, both ordinary as well as nested DO loops with statements manipulating dimensioned variables can be vectorized automatically.

The language permits the use of vector operands in the expressions. Also, two types of assignment statements are available; one for the creation of descriptors and the other for the updating of the elements of a vector.

The control statement takes the form WHERE(EXP) statement; here EXP is a vector bit expression and statement is a vector assignment statement. This statement allows the updating of a vector of operands subject to a vector condition.

Also, Cyber 200 FORTRAN provides for vector functions and a series of special subroutines which enable the user to specify machine instructions in the object code.

7.3.2 CFT (Cray 1 FORTRAN translator)

The CFT is also based on FORTRAN. The compiler detects which parts of a sequential program can be parallelized. However, unlike the situation in Cyber FORTRAN, in CFT the nested DO loops cannot be directly vectorized unless some rearrangement is performed

Five different vector functions are available for handling conditional statements. These are called conditional vector merge (CVM) functions; these can test for 'true', 'positive', 'zero', 'non-zero' or 'negative'.

The two different types of conditional statements used in CFT and Cyber FORTRAN make it difficult to move programs for the Cray 1 to the Cyber 205.

7.3.3 CFD FORTRAN (Illiac IV)

This language has a syntax that reflects the architecture of the Illiac IV. The Illiac consists of a control unit and 64 processing units. The control unit decodes an instruction; then it can either execute the instruction itself or broadcast it to one of the 64 processors. The control unit, however, has only a limited ability; it can execute only the integer arithmetic needed for address and loop computations. All the other calculations are to be sent to the processors. Since there is only one instruction stream directed by the control unit and there are 64 data streams, we say that the Illiac IV is of the SIMD type.

CFD directly reflects the 64 processors and the single control unit. When a variable is declared the programmer should decide whether one of the processors of the control unit would manipulate it. Thus each variable declaration is prefixed by CU (for control unit) or PE (for processor) together with its corresponding index (or name).

The conditional statement IF is available in CFD. It can be used, for instance, to update the elements of an array as a result of comparison between other array values.

Also, the logical connectives AND, OR and NOT and the quantifiers ANY and ALL are available. The quantifiers allow a test to be applied across the elements of an array.

The 64 processors of the Illiac IV form an 8×8 array ($0 \leqslant i \leqslant 7$, $0 \leqslant j \leqslant 7$) configuration. Each internal processor (i, j), for $1 \leqslant i \leqslant 6$, $1 \leqslant j \leqslant 6$, is connected to its east $(i, j + 1)$, west $(i, j - 1)$, north $(i - 1, j)$ and south $(i + 1, j)$ neighbours. The processors $(0, j)$ in the top row are connected to $(7, j)$ in the bottom row, and $(0, j + 1)$, $(0, j - 1)$, $(1, j)$ for $1 \leqslant j \leqslant 6$. The processors $(i, 0)$ in the left boundary are connected to $(i - 1 \bmod 8, 7)$ in the right boundary, $(i - 1)$, $(i - 1 \bmod 8, 0)$, $(i + 1 \bmod 8, 0)$ for $0 \leqslant i \leqslant 7$. Also, the processors $(7, j)$, $1 \leqslant j \leqslant 6$ are connected to $(7, j - 1)$, $(7, j + 1)$ and $(6, j)$. All these connections are two way or symmetric.

CFD provides index modifiers to route the data values through the interconnected network. The moving of the data to ensure that the right data is available to the right processor at the right time requires special skill and ingenuity in programming.

The Illiac interconnection scheme provides for certain special kinds of matrix operations.

CFD provides READ, WRITE, DISK statements for moving the data between the main and backing stores. Also, it provides a WAIT statement for synchronizing data transfer from the memory.

For further details, see Stevens (1975).

7.3.4   DAP FORTRAN

The language used in the ICL distributed array processor (DAP) is known as DAP FORTRAN. As in CFD, DAP FORTRAN is strongly machine dependent.

The ICL DAP consists of 64×64 processors. There is a master control unit to coordinate these array of processors; thus the DAP is an SIMD machine.

DAP FORTRAN contains three basic types; scalars, vectors and matrices; the size of vectors is 64×1 and the matrix size is 64×64. Declarations of variables of the above three types are possible; since the dimensions are predetermined, they are omitted in a declaration statement.

Arrays of vectors and matrices can also be declared by using higher dimensional variables.

Also, provision exists for forming expressions using matrices or vectors; the assignments can be made to a variable of similar type.

All the processors in the array of the DAP are activated unless excluded by an external inhibiting condition. DAP therefore provides for an instruction in which we can use a logical matrix of truth values. This logical matrix can be used as a conditional to mask an assignment statement suitably to achieve the required effect.

The interconnection structure of DAP is different from that in

Illiac IV. The DAP connection scheme has a torus structure. That is, the mesh-connected network is rolled to a horizontal cylinder by connecting the top and bottom row processors; the left and right column processors (see Section 5.3.4) are then connected end-around to form a torus.

To route the data to different processors DAP FORTRAN provides for shift operators – these can shift a matrix by one place north, south, east or west. Together with suitable indexing these operators can be used to make appropriate shifts.

DAP FORTRAN also provides a set of functions that take vectors and matrices as arguments. These are extremely powerful for matrix computations.

For example, DAP FORTRAN offers two very useful matrix functions called MATC and MATR. MATC replicates an $n \times 1$ vector n times to produce an $n \times n$ matrix:

$$\text{MATC} \begin{bmatrix} a \\ b \\ c \end{bmatrix} = \begin{bmatrix} a & a & a \\ b & b & b \\ c & c & c \end{bmatrix}$$

The MATR function replicates a $1 \times n$ row vector n times to produce an $n \times n$ matrix:

$$\text{MATR} [a\ b\ c] = \begin{bmatrix} a & b & c \\ a & b & c \\ a & b & c \end{bmatrix}$$

These functions are very useful for multiplying matrices using the algorithm described in Section 5.3.5.3 for a systolic matrix multiplier.

Also there is a special function TRAN for transposing a matrix.

DAP FORTRAN provides a very useful set of instructions for declaration and manipulation of data structures, flexible shift operators and masking logical matrices. Thus specialized matrix algorithms can be implemented with a very high degree of parallelism.

7.3.5 Actus: a Pascal-based language

As already mentioned, Actus based on Pascal was designed by Perrott (1979). This language follows the programming philosophy of sequential machines, namely the language should be machine independent.

Actus has the following main features:

(1)   user-constructed data types and program structuring facilities;

(2)   provision for describing the parallelism at the data declaration and statement level;

(3)   static control of the extent of parallelism by using index sets;

(4)   dynamic control of parallelism;

(5)   alignment of operands and independent indexing;

(6)   extension of Pascal conditional and repetitive statements to parallel array variables.

We shall now provide some explanation of these features; however, for a complete treatment of Actus reference is made to the excellent text by Perrott (1987).

(1)   **Data types**

In Actus the array is the only data structure that can be declared to have an extent of parallelism, that is whose elements may be simultaneously manipulated at data level. Hence all the parallel actions are confined to this structure. However, unlike all the previous FORTRAN-based languages, Actus allows the declaration of a parallel array having elements which are primitive or structured.

Also, Actus permits a complete row or part of a row of a matrix to be selected for parallel processing.

(2)   **Parallel constant**

Constant identifiers can be defined which have more than one value and can subsequently be used in expressions or assignments to parallel variables.

(3)   **Parallelism manipulation**

An index set is provided to vary the range or extent of manipulation of the arrays. The index set identifies the data elements that can be altered by indicating the appropriate lower and upper indices.

(4)   **Data alignment**

Two operators (rotate and shift) are available to move the data within the array data structure.

The shift operator works on a parallel variable and permits right, left, down or up movements. The rotate operator also works on a parallel variable and permits circular shifts.

(5)   **Assignment, conditional and repetitive statements**

Each assignment statement in Actus that contains a parallel variable must have associated with it a single extent of parallelism. Assignment statements can be used for several conventional purposes and also for the data alignment.

The conditional and repetitive statements are the extensions of **if**, **case**, **for** and **while** statements of Pascal, except that the extent of parallelism is taken into account when dealing with parallel variables.

(6)   **Subprograms**

Actus permits functions with scalar or vector parameters for the parallel variables.

Procedures, like functions, can be used as abstraction mechanisms. These procedures can return scalar, parallel or mixed types as values. Also, the procedures can be called recursively.

In summary, Actus seems to be the only language available currently for synchronous parallel programming that expresses problem parallelism independent of the machine, enables the structuring of the program and data and offers instructions for data alignment (see also Perrott *et al.* (1987)).

7.3.6   Data level parallelism languages

The connection machine (Section 5.8) utilizes existing programming languages and environments as much as possible. The languages are based on well-known standards – such as FORTRAN, C and LISP – with a minimal amount of extensions to support data parallel constructs.

FORTRAN 8X is an extension of FORTRAN 77. The most important extension is that expressions in FORTRAN 8X treat entire arrays as atomic objects; for example, the expression A = B + C adds every element of C to the corresponding element in B and stores the result in A. B and C may be scalars, vectors, matrices and many-dimensional arrays. Also, special instructions exist for selecting array sections as in Actus.

The C* language is a data parallel extension of C.

*LISP and CM-LISP are data parallel dialects of common LISP. These languages offer a productive programming environment for easy exploitation of the massive power of the connection machine.

7.4   Asynchronous parallel programming

In the previous two sections we studied the synchronous parallel programming used in synchronous processor systems. The two other categories of programming earlier mentioned, namely concurrent and distributed programming, both belong to the class of asynchronous parallel programming activities since they are both suitable for asynchronous multiprocessor systems.

The asynchronous programming languages can be classified into four major groups depending upon the answers to the following questions:

(1)   Is parallelism explicitly included in the semantics of the language?

(2)   Does the language have side effects?

(3)   Is the language implemented in a shared-memory or message-passing mode?

The four major groups are:

- Group 1: shared-memory, side effect, no explicit parallelism languages. These are the conventional sequential imperative programming languages such as FORTRAN, Pascal, Modula-2.

- Group 2: shared-memory, side effect, explicit parallelism languages. This group includes Ada, Pascal Plus, Concurrent Pascal, Modula-2. They are collectively known as 'shared-variable parallel languages' and are suitable for concurrent programming.

- Group 3: message-passing, side effect and explicit parallelism languages. Languages such as Ada, CSP and occam belong to this group. This group is called 'message-passing parallel languages' and is suitable for distributed and concurrent programming.

- Group 4: shared-memory, no side effect and no explicit parallelism languages. This group includes functional languages such as Pure LISP, FP and dataflow languages such as VAL, Loral Dataflo, LUCID.

In designing parallel programming languages, the three different features that we mentioned, namely the explicit parallelism, side effects and shared-memory or message-passing mode play a very important role.

For instance, the side effects (although harmful when used carelessly) add to the expressive power of the language. Also, if memory is not shared, it is quite difficult to exploit parallelism at the medium or fine level of granularity, since the act of copying shared data from one process to another is troublesome and error prone.

If explicit parallelism is not used then special methods need to be used to detect parallelism. This becomes difficult if side effects are present. That is why in dataflow languages, where explicit parallelism is not used, we have the single-assignment rule without side effects; this rule facilitates the drawing of a graph for detecting parallelism (see Section 7.7).

In a typical programming situation one has to attempt to exploit parallelism at all levels – ranging from instruction or primitive operation level to large program modules. Therefore the choice of architecture and the choice of an appropriate language for that architecture is a very difficult problem. At present a considerable amount of research is being carried out in this area (Chandy and Misra, 1988; Gehani and

McGettrick, 1988; Bell *et al.*, 1983; Whiddett, 1987). We shall not be able to deal with these aspects in this book.

In the following sections we shall describe the representative languages in groups other than group 1 in order to understand how asynchronous parallel programming is realized using each language.

7.5 Shared-variable parallel languages

We now consider shared-variable parallel languages such as concurrent Pascal, Modula 2, and Pascal Plus.

7.5.1 Concurrent Pascal

This language was developed by Brinch Hansen (1975). It is an extension of Pascal with features permitting concurrency.

The main new features are processes, monitors (Section 2.6.4), classes, statements **init**, **delay** and **continue** and the data type **queue**.

A process is a sequential program which may be executed with other processes. A monitor (as already described in Section 2.6.4) is a mechanism that encapsulates data which is shared among processes and for synchronizing the access for the shared data. A class defines a data structure and the operations that can be performed on it by a single process or monitor, thus providing for mutual exclusion.

The monitor essentially puts a wall around a collection of commonly shared resources so that concurrent processes will not have collisions in accessing these resources. Also, it provides a means for invoking procedures, a way of scheduling the various calls made by outside procedures (by keeping them in a queue) and a mechanism to delay or continue procedures initiated by processes.

The monitor contains local data, a set of procedures and some initialization statements. When a monitor is invoked, it can execute only if it is free; otherwise, the user is kept in a queue for its turn.

The monitor is useful for a shared memory uniprocessor to simulate concurrency but is not well suited for distributed computing. For a detailed study of concurrent Pascal, see Perrott (1987) and Brinch Hansen (1975).

7.5.2 Modula-2

The language Modula-2 combines the features of Pascal and Modula; all these languages were developed by Niklaus Wirth.

Modula is based on Pascal, except that it includes an additional structuring feature known as the 'module'. This is a data abstraction facility. It is a collection of declarations (of constants, variables, types and procedures) and a sequence of statements which constitute the initialization code. A module forms a closed scope and any identifiers brought in from the outside (called imported) must be listed in a **use** list. Any identifiers which are to be available outside must be listed in a **define** list (called exported).

A program can be partitioned into several modules, each module containing its own constants, variables, procedures, types, import and export lists.

Modula-2 was primarily designed for a single-processor system and hence does not possess sophisticated concurrency features. Modula-2 assumes that a program is used to describe several processes that interact relatively infrequently and are therefore loosely coupled.

Communication between processes occurs in two distinct ways, namely either through shared variables or by signals. Shared variables are encapsulated in monitors as in concurrent Pascal.

Signals, exported as a data type from the module processor, themselves carry no data but serve to synchronize processes. Apart from initialization, only two operations are applicable to signals; a process may send a signal, and it may wait for some other process to send a signal to it. Sending a signal activates at most one waiting process. These signals differ from semaphores in that sending a signal for which no process is waiting is considered as a null operation.

Modula-2 also provides co-routines (Section 1.2.3) to simulate quasi-parallelism (that is time multiplexing, where only one process is acting at any time and switching among processes happens at different times).

7.5.2.1   Example

We now give an example in Modula-2 for using the co-routine for computing a binomial coefficient

$$C(n, k) = \frac{n(n - 1)\ldots(n - k + 1)}{1 \times 2 \times \ldots \times k}$$

for integers n and k such that $0 \leqslant k \leqslant n$.

The following Modula-2 program computes the denominator and numerator concurrently by transferring the control from the main process to the co-routine (computation of numerator – called co) and back until both have performed $k - 1$ multiplications. This synchronization ensures exact divisibility.

```
MODULE Binomial ;
(* This Modula program calculates the binomial coefficient c (n, k)
   concurrently.
        Inputs : n, k which are cardinal numbers.
        Output : Binomial which is a cardinal number.          * )
FROM SYSTEM IMPORT
   PROCESS, (* Data type to describe execution status
                  of coroutine * )
   TRANSFER, (* Procedure to activate or resume execution
                  of coroutine * )
   NEWPROCESS, (* Procedure to create a coroutine * )
   ADR, SIZE ;
FROM InOut IMPORT
   ReadCard, WriteCard ;
VAR
   co, main : PROCESS ;
   workspace: ARRAY [1..200] OF CARDINAL ;
   Binomial, n, k, num, ProdN, ProdD : CARDINAL ;
PROCEDURE Numerator ;
BEGIN
   ProdN := 1 ;
   LOOP
      ProdN := ProdN * n ;
      n := n – 1 ;
      TRANSFER (co, main) ;
   END (* loop * ) ;
END Numerator ;
BEGIN
   ReadCard (n) ;
   ReadCard (k) ;
   NEWPROCESS(Numerator, ADR(workspace), SIZE(workspace), co) ;
   ProdD := 1 ;
   num := 1 ;
   WHILE num <= k DO
      ProdD := ProdD * num ;
      num := num + 1 ;
      TRANSFER(main, co) ;
   END (* while * ) ;
   Binomial := ProdN DIV ProdD ;
   WriteCard(Binomial, 6) ;
END Binomial.
```

For a detailed study of Modula-2 see Wirth (1985), Terry (1987) and Sale (1986).

7.5.3 Pascal Plus

This language is a superset of Pascal. It has features for program modularization and data abstraction as in Modula-2. Further, monitors and conditions are available for synchronization and mutual exclusion.

For a detailed account of Pascal Plus, see Perrott (1987) and Welsh and Bustard (1979).

7.6 Message-passing parallel languages

The message-passing approach to synchronization is used in Ada, CSP and occam. Such an approach is best suited for a distributed system in which each processor has its own local memory.

Although both Ada and occam are classified under the group of message-passing languages, Ada is much more powerful than occam since occam lacks many high level programming features such as recursion, and the pointer data type. However, both of these languages use similar concepts for concurrency and communication. (Recall that in Section 1.7.1.1 we classified Ada as an operation-oriented language with a remote procedure call facility. In fact the message-passing feature in Ada is a particular form of a remote procedure call; see Andrews and Schneider (1983) and also Section 7.6.1.)

The message-passing approach requires four basic features:

- Process naming
- Synchronization
- Message structure
- Handling failure of communication.

(1)   **Process naming**

The process naming can be either direct or indirect. In direct naming, the sender of a message explicitly names the receiver; in indirect naming, the sender names an intermediate object such as a channel, mailbox, pipe etc. from which the receiver picks up the message eventually. Direct naming is simpler but indirect naming allows flexibility of choice among receivers.

We say that a naming scheme is symmetric if the receiver and sender call each other directly or indirectly by a name; the naming scheme is asymmetric if only the sender names the receiver and the receiver accepts messages from many senders. The asymmetric naming system is useful in client–server processes where the server process provides services for many clients.

(2)   **Synchronization**

The synchronization can be of three kinds:

- Asynchronous (no wait): the sender after sending the message proceeds further without waiting to know whether the message is received or not. Many operating systems use this principle.
- Synchronous: the sender proceeds only when the message is received by the receiver; CSP and occam use this concept.

- Remote call: the sender proceeds only when a reply has been returned from the receiver. Ada uses this concept.

(3) **Message structure**
This can vary within a very wide range from simple tasks to a large database search and query.

(4) **Handling failures of communication**
There should be a provision for handling deadlocks and starvation.

The Ada language uses asymmetric, direct naming and the remote call method for message passing. Such a method is called 'rendezvous' as mentioned earlier (Section 2.7.2.4).

CSP and occam use symmetric, direct naming and the synchronous method for message passing. This means that the communication is restricted to one way from the sender to the receiver and the receiver does not acknowledge the receipt of the message as it does in a rendezvous.

7.6.1 Ada

There is a very long history associated with the development of Ada by the US Department of Defense. The name Ada was chosen for this language in honour of Augusta Ada Byron, Countess of Lovelace, who worked with Charles Babbage and is regarded as the world's first programmer.

Numerous books are available on Ada. The principal source is the *Ada Language Reference Manual* written by a team under J. Ichbiah. This manual is published by the American National Standards Institute (ANSI-MIL-STD-1815); for a detailed study see Burns (1986), Cherry (1984) and Perrott (1987).

The basic structuring feature in Ada is known as a package which is similar to a module in Modula-2. It serves as a logical building block for complex programs. A package has two parts: the specification and the body; the body contains the code necessary to implement the specification.

Ada also uses the word task for a process to indicate a sequence of actions which are conceptually executed in parallel with other actions. Every task is written in the declarative part of some enclosing program unit, which is called its parent. Different tasks proceed independently, each with its own thread of control, except at points where they synchronize.

The task has two parts: the specification and the body. It has a similar syntactical structure to that of the package. If several tasks are written in the same declarative part they are executed in parallel with one another and their parent.

Intertask communication in Ada can take place in either of two ways:

(1)   shared variables;
(2)   the message-passing mechanism called the rendezvous.

Although shared variables are allowed, no protection primitives such as semaphores or monitors are provided. Further, since all the necessary interprocess communications can be achieved using rendezvous, use of shared variable communication is discouraged (Nissen and Wallis, 1984). Also, it is possible to construct monitors using rendezvous. Therefore, we classify Ada as a message-passing parallel language. In fact Ada's main innovations are the very powerful rendezvous form of communication which we briefly introduced in Section 2.7.2.4 and the select statement that introduces non-determinism and flexibility in the language.

7.6.1.1   Rendezvous

The term rendezvous refers to Ada intertask communication. In order to achieve intertask communication Ada uses the following method.

In each task the procedures that are callable externally are defined as entries and declared in the task specification. A calling task issues an 'entry call' on the called task which either 'accepts' this request or not. If the call is accepted the rendezvous takes place.

To achieve such a rendezvous, the calling task names the called task explicitly. However, the called task does not know where the call is coming from. (This is analogous to dialling a telephone where the caller knows whom he is calling whereas the receiver does not initially know who is calling.) Thus a task can accept a call on its entry from any task without knowing the origin.

In order to synchronize the acts of calling and accepting, the following method is adopted. If the calling task calls the entry first before its owner reaches its accept statement, the calling task is suspended until the called task reaches its accept statement in its program; however, if a task reaches its accept statement in its program, and has not so far received any entry call, it is suspended until an entry call arrives from some caller.

The rendezvous can be used to communicate data between tasks via the parameters defined in the entry specification.

An accept statement specifies the action to be done when a call of an entry is made. The description in the accept statement must match the entry in the task specification. Also, an accept statement may appear only in the task body. Thus a task may only execute accept statements for its own entries.

The accept statement is similar to a procedure. Once a match between an entry call and the corresponding accept occurs, the caller is suspended until the accept body is executed by the called task. The accept body is the only place at which the parameters of the entry are accessible. At the execution of the accept body the possible 'out' parameters are passed on to the caller. This is the end of the rendezvous; then the two tasks can proceed in parallel.

Since a task can accept calls from more than one task, a queue is associated with each entry. A task that is suspended on an entry call is placed on the queue associated with that entry. Each task can therefore be present only on one queue at a time. The calls are then processed in the order in which they arrive.

7.6.1.2   Select statement

This is one of the most important statements in Ada and is based on Dijkstra's guarded command. Thus it introduces non-determinism in the selection of only one among a number of alternatives that may arise in a particular situation.

In particular, if accept statements are used as a sequence of alternatives to a select statement, a task can be made to wait for a call to any of the specified entries. This means we can make a task accept any one of a number of possible entry calls. Such an approach allows a task to accept entry calls in the natural order dictated by the non-deterministically evolving computations rather than by some predefined structure; also, it enables a task making an entry call not to be inevitably committed to the ensuing rendezvous.

The select statement can be structured so that, in the absence of an outstanding entry call, one of the following actions can occur:

(1)   indefinite waiting for a call to be made;

(2)   waiting for a call to be made or a time-out to expire (the delay alternative);

(3)   execution of another piece of code (the else clause) instead of waiting;

(4)   termination of the task.

For a detailed study of Ada tasking see Burns et al. (1987).

Also a guard (a boolean expression) can be attached with each branch of the select statement except the else clause. The absence of a guard is equivalent to a constant guard which is true.

In such a case, on the execution of the select statement the guards are first evaluated. If a guard is false (called closed) the corresponding branch is not chosen. If all the branches have closed guards and there is no else part, error is indicated.

When there are several open alternatives, the select statement determines which accept statements are waiting for rendezvous; if there are several open alternatives, one of these is selected arbitrarily.

If there are neither open alternatives nor waiting processes, the else clause is executed, if there is one.

If there are neither waiting processes nor else clauses, the select statement waits for the first process to attempt a rendezvous with an accept statement in one of the open alternatives (see Section 2.7.2.4).

7.6.1.3 Richness of Ada

Ada is a very large, rich and powerful language. It has all the desired Pascal-like control features, type constructs, package structure, facilities for low level programming and the most sophisticated interprocess communication. The main purpose of its design is to program real-time systems. However, it is still under debate whether some of its features are effective; in particular, it is not known whether the tasking model is a natural and effective one. Some believe that Ada programming style is too complex and reserved for the ivory tower crowd; hence it is merely of academic interest and would need a lot more experimentation and analysis before it becomes a popular and a user-friendly language.

7.6.2 Communicating sequential processes

Communicating sequential processes (see Section 2.7.2.1), popularly known as CSP, was developed by Hoare (1978). In CSP the naming scheme is direct and symmetric and the sender proceeds only when the message is received by the receiver. That is, synchronous message passing is used. Together with such message passing, selective communication is achieved using Dijkstra's guarded commands.

A process P sends a message to process Q by executing a statement of the form

  Q!x   (meaning: send x to Q or output x to Q)

Process Q receives the message by having a command of the form

  P?y   (meaning: receive y from P or input y from P).

The effect of these statements is the assignment x := y.

Selective and repeated selective communciation takes place as described in Section 2.7.2.1.

CSP provides a powerful mechanism for programming process interaction. It is amenable to formal proof techniques by using the mathematical model TCSP (discussed in Section 3.8).

CSP was not intended to be a complete concurrent programming language. Its ideas have been used as the basis for a programming language known as occam.

7.6.3 occam

occam is a direct descendant of CSP; it derives its name from the 14th century English scholastic philosopher who believed in the principle of simplicity in the structure of entities. It is a simple language essentially consisting of only the basic primitives needed to program a distributed system; and as already mentioned, it lacks many high level features such as recursion and the pointer data type. Thus it is a very small language in comparison with Ada. For a detailed comparison with Ada, see Burns (1988).

occam was developed for use in a single-chip computer with a processor, local RAM memory and four dedicated input–output links. Such a computer is called a transputer (for *trans*istor for multicom*puter* architectures). Typically, it has an internal memory of 2 Kbytes with a 32-bit processor with 50 nanosecond addition time and 950 nanosecond multiplication time.

occam provides a powerful method for implementing parallel algorithms on a transputer-type network architecture. occam programs can, however, be used for programming distributed systems independent of the transputers (see May and Taylor (1984)).

7.6.3.1 Basic constructs

Two fundamental concepts are used in occam: processes (PROC) and communication channels (CHAN).

A process is a group of statements or a statement or a composition of processes. A channel is a basic communication link that enables interprocess communication via message passing.

In occam, like Ada, concurrency is handled at the process level (or large granularity); this is unlike the dataflow languages (Section 7.7) which have a much lower level of granularity.

occam uses three primitive processes:

(1) assignment: for example, x := x + 1;

(2) input: receiving a value from a channel and assigning it to a variable, for example Chan1 ? y;

(3) output: sending a value to a channel, for example Chan1 ! x.

These primitive processes can be suitably combined with the following six basic program constructors to build a complex program:

(1)   **Sequential constructor** (SEQ)
Here the component processes are executed one after another.

(2)   **Parallel constructor** (PAR)
Here the component processes are executed together simultaneously, terminating when all the components have terminated.

(3)   **Alternative constructor** (ALT)
This chooses one of its component processes from among several processes for execution terminating when the chosen component terminates.

A guard can be associated with each component process to introduce a choice criterion of each component. The guard consists of a boolean expression followed by an input. If the boolean expression is true then that component is selected for input. In the absence of a boolean expression the guard is considered true.

An alternative process waits until at least one of the guarded processes is ready to execute. One of the ready processes is then selected at random and executed. The construct then terminates.

ALT can be used in a way similar to the **select** statement in Ada to perform selective communication (see Inmos (1984) and Jones (1987)).

(4)   **Conditional constructor** (IF)
This executes the component process for which the boolean expression evaluates TRUE.

(5)   **Repetitive constructor** (WHILE)
This executes the component process repeatedly as long as the boolean expression controlling the repetition evaluates TRUE. When the expression evaluates FALSE it terminates; if the expression evaluates FALSE initially, the component process is not executed at all.

(6)   Replicator (FOR)
A replicator is provided to replicate a process a fixed number of times from 0 to n. This construct can be combined with SEQ, PAR and ALT to achieve the required effects:

- SEQi = [1 FOR n] provides a for loop;
- PARi = [0 FOR n] provides an array of parallel processes;
- ALTi = [1 FOR n] provides for an input from an array of channels.

7.6.3.2 Declarations – variable, process and channel names

Declaration introduces an identifier (a name) for a variable, process or a channel. For example, VAR x : introduces identifier x. The variable declaration is of the form:

```
declaration = VAR var { , var } :
```

where var denotes an identifier. The declarations are linked to the following process by a colon (:).

If a particular process is going to be re-used many times, in different channels, it is essential to give it a unique name. A process declaration allows a name to be given to a process. This is declared thus:

```
PROC name =
```

The text so declared will then be automatically substituted for all occurrences of the name in a subsequent process.

A channel declaration introduces an identifier to be used as a channel.

```
declaration = CHAN chan (, chan)
```

where chan denotes an identifier.

7.6.3.3 Examples

EXAMPLE 7.1 _____

The process of squaring can be described by:

```
PROC square (CHAN chan1, chan2) =
  VAR y:
  SEQ
    chan1 ? y
    chan2 ! y * y
```

EXAMPLE 7.2 _____

We now give an example for the PAR construct. In this example a single buffer process is declared; then the text for this is substituted in the two components of a parallel construct to give a process from channel in1 to channel out1 buffering up to two values at a time.

```
PROC buffer (CHAN in, out) =
  WHILE TRUE
    VAR x :
    SEQ
      in ? x
      out ! x:
CHAN c:
PAR
  buffer (in1, c)
  buffer (c, out1)
```

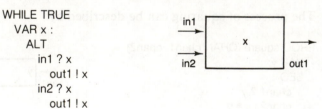

EXAMPLE 7.3

We now give an example for the use of the ALT construct. Here we have two channels in1 and in2 and the process non-deterministically interleaves (Section 2.2.1) data coming from in1 and in2 and outputs in out1.

```
WHILE TRUE
  VAR x :
  ALT
    in1 ? x
      out1 ! x
    in2 ? x
      out1 ! x
```

EXAMPLE 7.4

We now provide a more realistic example of distributed programming using occam. This program finds the multiplicative inverse of an element over a finite field modulo a prime number *p*. The basic algorithm used is the extended euclidean algorithm (Krishnamurthy, 1985) given below.

Remark

Given p and an element x we compute $x^{-1} \bmod p$ such that $x \times x^{-1} = 1 \bmod p$.

```
begin
      a ← p; a0 ← x;
      b ← 0; b0 ← 1;
   while a0 ≠ 0 do
      begin
           q ← quotient (a, a0)
          ra ← a − q*a0
          rb ← b − q*b0
            a ← a0; a0 ← ra;
            b ← b0; b0 ← rb;
      end;
      x⁻¹ ← b mod p
end.
```

In the occam program below, <> means not equal to and p\q stands for the remainder when p is divided by q; the sign of the remainder is the same as the sign of p.

```
— multiplicative inverse process
PROC multinv(VALUE num, VAR inv) =
   — Process to find the multiplicative inverse of a number with respect
   — to a given field.
   — 'field' is defined as a main constant and is the maximum value able
   — to be used without an overflow.
VAR a, a0, q, ra, rb, b, b0, p:
SEQ
   PAR
      a0 := num
      a0 := field
      b0 := 1
      b  := 0
   WHILE (a0 <> 0)
      SEQ
         q := a/a0
         PAR
            ra := a − (q*a0)
            rb := b − (q*b0)
         PAR
            SEQ
               a := a0
               a0 := ra
            SEQ
               b := b0
               b0 := rb
```

```
    b := b\field
IF
   b < 0
      inv := b + field
   TRUE
      inv := b:
```

EXAMPLE 7.5

As another example in occam, we consider the computation of $C(n, k)$ (Section 7.5.2.1), the binomial coefficient.

```
— This occam program calculates the binomial coefficient C(n, k)
— concurrently.
—     Inputs: n, k which are positive integers
—     Output: binomial which is outputted to channel c3
— PROGRAM Binomial
CHAN c1, c2, c3:
VAR n, k, num:
— read a positive integer
PROC read (VAR x) =
. . .
— Evaluate numerator
PROC Numerator (CHAN c) =
   VAR prodn, num, i:
   SEQ
      prodn := 1
      num := n
      SEQ i = [1 FOR k]
         SEQ
            prodn := prodn * num
            num := num − 1
      c ! prodn:
— Evaluate denominator
PROC Denominator (CHAN c) =
   VAR prodd, num, i:
   SEQ
      prodd := 1
      num := 1
      SEQ i = [1 FOR k]
         SEQ
            prodd := prodd * num
            num := num + 1
      c ! prodd:
— Divide numerator by denominator, output to channel c3
PROC Division (CHAN cl, c2, c3) =
   VAR binomial, prodn, prodd:
```

```
SEQ
  PAR
    c1 ? prodn
    c2 ? prodd
    binomial := prodn/prodd
    c3 ! binomial:
  SEQ
    read (n)
    read (k)
    PAR
      Numerator(c1)
      Denominator(c2)
      Division(c1, c2, c3)
```

7.6.3.4 Uses of occam

occam has several useful properties. It supports a hierarchical structure and is applicable for systems built from a large number of concurrently operating processes.

occam is useful for programming wavefront arrays (Chapter 5) and other related hardware structures.

A new version of occam – occam 2 – provides new data types and other capabilities for multidimensional array processing and user-defined data types. For a detailed study of occam 2, see Burns (1988).

It is expected that occam-like languages will be developed further with a view to applications in very large scale distributed systems.

7.7 Dataflow programming languages

In Section 3.9.2 we described the dataflow computing model and in Section 5.7 we briefly mentioned the dataflow architecture. In this section we briefly describe the advances that have been made in dataflow programming: see Gurd *et al.* (1987).

In control flow programming, an execution of the sequence of statements is dictated by the order in which the statements are textually composed by the programmer, whereas in dataflow programming every instruction is scheduled for execution only after all its run-time input values are available (because they are the outputs from other preceding processes). Therefore the sequence in which the instructions are textually composed need not necessarily be the order of execution. Further, if several of the instructions have their inputs simultaneously available, these instructions can be executed concurrently.

The concurrency associated with dataflow programming is at the primitive instructional level and hence is at a much lower level than the process level. This means that languages such as Ada and Modula-2 are not well suited for this purpose.

The basic step in dataflow programming is to identify those parts of the program that can be executed concurrently for available inputs. This is usually carried out by drawing a directed graph, called a dataflow graph, that exhibits the activities. Such an approach resembles the dataflow analysis used in the optimization of arithmetic expressions for compilation in a sequential machine.

For example, consider a program that consists of the following instruction sequences:

(1) $a = p - q$

(2) $b = a / p$

(3) $c = q * b$

(4) $d = a + b$

(5) $e = (a / b) - c$

(6) $f = d - e$

The data dependences in this program can be exhibited using the dataflow graph in Figure 7.1.

In this dataflow graph each operation is assigned a node. Each node is enabled for execution (or fires as in a Petri net) when data (or tokens) arrive at the directed input arcs of that node.

This means that a directed graph has to be constructed for every

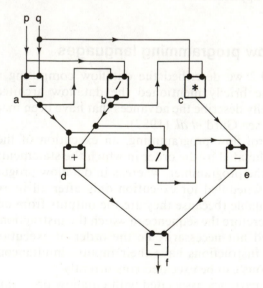

Figure 7.1 A dataflow diagram.

dataflow program to be executed. However, this is not a very practicable scheme for every problem. Hence languages have to be designed in which a programmer can write code following certain guidelines so that this code is automatically translatable into a dataflow graph by the machine (to detect data dependences and provide concurrency) and is executed. Such languages are called dataflow languages (see Gurd *et al.* (1987)).

7.7.1 VAL

The basic requirements for the design of one such dataflow language called VAL is described in Ackerman (1982). These are as follows:

(1) **Side-effect free**
     The language is functional and, once the values of all the inputs are available to an expression or a function, the execution cannot influence the results of any other operations that are ready to execute.

(2) **Locality of effects**
     The scope of a variable is to be restricted to ensure that operations do not have far-reaching data dependences.

(3) **Single assignment rule**
     A variable may appear on the left-hand side of an assignment only once within its scope and the same variable does not appear on both sides of any assignment statement; that is, we cannot write statements such as $X := X + 1$. In other words, the assignment statements are converted to mathematical equalities. It is this feature that makes the language functional and enables us to obtain the dataflow graph from the program directly.

(4) **A construct for parallel repetition**
     There is a loop-free repetition statement for calculations which do not depend on each other and can be calculated in parallel; this statement is called forall in VAL.

7.7.2 Features of VAL

The dataflow language VAL is a value-oriented language or a functional language. The main vehicles for calculations are expressions and functional operators. In this sense it is like pure LISP. However, VAL does not permit recursion which is basic to a functional language.

Also, the concurrency in VAL is implicitly achieved without any explicit features for describing the synchronization. This is a great advantage for error-free programming.

The built-in data types of VAL are the standard types usually available; aggregate data types can be constructed using array, record and the discriminated union.

In the usual programming languages, a function can only return a single value as a result of its execution. However, a VAL function can return more than one value and each of different types as a result of its parallel action.

VAL provides for the construction of functions and expressions without side effects.

Parallel expressions can be constructed in VAL. These consist of three parts; a range specification, environment expansion and result accumulation. These expressions permit parallelism among independent computations.

There are, of course, sequential constructs such as If – then – else, case; also, the for–iter expression is available to carry out sequential loops in which a value at a preceding step is consumed at a succeeding step.

Two serious drawbacks of VAL are the absence of input–output and the lack of recursion facilities.

7.7.3   Other dataflow language

The language VAL is at the primitive instructional level. Recently dataflow languages with much larger grain size have been proposed. One such language is the Loral Dataflo LDF 100 (see Di Nucci (1987)); yet another language is LUCID – see Wadge and Aschroft (1985).

7.8   Parallelism in functional programming

All the functional programming languages use λ-calculus as the basis (Chapter 3). For a general introduction to functional programming, see Henderson (1980).

Functional programs deal with expressions. These expressions consist of rewritable functions and constructor functions as in a recursive function definition (Chapter 3).

Functional programs have no side effects: a subexpression in a total expression can be replaced by any other equivalent expression with the same value without affecting the value of the total expression. This property is called **referential transparency**.

The execution of a functional program consists of reduction and evaluation of expressions. While evaluating, a choice is made according to the following computational rules (Manna, 1974; Manna and Waldinger, 1985):

(1)   leftmost innermost rule (*call by value*) (Section 3.3.7.5);

(2)   parallel innermost rule;

(3)   leftmost (*call by name*) rule (Section 3.3.7.5);

(4)   parallel outermost rule;

(5)   free argument rule;

(6)   full substitution rule.

Such a choice affects the behaviour of the evaluation. However, the only way non-determinism can arise here is in the order in which some of the subexpressions are reduced. Also, the only way parallelism can be introduced is by using parallel reduction and evaluation schemes. Hence all parallel functional programming consists in finding the quickest evaluation schemes that are guaranteed to terminate.

Two of the most important schemes are the **lazy** and **eager evaluation** schemes (Section 3.3.7.7).

In the lazy evaluation scheme (call by need), a functional expression may be reduced before all its arguments are completely evaluated, the arguments being reduced only on demand. Several languages such as HOPE, SASL and KRC are based on this scheme (Henderson, 1980). Lazy evaluation is applicable to stream processing where an unbounded input is processed to generate an unbounded output.

Kahn and McQueen (1977) generalized the notion of lazy evaluation to include parallelism. Here each function call in an expression is viewed as a process in a network. Such a process can be modelled as a producer–consumer process to evaluate arguments. It is amenable for multiprocessing since several producer–consumer processes can be made to run in parallel. This scheme is called the **eager** or **parallel evaluation** scheme.

For a recent survey of parallel functional programming, see Burton (1987).

7.8.1   Example

A typical SASL program resembles a recursive function definition (Chapter 3). For example,

```
FIB = f11
fab = a : fb(a + b)
```

where : denotes append, is an SASL program that generates the infinite list of Fibonacci numbers 1, 1, 2, 3, 5, . . . where each number is the sum of the preceding two numbers.

7.8.2 Reduction strategies

Various schemes have been proposed for reduction (Georgeff, 1984). Also, reduction machines have been designed. We shall not be able to deal with these aspects any further. For a recent survey, see Kluge and Schmittgen (1987).

7.8.3 Multilisp

Recently a new language called Multilisp has been proposed by Halstead (1985) for concurrent symbolic computation. This language includes side effects to improve the expressive power of the functional language. Interested readers should refer to the paper cited.

7.9 Parallel logic programming

The most commonly used sequential logic programming language is PROLOG. A PROLOG program is a set of statements in the first-order predicate calculus. These statements can be divided into facts and rules. The set of facts serves as a database of relations among the objects under question. This database can therefore be queried to obtain information about the relationship among specific objects by suitably matching the rules. Since there are many different ways of matching the rules simultaneously or in parallel, the PROLOG system is well suited for parallelism of different kinds. Several researchers have developed different parallel–concurrent logic programming languages; see Conery (1986), McCabe *et al.* (1982), Sato and Sakurai (1984), Clark and Gregory (1986), Gregory (1987), Ueda (1986), Shapiro (1984, 1987), IEEE (1988), Tick (1988) and Campbell (1984).

SUMMARY

In this chapter we introduced the basic principles of synchronous and asynchronous parallel programming languages.

The three different approaches used for the design of synchronous parallel programming, namely the parallelism detection, direct specification and problem parallelism approaches, were described together with some representative languages – CFT, CFD FORTRAN, DAP FORTRAN and Actus; also, we briefly mentioned the architectural configuration that is compatible with each language.

We then classified the asynchronous programming languages on the basis of the three features: explicit parallelism, side effects and shared memory–message passing. This results in four groups: sequential imperative, shared-variable, message-passing, functional–dataflow languages.

We then introduced the features of some of the important shared-variable languages – concurrent Pascal, Modula-2, and Pascal Plus – and the features of the message-passing languages Ada, CSP and occam.

A brief description of dataflow languages was then given together with an example of the dataflow language VAL.

Finally, we gave a brief account of developments in parallel functional and logic languages.

EXERCISES

7.1   Study how CFT vectorizes a do loop in FORTRAN.

7.2   Using a vector processor explain how to find the transitive closure of a directed graph.

7.3   Study the Actus language and Pascal Plus. Compare and contrast.

7.4   Study the VAL language and use it for programming wavefront arrays, which are asynchronous and data driven.

7.5   Write a VAL program to invert a matrix based on the algorithm given in Exercise 2.8.

7.6   Write an Ada program to compute the binomial coefficient $C(n, k)$ (Section 1.9.4.3).

7.7   Use Ada to compute the convergents of a continued fraction described in Exercise 2.7.

7.8   Generate the mutual recursion in Section 1.9.4.4 using a producer–consumer model. Program it in Ada.

7.9   Write an Ada procedure for the Petri net multiplier (Chapter 3).

7.10   Devise a parallel algorithm for Chinese remaindering (assume n residues and n processors are available). Extend it to polynomial interpolation (Chapter 1).

7.11   Write an Ada program for the dining philosophers' problem.

7.12   Write an occam program for generating the sequence given in Exercise 1.15.

7.13   Write an Ada program for sieving primes using the Eratosthenes method (Section 1.9.4.5).

7.14   Write a program in occam for sorting n positive numbers using n processors.

7.15   Write an occam program for computing the Moore–Penrose inverse using the algorithm given in Exercise 2.8.

7.16   Program the Petri net given in Exercise 4.3 for detecting whether it deadlocks.

7.17   Construct an Ada or occam program to determine the well formedness of a set of two different types of pairs of parentheses using a simulated systolic mesh of processors.

7.18   Read about SASL. Write an SASL program for 'quicksort'.

7.19   Study Multilisp and its application to concurrent symbolic computation.

7.20   Read about combinators and their reduction in the SECD machine (Revesz, 1988).

7.21   Write a PROLOG program to simulate a Petri net.

7.22   Read about PARLOG and use it for programming any parallel algorithm for sorting.

7.23   Read about concurrent PROLOG (Shapiro, 1987). How does it differ from PARLOG?

7.24   How is systolic programming carried out using concurrent PROLOG?

7.25   Examine how concurrent PROLOG can be used to carry out systolic matrix multiplication in a mesh-connected processor array.

References

Ackerman W.B. (1982). Dataflow languages. *IEEE Trans. Computers*, **15**, 15–25
American National Standards Institute (1983). *Ada Language Reference Manual* (ANSI–MIL–STD–1815)

Andrews G.R. and Schneider F.B. (1983). Concepts and notations for concurrent programming. *ACM Computing Surveys*, **15**, 3–43

Bell D.H., Kerridge J.M., Simpson D. and Willis N. (1983). *Parallel Programming – a Bibliography*. London: Wiley–Hayden

Brinch-Hansen P. (1975). The programming language concurrent Pascal. *IEEE Trans. Software Engineering*, **1**, 199–207

Burns A. (1986). *Concurrent Programming in Ada*. London: Cambridge University Press

Burns A. (1988). *Programming in occam 2*. Wokingham: Addison-Wesley

Burns A., Lister A. and Wellings A. (1987). Ada tasking. *Lecture Notes in Computer Science*, **262**

Burton F. (1987). Functional programming for concurrent and distributed computing. *Computer J.*, **30**, 437–50

Campbell J.A. (1984). *Implementations of Prolog*. Chichester: Ellis Horwood

Chandy K.M. and Misra J. (1988). *Parallel Program Design – a Foundation*. Reading MA: Addison-Wesley

Cherry G.W. (1984). *Parallel Programming in ANSI Standard Ada*. Englewood Cliffs NJ: Prentice-Hall

Clark K.L. and Gregory S. (1986). PARLOG: parallel programming in logic. *ACM Trans. Programming Languages Systems*, **8**, 1–49

Conery J.S. (1986). *Parallel Execution of Logic Programs*. Boston MA: Kluwer

Di Nucci D.N. (1987). In *Programming Parallel Processors* (Babb II R.G., ed.). Reading MA: Addison-Wesley

Gehani N. and McGettrick A.D. (1988). *Concurrent Programming*. Wokingham: Addison-Wesley

Georgeff M. (1984). Transformations and reduction strategies for typed lambda expressions. *ACM Trans. Programming Languages Systems*, **6**, 603–31

Gregory S. (1987). *Parallel Logic Programming in PARLOG*. Wokingham: Addison-Wesley

Gurd J.R., Barahona P.M.C.C., Bohm A.P.W. *et al.* (1987). Fine grain parallel computing: the data flow approach. *Lecture Notes in Computer Science*, **272**, 82–152

Halstead R.H. (1985). Multi-Lisp: a language for concurrent computation. *ACM Trans. Programming Languages Systems*, **7**, 501–38

Henderson P. (1980). *Functional Programming*. Englewood Cliffs NJ: Prentice-Hall

Hoare C.A.R. (1978). Communicating sequential processes, *Comm. ACM*, **21**, 666–77

IEEE (1988). *Proc. 1987 Symp. on Logic Programming*. New York NY: IEEE

Inmos (1984). *occam Programming Manual*. Englewood Cliffs NJ: Prentice-Hall

Jones G. (1987). *Programming in occam*. Englewood Cliffs NJ: Prentice-Hall

Kahn G. and McQueen D. (1977). Coroutines and networks of parallel processes. In *Information Processing '77*. Amsterdam: North-Holland

Kluge W. and Schmittgen C. (1987). Reduction languages and reduction systems. *Lecture Notes in Computer Science*, **272**, 153–84

Krishnamurthy E.V. (1985). *Error-free Polynomial Matrix Computations*. New York NY: Springer

Manna Z. (1974). *Mathematical Theory of Computation*. New York NY: McGraw-Hill

Manna Z. and Waldinger R. (1985). *The Logical Basis for Computer Programming*, 2 vols. Reading MA: Addison-Wesley

May D. and Taylor R. (1984). occam – an overview. *Microprocessors and Microsystems*, **8**, 73–9

McCabe F.G., Clark K.L. and Gregory S. (1982). IC–PROLOG language features. In *Logic Programming* (Clark K.L. and Tarnlund S.A., eds.). London: Academic Press

Nissen J. and Wallis P. (1984). *Portability and Style in Ada*. London: Cambridge University Press

Perrott R.H. (1979). A language for array and vector processors. *ACM Trans. Programming Languages Systems*, **2**, 177–95

Perrott R.H. (1987). *Parallel Programming*. Wokingham: Addison-Wesley

Perrott R.H., Lyttle R.W. and Dhillon P.S. (1987). The design and implementation of a Pascal-based language for array processor architecture. *J. Parallel and Distributed Computing*, **4**, 266–87

Revesz G. (1988). *Lambda Calculus, Combinators and Functional Programming*. Cambridge: Cambridge University Press

Sale A. (1986). *Modula-2: Discipline and Design*. Wokingham: Addison-Wesley

Sato M. and Sakurai T. (1984). Qute – a functional language based on unification. In *Proc. Int. Conf. on Fifth-Generation Computer Systems* (Aiso H., ed.). Amsterdam: North-Holland

Shapiro E. (1984). Systolic programming: a paradigm of parallel processing. In *Proc. Int. Conf. on Fifth-Generation Computer Systems*, Tokyo, pp. 45–7

Shapiro E. (1987). *Concurrent Prolog – Collected Papers*, 2 vols. Cambridge MA: MIT Press

Stevens K. (1975). CFD – A FORTRAN like language for the ILLIAC IV, *SIGPLAN Notices*, **10**, 72–80

Terry P.D. (1987). *An Introduction to Programming with Modula-2*. Wokingham: Addison-Wesley

Tick E. (1988). *Memory Performance of Prolog Architectures*. Boston MA: Kluwer

Ueda K. (1986). *Guarded Horn Clauses, a Parallel Logic Programming Language with the Concept of a Guard*. Technical Report TR–208, ICOT, Tokyo

Wadge W.W. and Aschroft E.A. (1985). *Lucid, the Dataflow Programming Language*. New York NY: Academic Press

Welsh J. and Bustard D.W. (1979). Pascal Plus – another language for modular multiprogramming. *Software Practice and Experience*, **9**, 947–57

Whiddett D. (1987). *Concurrent Programming for Software Engineers*. New York: John Wiley

Wirth N. (1985). *Programming in Modula-2*. New York NY: Springer

Chapter 8
Parallel Processing of the Database

8.1 Introduction

Our studies so far have been confined to parallel, concurrent and distributed processing techniques that relate to the design of operating systems, languages and processors. A very closely related area of great practical importance is the design of efficient multiuser database management systems. During the last several years this area has advanced independently, leading to new techniques for the parallel processing of the information about the databases. Such techniques permit simultaneous processing of the information about the database and concurrent processing of the user requests. These database management systems are known as 'multiple-request multiple-datastream' systems.

Both software and architectural aspects of these systems have been studied recently in very great depth. It is our intent in this chapter to introduce the basic principles of these systems. For a detailed study reference is made to the following excellent treatises on this subject: Bernstein *et al.* (1986), Ceri and Pelagatti (1984), Date (1983, 1987), Ullman (1982), Papadimitriou (1986), Alagic (1986), Hsiao (1983), Moss (1985) and Su (1988).

8.2   Multiuser database management system

A database is a collection of data stored in a computer system, where the data is closely related. For example, a database might consist of information relating to the passengers in a particular flight or information relating to the fertilizers for horticultural applications. In such a database, each item is stored using a suitable data structure to allow efficient storage, manipulation and retrieval. To enable ease of manipulation of data structures a data model is used. Three different kinds of models are widely used (Date, 1983):

(1)   the hierarchical model,

(2)   the network model, and

(3)   the relational model.

The hierarchical model represents information in a hierarchy with logical records of information having subrecords which themselves may have subrecords and so on, thus resembling a rooted tree. The network model represents information as a graph (connected or disconnected). The relational model uses tables for representing the information.

Most commercial systems use the hierarchical or network models; however, recently the relational model has been gaining in importance owing to its mathematical precision and practical value.

For a given model, the language of the high level operations of the data model is called the query language. Using this language users can access and update the database directly. Usually, conventional programming languages can be used to write programs.

The computer program that interfaces between the user and the database is called the database management system (DBMS). The DBMS is a very user-friendly system that allows the user to specify what must be done with little or no attention on the user's part to the detailed algorithms or data representation used by the system. In addition, the DBMS is responsible for the following important functions:

(1)   **Security**
Only authorized people are allowed to have access; the DBMS takes care of this.

(2)   **Integrity**
Certain consistency constraints are to be satisfied while dealing with the properties of data. For example, in an airline reservation system, a flight should have no more passengers than the capacity of the particular aircraft used.

(3)   **Concurrency control**
Often many users run programs that access the database at the same time. The DBMS should monitor and control the concurrent

execution of the programs so that overall correctness is maintained. This is called concurrency control; it permits simultaneous processing of the information about the database and concurrent processing of the user requests.

(4) **Crash protection and recovery**
Regular backup copies of the database are to be made to reconstruct or restore the database after a hardware or software error causes a crash of the system. This restoration operation is also called 'roll forward'.

8.3 Database manipulation – transactions

A resource that is of primary interest in the DBMS is the data. Hence every process initiates operations which manipulate data. These operations are to be carried out in such a way that they keep the database system consistent, thereby preserving integrity. In a multiuser system, there could be multiple requests from different users requiring a multiple datastream. These processes interact with each other and can produce both desirable and undesirable effects. To understand these processes, their interactions and effects we introduce certain basic definitions and terminology.

Remark
The terminology used in the concurrent processing of databases differs from the terminology used so far for parallel–concurrent processing. The reason for this may perhaps be attributed to the independent evolution of the two subjects.

A database is a finite set of objects which are assigned values. Every object may be addressed, either directly or indirectly. The set of values taken by all the objects is defined as the state of the database.

At the lowest level in the hierarchy, operations on data objects are called actions. For example the following actions occur in a database:

(1) Delete: this deletes all the records satisfying a query.

(2) Insert: inserts a record into a memory space reserved.

(3) Update: specifies the new value to be taken by the object being modified.

(4) Retrieve: fetches the relevant data satisfying a query from a memory space.

A database is in one of the following three possible states: {open, closed, active}. When processing is to be carried out the database is in the open state; then it goes into the active state until all the processes end. One may then close the database in which case no processing is allowed.

The actions required by a user are called requests. A finite sequence of such requests is called a transaction. Such a transaction is created by a command begin transaction.

The effect of a transaction on the database is the result of actions on the data objects. Such an effect is postponed until its validation.

If the transaction ends successfully (by certain criteria) the end transaction is executed, validating the effects; that is, all the effects are committed and made permanent.

If the transaction is unsuccessful it is 'aborted' and will have no effect on the database. In this case all the tentative updates are to be undone or rolled back.

Note that the database operations are extremely simple and each of the operations can be undone, unlike the situation in scientific–math-ematical–symbolic computing. Thus in all our future discussion we always assume that undoing is possible.

In order to facilitate all the above actions, every transaction is archived; that is, a sequential journal will record all the operations and the input data for each transaction.

The user can also create a safety copy of the database. A command restore will give the database the value contained in the copy. Finally, the transactions recorded in the journal may be rerun using a command restart which will empty the journal.

Systems such as Ingres use the principles described above (Date, 1987).

It is assumed that a database is consistent before and after each transaction.

There is a major difference between the conventional concurrent programming and concurrent transactions on a database. In the case of a program the entire set of instructions is already fully predefined or completely specified whereas, in the case of a transaction, users may want execution of a transaction to begin before all the requests in the transaction have been provided to the DBMS. Such a transaction is called 'incompletely specified'. Special facilities are needed to deal with such transactions; in our discussion, we assume that every transaction is completely specified.

8.4 Schedules and schedulers

When several users use a DBMS, the transactions are submitted and run concurrently, with their steps interleaved. An interleaved execution of several transactions is called a 'schedule' – also called a 'history' or 'log'. Thus a schedule is a shuffle of the sequences of requests by different users.

A **serial schedule** is a schedule consisting of a succession of transactions without any interleaving. For example, if there are two users A and B, each with requests a_1, a_2, a_3, a_4 and b_1, b_2 respectively a serial schedule is $a_1, a_2, a_3, a_4, b_1, b_2$.

The serial schedules are like independent sequential programs causing no side effects. Since each such transaction is assumed to run correctly (that is, leaving the database consistent), a schedule is called correct if it has the same property as a serial schedule. Such an assertion is trivially true since a serial schedule is a special case of a schedule.

If a schedule is equivalent to some serial schedule in the sense of producing the same effects on the database, we say it is **serializable**. Since we assume that serial schedules are correct, we are led to the principle 'a schedule is correct if it is equivalent to a serial schedule'. Unfortunately, this principle does not help us to prove the correctness. In fact, establishing such equivalences turns out to be NP-complete (Papadimitriou, 1986).

We now proceed to describe the part of the database that is used for scheduling. This is called a scheduler. The scheduler is the part of the DBMS responsible for concurrency control. All the user requests are routed through the scheduler. The scheduler then grants or delays the requests so as to keep the database consistent. In other words, the scheduler coordinates the transactions for maximal concurrency ensuring consistency. This act of the scheduler resembles a program prover that checks for consistency before and after a non-deterministic interleaved execution of transactions. Therefore design of a scheduler turns out to be a key issue. Also, the design of a scheduler depends on the manner in which the DBMS is organized – centralized or distributed.

8.5 Centralized and distributed DBMS

A centralized database system consists of:

(1)   a database;
(2)   a database manager module (DM);
(3)   a transaction module (TM) that controls concurrent execution of transactions;
(4)   a set of transactions (inputs) from users.

Both DM and TM together form the DBMS.

A distributed database system consists of:

(1)   the database stored as records (not necessarily disjoint) at various locations – called database modules;
(2)   a network module that provides a two-way communication link between the different TMs and database modules;
(3)   a TM for each location;
(4)   a set of transactions associated with each TM.

In other words, a distributed database is a collection of data stored in a computer network.

Because of communication costs, delays and failures, distributed database systems together with associated concurrent control are very hard to design. As we mentioned in earlier chapters, the actions taking place at different places in a distributed system will not be linearly ordered. They form a partially ordered multiset (Section 3.9.1). Hence the distributed database design presents a lot of design problems.

Most commercial systems are centralized. However, new systems are under development. Ingres (Date, 1987) has been recently developed at the University of California as a distributed system.

Also, some restricted forms of distributed systems are currently under development (Hsiao, 1983; Wolfson, 1987).

There are of course a variety of software products supplied by IBM which include DBMS and transaction handlers. They provide a very complex environment for the designer of a distributed database. The most important of these tools is the Inter System Communication (ISC) and the CICS.

CICS executes application programs (which are, in general, database accessing programs) at the request of users at the terminals and manages the system resources. CICS can carry out function shipping, asynchronous transaction processing and distributed transaction processing.

Function shipping consists of sending a single data access primitive to a remote site. In asynchronous transaction processing, a local transaction starts a named transaction at a remote site which proceeds asynchronously with respect to its initiator. In distributed transaction processing, a local transaction can start a remote transaction as in asynchronous transaction processing.

The CICS system is considered to be a positive step in the direction of the development of an integrated database management environment.

8.6   Data integrity and concurrency

A database is said to be in a consistent state if it satisfies a set of explicit logical conditions called integrity constraints. These constraints are specified when the model is chosen and are expressed in the form of boolean expressions. If the expression is true then the constraint is valid; else it is invalid.

When a user interacts with a database through a transaction, the database must be transformed from one consistent state to another; otherwise, the updates carried out should be rejected and the original database should be restored.

Three different kinds of inconsistencies arise. These are called

(1)   lost action;
(2)   uncommitted dependency;
(3)   inconsistent analysis.

Usually, in conventional programming we say that these inconsistencies are caused by **side effects**. We can categorize these side effects in the context of database processing into three types thus:

(1)   type ru: user U_i retrieves an object and user U_j updates the same object;
(2)   type ur: user U_i updates an object and user U_j retrieves the same object;
(3)   type uu: user U_i updates an object and user U_j updates the same object.

(Note that the use of only retrieval operations will not cause side effects.)

All three inconsistencies listed above arise from one or more of these three types of side effects. These inconsistencies are illustrated below with examples.

8.6.1   Lost action

Here a user U_1 retrieves an object A at the time step 0; user U_2 retrieves the same object A at time step 1; then U_1 updates A at time step 2; then U_2 updates the same object A at time step 3.

As a result of these transactions we find that U_1 has lost its update at time step 3 since U_2 has overwritten it (Table 8.1). This is called a **lost action**. It is a combination of the side effects of type ru and type uu on the same object A.

This 'lost action' of U_1 results in inconsistency if the state of the database system includes the value of A as well as a boolean condition for

Table 8.1   Lost action.

Time step	U_1	U_2
0	Retrieve A	$\cdots$
1	$\cdots$	Retrieve A
2	Update A	$\cdots$
3	$\cdots$	Update A

whether or not a transaction has been completed. In this example, the boolean for U_1 was set 'true' but the action 'update A' of U_1 has been lost.

This example illustrates a conflict that arises when the same data object is accessed by different transactions and an update operation is performed. To resolve this conflict, object A should be accessed by one and only one transaction. This leads to the concept of a lock.

Locks are set on objects. A lock serves the purpose of prohibiting transactions on a given object that is currently used by another transaction. (This is mutual exclusion.) We shall study locks a little later.

8.6.2 Uncommitted dependency

If one transaction U_1 is allowed to update a record that has been updated by another transaction U_2 but has not been committed by U_2 then inconsistency arises (Table 8.2). This is called **uncommitted dependency**; it is a type ur side effect on object A.

In Table 8.2 transaction U_2 updates A at time step 1; at time step 2, U_1 retrieves this information on A, which is not yet committed. At time step 3, U_2 is aborted and so update of A is undone. The actual value of A is then what it was prior to time step 1. Hence U_1 is under a false assumption.

Note that this example is quite realistic, since U_2 might have been aborted because of a crash and the transaction U_1 may have terminated.

As another example, we may consider again Table 8.2 in which, at time step 2, U_1 also updates A. Now, at time step 3, this update will be lost and A has the same value it had at time step 0. Here we have a type uu side effect.

8.6.3 Inconsistent analysis

This case arises when two transactions function as in Table 8.3. The transactions U_1 and U_2 operate on three different accounts – F, C, H.

The transaction U_1 is asked to find the total sum of the three accounts. Let us assume F = \$100, C = \$200, H = \$300.

Table 8.2 Uncommitted dependency.

Time step	U_1	U_2
0	. . .	. . .
1	. . .	Update A
2	Retrieve A	. . .
3	. . .	Abort

Table 8.3 Inconsistent analysis.

Time step	U_1	U_2
0		
1	Retrieve F (total = $100)	
2	Retrieve C (total = $300)	
3		Retrieve H
4		Update H (H := H − $100)
5		Retrieve F
6		Update F (F := F + $100)
7		End transaction
8	Retrieve H (total = $500)	

Let the transaction U_2 be as follows:

(1)   Retrieve the balance in H at time step 3 and withdraw $100 at time step 4 from H.

(2)   Retrieve the balance in F at time step 5 and update F by putting in $100, at time step 6. At time step 7, U_2 ends transaction.

At time step 8, if U_1 is asked to read the total of all the three accounts, it yields a disastrous result. The actual balance should be $600; but the balance retrieved will be $500.

The reason is that the update of F is not known to U_1, which is under the false assumption that F has the value $100 read at time step 1.

In this case we have a side effect of type ru on object F and a side effect of type ur on object H. The net effect is a combination of these two side effects.

8.6.4 Inferences from examples

From the above examples we infer the following points:

(1)   Two transactions when shuffled need not necessarily produce the same effect that they would produce when they are serial.

(2)   The retrieve and update operations should be controlled to avoid inconsistencies.

(3)   There should be a mechanism (scheduler) that restricts the possible sequences of retrieve–update operations by suitably locking them in or out, so that the net effect is a 'serializable schedule' with no inconsistencies.

(4)   In the event that the scheduler fails to achieve the desired serializable schedule, there should be an externally visible phenomenon so that a corrective action can be taken.

The consideration of these points led to the theories of locking, reliability and recovery of systems (Papadimitriou, 1986; Alagic, 1986; Stonebraker, 1985).

8.7   Design of schedulers

Basically two different methods are used for designing the concurrency control in the scheduler. These are:

(1)   the locking method,
(2)   the timestamp ordering method.

Of course a mixture of these methods can also be used (Bernstein *et al.*, 1986; Casanova, 1981).

In the locking method serializability is achieved by dynamic locking and unlocking of objects in a database. Locking is an action which a transaction executes on an object to prevent other transactions from accessing that object while it is in a state of temporary inconsistency. This enables control of the orderings when conflict arises.

As we indicated earlier in Section 2.6.2, locking and unlocking actions have the same atomicity properties as a semaphore; that is, these sequence of actions are performed in entirety or not at all.

In the timestamp ordering method a serialization order is selected *a priori* and transaction execution is forced to obey this order. Each transaction is assigned a unique timestamp by its TM and when conflict arises timestamp order is used.

8.7.1   Locking approaches

We mentioned that locks can be set on objects in a database. This immediately raises an issue of the 'granularity' or 'unit' of the lock – whether it is going to lock the finest unit or a coarse unit. Three kinds of locks are commonly used:

(1)   object locking – fine level lock;

(2)   predicate locking – higher level lock;

(3)   structured locking – hierarchical lock.

In object locking, concurrency is increased at the expense of the setting of numerous locks. Also, it may sometimes happen that a transaction creates a new object whose existence may not be known to another transaction. This may lead to inconsistency.

In predicate locking, predicates which express conditions on entities are used as the unit of locking. This is at a higher level than object locking. However, if the predicates are not simple enough, it may become an undecidable problem to determine overlapping sets of objects.

In structured locking, the database is organized into a tree hierarchy and several granularities of locks are used. Each node of the tree can be locked; this implicitly locks its descendants in the tree. Such a scheme is called a **tree protocol**.

8.7.2   Locks – types, protocol, allocation

The basic principle of a lock is very simple. When a transaction is about to deal with an object, it acquires a lock on that object, provided that the lock is granted by a protocol mechanism. This locks out other transactions and so no changes can be made.

8.7.2.1   Types of locks

Two types of locks are used: the exclusive lock (X) and shared lock (S). The S lock is also called a read lock and the X lock is also called a write lock.

The X lock is a mutual exclusion mechanism. It can be realized by the use of spinlock or a binary semaphore (Chapter 2). The S lock is shared by more than one transaction. One can use a general semaphore for this purpose or the shared reading scheme used in the readers–writers' problem (Section 3.6.6). Thus writing or updating is a mutually exclusive operation, while reading or retrieving is a shared operation.

These two locks together constitute what is known as a **two-phase locking system** (2PL). This terminology arises from the manner in which the locks are allocated. In the first phase, called the growing phase, a transaction can acquire an S lock and then can be promoted to acquire the X lock (if it is free); in the shrinking phase the locks are released by the ending transaction.

For setting these locks a lock protocol is used to avoid conflicts.

Table 8.4 Lock compatibility matrix.

Transaction	U_1 holds		
	X	S	*None*
U_2 requests			
X	Wait	Wait	Granted
S	Wait	Granted	Granted

8.7.2.2 Lock protocol

The following rules constitute the lock protocol:

Rule 1

If a transaction U_1 holds an X lock on object A, then a request for a lock of X or S type to object A by another transaction U_2 will be delayed until U_1 releases the X lock. Thus U_2 waits.

Rule 2

If U_1 holds an S lock on object A then a request for an S lock on A by U_2 will be granted; however, a request for an X lock on A by U_2 will not be granted until U_1 releases the S lock on A.

These rules are represented by a lock compatibility matrix (Table 8.4).

8.7.2.3 Implicit allocation rules

Initially the following scheme is used for the allocation of locks. If a conflict arises the lock protocol overrides.

(1)   Before a transaction retrieves an object, it automatically acquires an S lock on that object (if the lock is granted).

(2)   Before a transaction updates an object, it automatically acquires an X lock on that object (if the lock is granted).

(3)   If, however, the transaction already holds an S lock, the update will give it an X lock (if the lock is granted).

(4)   It is also understood that each transaction holds its locks until it ends.

We also further enforce that all the transactions obey the following rules:

(1)   A transaction never relocks the same object (which it has already locked).

(2)   A transaction never unlocks an object which it has not locked.

(3)   On its completion, a transaction unlocks all objects it locked.

Transactions obeying these rules are called well-formed transactions.

8.7.3   Use of locks and consequences

We now invoke the three problems earlier described in Section 8.6 and explain how the locks may be used to solve the problems partially (by partial we mean that the solution may lead to a deadlock).

8.7.3.1   Lost action

We now reinvoke Table 8.1. The rules described for locks are now used. This results in Table 8.5, which is a deadlock.

In Table 8.5, we see that, while the action was not lost, transactions are deadlocked. The use of locks can thus result in deadlocks. Hence we need a method to detect and rectify deadlocks or to prevent them occurring. We shall deal with this aspect later.

8.7.3.2   Uncommitted dependency

We now reinvoke Table 8.2. The results described are then applied. This results in Table 8.6.

In Table 8.6, the uncommitted dependency is removed since U_1 sees only a committed value (if U_2 is aborted it sees the pre-value; else, it sees the post-value).

Table 8.5   Deadlock.

Time step	U_1	U_2
0	Retrieve A (acquire S)	· · ·
1	· · ·	Retrieve A (acquire S)
2	Update A (request X)	· · ·
3	Wait	Update A (request X)
4	Wait	Wait

Table 8.6 Locking for uncommitted dependency.

Time step	U₁	U₂
0	...	...
1	...	...
		Update A
		(acquire X)
2	Retrieve A	...
	(request S)	
3	Wait	Abort
		(release X)
4	Retrieve A	
	(acquire S)	

8.7.3.3   Inconsistent analysis

We now reinvoke Table 8.3 where we encountered inconsistency. The use of locks again results in a deadlock; see Table 8.7.

Table 8.7 Use of locks – inconsistency analysis.

Time step	U₁	U₂
0	...	...
1	Retrieve F	...
	(acquire S on F	
	– total = \$100)	
2	Retrieve C	...
	(acquire S on C	
	– total = \$300)	
3	...	Retrieve H
		(acquire S on H)
4	...	Update H
		(acquire X on H;
		H := H – \$100)
5	...	Retrieve F
		(acquire S on F)
6	...	Update F
		(request X on F)
7	...	Wait
8	Retrieve H	Wait
	(request S on H)	
9	Wait	Wait
	Deadlock	

8.7.4 Deadlock detection and resolution

Deadlocks are very undesirable as they result in waste of effort, time and money. Therefore it is better to detect and remove them.

To detect the deadlock we construct a directed graph that represents the 'waiting for' relationship among the transactions. In this graph each node i represents a transaction U_i and a directed arc i–j denotes that U_i is waiting for U_j to acquire a lock. Naturally, such a graph will contain a cycle if there is a deadlock. Then one of the transactions can be aborted.

Such an algorithm functions like the umpire in Dekker's algorithm (Section 2.6.1.1). When a lock request is denied, the umpire tests the requesting transaction (say U_i) and the transaction that currently owns the lock (say U_j). If the waiting is for a genuine cause (as in Table 8.6), the transactions proceed; otherwise, either U_i or U_j is chosen as a victim and aborted. All the actions of U_i (or U_j) are then undone; then U_i (or U_j) is restarted. If U_i is aborted it is called a **non-pre-emptive abort**; if U_j is aborted it is called a **pre-emptive abort**.

The detection of deadlocks as well as the choice of the victim are computationally very complex problems when there are many users (Papadimitriou, 1986).

Remark

The close relationship between the above method and Dekker's algorithm (Chapter 2) can be easily seen. In fact the principles are the same. Dekker's algorithm gives priority to only one of the processes to proceed when conflict arises and restarts the other process. Only the manner in which the principles are applied differs.

The priority methods have also found applications (see Section 3.6.6 – readers–writers' problem) for 'concurrent control in databases'. These are called **timestamp ordering** methods.

8.7.5 Timestamp schedulers

The use of locks results in deadlocks that can be removed only by using priorities. This suggests another method for scheduling, based on temporal ordering of the events in transactions.

In this method, a transaction U_1 whose first step arrives earlier than another transaction U_2 is considered older. Whenever a conflict arises, the older transaction is assigned a priority.

Such a method is known as the timestamp method. It can be shown that this method produces serializable transactions (Papadimitriou, 1986).

8.7.6   Other schedulers

Several other approaches are also used for serialization. Two of these methods are the multiversion method and the optimistic method (Papadimitriou, 1986; Bernstein and Goodman, 1981, 1983; Bernstein *et al.*, 1986; Moss, 1985). These methods are too specialized for treatment within the scope of this book.

8.8   Modelling and analysis of concurrency in database systems

There have been attempts to model concurrency in database systems by using Petri nets (Voss, 1980, 1987) and other methods (Sethi, 1981; Sevcik, 1983). Unfortunately, these models are not easy to analyse to yield practical results.

Many problems concerning concurrency in distributed systems are too complex to solve. In particular, the study of conflicts turns out to be PSPACE-complete (Chapter 6). It seems unlikely that such problems are solved efficiently for practical applications (Papadimitriou, 1986; Wolfson, 1987).

8.9   Database architecture and languages

At present a large number of researchers are working in the area of database architecture in the USA, France, Germany, Italy and Japan. All these architectures are in the prototype stage.

Efforts are underway to use both the shared-variable and the message-oriented approaches to design new database architectures (Hsiao, 1983; Su, 1988).

Also, currently a substantial amount of effort is being made to interface Ada to relational DBMS. More specifically, there are several projects to create a binding between Ada and the standard database language SQL (Brykczynski, 1988).

The use of CSP and PROLOG transaction processing is also under study (Woodcock, 1987).

SUMMARY

In this chapter we introduced the principles of parallel–concurrent processing of the database. After a brief introduction to DBMS, we described the basic properties of transactions. Then we described the concepts of schedules and schedulers. Following this we explained how the side effects that arise from concurrency can affect the integrity of the database.

Then the two different methods – the locking method and the timestamp ordering method – for the design of schedulers were introduced. We described the locking method in detail and explained how it can solve the integrity problems arising from concurrency.

The use of locks, unfortunately, may lead to deadlocks. Briefly we mentioned how such deadlocks are detected and removed. Also, we described in brief the recent developments in the design of other types of schedulers.

Finally, we made a passing reference to the modelling of distributed database control and the design of new architectures and languages exclusively for database management.

EXERCISES

8.1   Study the different data models and the commercial systems that use these different models.

8.2   Study how the various commercial systems handle concurrent transactions.

8.3   Model S and X locks using Petri nets.

8.4   Model the lock compatibility operational matrix (Table 8.4) using a Petri net.

8.5   Study the relation between Dekker's algorithm and the use of 2PL with deadlock abort and restart.

8.6   Study how a structured lock is designed. How do you relate this to a nested monitor?

8.7   What is a timestamp scheduler? Study the use of timestamps for the transactions in Tables 8.5, 8.6 and 8.7.

8.8   Explain how Ada can be used for concurrent database control.

8.9   Write a program in Ada to simulate X and S locks.

8.10 What is a multiversion scheduler?

8.11 What is an optimistic scheduler?

8.12 Are dataflow machines suitable for concurrent database work?

8.13 List some of the NP-complete problems that arise in database concurrency control.

8.14 Study SQL and its environment.

8.15 Study the binding of Ada to SQL.

References

Alagic S. (1986). *Relational Database Technology*. New York NY: Springer

Bernstein P.A. and Goodman N. (1981). Concurrency control in distributed database systems. *ACM Computing Surveys*, **13**, 185–222

Bernstein P.A. and Goodman N. (1983). Multiversion concurrency control: theory and algorithms. *ACM Trans. Database Systems*, **8**, 465–83

Bernstein P.A., Goodman N. and Hadzilacos V. (1986). *Concurrency Control and Recovery in Database Systems*. Reading MA: Addison-Wesley

Brykczynski B. (1988). Methods of binding Ada to SQL: a general discussion. *ACM Ada Lett.*, **8**, 38–51

Casanova M.A. (1981). The concurrency control problem for database systems. *Lecture Notes in Computer Science*, **116**

Ceri S. and Pelagatti G. (1984). *Distributed Databases, Principles and Systems*. New York NY: McGraw-Hill

Date C.J. (1983). *An Introduction to Database Systems*. Reading MA: Addison-Wesley

Date C.J. (1987). *A Guide to Ingres*. Reading MA: Addison-Wesley

Hsiao D.K. (1983). *Advanced Database Machine Architecture*. Englewood Cliffs NJ: Prentice-Hall

Moss J.E.B. (1985). *Nested Transactions*. Cambridge MA: MIT Press

Papadimitriou C. (1986). *The Theory of Database Concurrency Control*. Rockville MD: Computer Science Press

Sethi R. (1981). A model of concurrent database transactions. *Proc. IEEE, Foundations of Computer Science*, **22**, 175–84

Sevcik K.C. (1983). Comparison of concurrency control methods using analytic models. *Information Processing*, **83**, 847–58

Stonebraker M. (1985). *The INGRES Papers: Anatomy of a Relational Database System*. Reading MA: Addison-Wesley

Su S.Y.W. (1988). *Database Computers*. New York NY: McGraw Hill

Ullman J.D. (1982). *Principles of Database Systems*. Rockville MD: Computer Science Press

Voss K. (1980). Using predicate/transition-nets to model and analyze distributed database systems. *IEEE Trans. Software Engineering*, **6**, 539–44

Voss K. (1987). Nets in databases. *Lecture Notes in Computer Science*, **255**, 97–134

Wolfson O. (1987). Overhead of locking (and commit) protocols in distributed databases. *ACM Trans. Database Systems*, **12**, 453–72

Woodcock J.C.P. (1987). Transaction processing primitives and CSP. *IBM J. Research Development*, **31**, 535–45

Index